# CONTEMPORARY ISSUES IN COMMERCE AND BUSINESS

# CONTEMPORARY ISSUES IN COMMERCE AND BUSINESS


*Edited by:*

**DR. V.K. BHALLA**
*Professor of Finance*
Faculty of Management Studies,
University of Delhi,
Delhi-110007

**DR. S. RATHORE**
*Head*
Department of Financial Studies
University of Delhi (South Campus),
Delhi-110021

**DR. Y.P. SINGH**
*Dean*
Faculty of Commerce and Business
University of Delhi,
Delhi-110007



**ANMOL PUBLICATIONS PVT. LTD.**
NEW DELHI - 1000 02 (INDIA)

**ANMOL PUBLICATIONS PVT. LTD.**
4374/4B, Ansari Road, Daryaganj
New Delhi - 110 002

*Contemporary Issues in Commerce and Business*



First Edition, 2000

ISBN 81-261-0667-0



PRINTED IN INDIA

---

Published by J.L. Kumar for Anmol Publications Pvt. Ltd., New Delhi - 110 002 and Printed at Mehra Offset Press, Delhi.

*In Honour of*

**Professor R. S. Nigam**

# PROFESSOR R.S. NIGAM

## *A Profile*

Born in July 1935 and educated in India, the Netherlands (Amsterdam) and Switzerland (Geneva). Professor R.S. Nigam has a doctorate degree in Commerce (International Business) in addition to International Diploma in European Integration (Europa Institute, University of Amsterdam), and Diploma and Certificate in International Commerce (I.T.C., Geneva). He has substantial university teaching and research experience in the fields of business and applied economics with specialization in International Business and Management, International Marketing, International Finance and allied areas. He is an eminent scholar and educationist, has to his credit substantial research, professional consulting, and published work, and has long association with educational planning, administration and training in India and abroad.

Dr. Nigam has been a tenured (permanent) professor at the Department of Commerce (Faculty of Commerce and Business University of Delhi, India) at Delhi School of Economics since 1974. In 1979-82 he worked as Professor in the Department of Management Studies (Faculty of Social Sciences), University of the West Indies at St. Augustine (Trinidad). He has been associated with a number of academic and professional institutions in India and abroad and is the founder president of Indian Society for Research in International Business, as also one of the founder members and senior consultant of the Transcaribbean Management Centre (West Indies).

Dr. Nigam has been participating and attending international conferences and programs in different parts of the world since 1968. He has presented papers and chaired sessions at national and international conferences in India, the U.S.A., South Korea, etc. dealing with issues of higher education, training, international business/management, policies and Commerce. He was awarded the Netherlands Government Fellowship which enabled him to devote one academic year at the University of Amsterdam in 1970-71 (Europa Institute). In 1976 Dr. Nigam was awarded Times (London) Third World Fellowship of the Comonwealth which enabled him to devote ten weeks in Malaysia to study the working of joint industrial and business ventures. He has been a Government nominee on the central councils of the Institute of Chartered Accountants of India and Institute of Company Secretaries of India and served on various committees of these two statutory bodies of professionals. Dr. Nigam has also been associated with the work of Federation of Indian Chambers of Commerce and Industry, Associated Chambers of Commerce, All India Management Association, Confederation of Indian Industries, PHD Chamber of Commerce, etc. He has been on academic bodies of various universities and institutions of higher learning in India and abroad, and has been special (nominee) director on four public limited companies. He has also served as member of various governmental committees in policy areas of higher education, research, economic and business planning. Dr. Nigam has supervised 49 doctoral and more than 50 M.Phil. research studies in functional areas of business and applied economics, especially with international dimensions.

In 1989-90 Dr. Nigam was an Indo-U.S. scholar at the University of Wisconsin (Marathon Centre) and the University of Nevada at Las Vegas. He worked as Visiting Professor of International Management at the College of Business and Economics, University of Nevada at Las Vegas (U.S.A.) in 1991. He has worked as Head, Department of Commerce, University of Delhi and Director of Delhi School of Economics for three terms each between June 1973 and September 1993 For 1993-95 he was selected National Fellow by the University Grants Commission of India. After 42 years of service Prof. Nigam has retired from the University of Delhi in July 2000.

विश्वविद्यालय अनुदान आयोग
नई दिल्ली-110 002
UNIVERSITY GRANTS COMMISSION
BAHADURSHAH ZAFAR MARG
NEW DELHI-110 002
Off. : (011) 323-7143 323-9337
Fax : (011) 323-6288
E-mail : drharigautam@hotmail.com

डा. हरि गौतम-अध्यक्ष
*Dr. Hari Gautam*
MS FRCS (EDIN) FRCS (ENG) FAMS
FACS FICS FIACS DSc (HON CAUSA)
CHAIRMAN

# FOREWORD

With the unprecedented developments in information technology, trade, investment and technology flows the demand for business education in the university system has got a big boost in the last thirty years. As an academic discipline Commerce education was initially concentrated in cities with business firms and entrepreneurial ventures, and most of the universities in our country concentrated at undergraduate work leading to B.Com. qualifications for graduates. It was in the later half of the twentieth century that Commerce has emerged as a strong academic discipline in the university system.

In giving the present shape to Commerce and Business education, roles and leadership of individuals is worth noting. Professor R.S. Nigam, in evolving, organising and updating the area of Commerce into International Business/ Management has been in the forefront in bringing his vast international experience of Europe, U.K., U.S.A., South-East Asia, and Latin America, has contributed significantly to the qualitative growth of education, research and professional training of various stake holders, functionaries and managers of national, regional and international business ventures and firms. It is in the fitness of things that on his retirement, a volume in the shape of the present publication is being brought out by his students, associates and admirers. I highly commend this gesture.

This volume has thrown innovative insight into various areas of today's and future interests of policy makers, business firms and researchers. Most of the contributions relate to international/global business and related to issues like disinvestments, W.T.O. working and globalisation perception, corporate governance, Human Resource Management and Development, Information Management and Information Technology. All these have been contributed by well known persons from a wide variety of academic and professional fields disciplines, and as such, are full of research input of recent years and also of new dimensions of professionalism, innovation and communication developments.

I am happy to join all associates of Professor R.S. Nigam in felicitating him on his attaining the age of 65 and commending the leadership role of his which inspired a good number of young men and women around the world in meeting their global career aspirations and taking the new developments as opportunities and challenges. This volume is both timely and the most appropriate commendation of Professor Nigam's popularity around the world.

**(DR. HARI GAUTAM)**

# PREFACE

With the acceleration of the process of economic reforms, liberalisation, opening up and strengthening of market oriented business environment and operations the international business community has come to be regarded as a global village. The collapse of centrally planned economies of the former U.S.S.R., East European countries and other highly regulated political and economic regimes, along with unprecedented developments in information technology, communication systems and dismantling of tariff and non-tariff barriers all around have made it possible to trade in commodities, options, futures and derivatives, and other economic value-additions on a twenty-four hour basis around the world. The coming up of e-Commerce with a host of variations has made our entry into the twenty-first century a revolutionary event far more important than any economic and political development in the recorded history of mankind. This has necessitated a major overhaul of Commerce and Business education in the areas of international business and management with innovations in course structure, educational technology and manpower resources. It is here a host of opportunity and challenges have come up before the young generation and teacher of Commerce and Business to have global career, teaching, researching and consulting aspirations.

Within nations, proper education is fast becoming an economic necessity for survival. The businessman coming to realise that education is to business what fertilizer is to farming. While affirming the role of commerce education in Indian industry and business, Professor R.S. Nigam always advocated that one should be a first rate specialist—but also be a good generalist as well. Or, to say, be like a doctor who's an excellent surgeon, but who also has the broad knowledge of a general practitioner. Of course, there is no substitute for strong functional expertise. But it's possible for financial engineers to become so functionally narrow that they don't have the capability for application. They may be great researchers—but poor in application, just because they are so narrow. So, even as knowledge increases exponentially, the key is to develop deep functional skills in one discipline (or sub-discipline) while maintaining a broad view of the world economics, business and management.

Today's world is smaller not just by virtue of digital communications, satellites, fax machines, and the like, but because of steady growth of truly global economy, which, far more thoroughly than any weapon of war, is tearing down political barriers that, a short time ago, seemed absolute and unbreachable. To survive in the rapidly changing world, global awareness programmes, covering global business issues, global market trends, political trade agreements, and trade barriers along with the case studies need to explore such things as cross-border components of team building, expatriation, legal issues, financial intermediation, and effective cross cultural teamwork, and subtle cultural differences that can make the difference between success and failure. These are critical to the process of innovation—and to the progress that follows. Why? Because in the world outside the university, the application of knowledge is far less compartmentalised than the acquisition of it. Finding an innovative solution to a problem may require the application of concepts and insights from two or three or more different fields. Hence, along with functional expertise and breadth, one should develop three separate but mutually enforcing sets of skills :analysis / problem solving, persuasion, and vision.

Technology is preparing a world in which we may be learners all life long. It is not surprising that many of the articles in this volume address the issues of competing, surviving and prospering in the market place. The contributions are made much more but this book restricts to twenty one articles selected on the basis of three fold rationale. In the first place in the field of commerce and business, as a body of knowledge, has emerged as a highly interactive process with economic reasoning and system thought calling for greater adoption of techniques imparting precision and measurement. Secondly, the institutional and instrumental options which have influenced in the recent years the strategy and operational planning in business and industry and eventually influenced research and pedagogtc efforts . Thirdly, this volume is brought out in honour of Professor R.S. Nigam who is soon superannuating and whose inspiration and promotion in research in these areas and their pedagogic integration has been tremendous. This three fold rationale is the basis of delimiting the scope of this book .

This publication entitled *Contemporary Issues in Commerce and Business* in which 24 scholars have contributed is humble and consolidated presentation of thoughts and research output of the teachers, scholars and friends, primarily to share information, perceptions and to seek suggestions directionally so that research interests are further argumented and continuity is maintained. The book has been brought out with feeling of emotions, willing cooperation and collective wish of all teachers, research scholars and friends in the honour of Prof. R.S. Nigam for his contributions in evolving, organising and updating the area of commerce into International Business spread over the last four decades .We owe a lot to him and wish him a long, healthy, happy and professionally most rewarding life.

**V.K. BHALLA**
**S. RATHORE**
**Y.P. SINGH**

# CONTENTS

# LIST OF CONTRIBUTORS

**Asthana, B.N.**
Former Professor and Head, Deptt. of Commerce & Management, University of Allahabad; and the former Vice-Chancellor of Kanpur University.

**Bansal, V.P.**
Reader, Department of Commerce, Satyawati College (Evening), University of Delhi.

**Bhalla, V.K.**
Professor, Faculty of Management Studies, University of Delhi, Delhi-110007.

**Goel, Ravinder**
Lecturer, Department of Commerce, Satyagi College (E), University of Delhi.

**Gupta, Chander Kanta**
Senior Lecturer in P.G.D.A.V. College and a research scholar in Department of Commerce at Delhi School of Economics, University of Delhi.

**Gupta, Chandra Prakash**
Reader, Shri Ram College of Commerce, University of Delhi, Delhi-110007.

**Gupta, Ravi**
Senior Lecturer, Shri Ram College of Commerce, Department of Commerce, University of Delhi, Delhi-110007.

**Jain, Nidhi**
Senior Lecturer, Department of Financial Studies, University of Delhi (South Campus), New Delhi-110021.

**Kumar, Devendra**
Reader, Department of Economics, Rajdhani College, University of Delhi.

**Kumar, Muneesh**
Professor, Department of Financial Studies, University of Delhi (South Campus), New Delhi-110021.

**Kumar, Satender**
Principal, Satyawati College (E), University of Delhi.

**Mahajan, Subhash**
Reader, Department of Commerce, Deshbandhu College (Eve.), University of Delhi.

**Narang, S.P.**
Secretary, The Institute of Company Secretaries of India.

**Navjot**
Research Scholar, Department of Commerce, Delhi School of Economics, University of Delhi.

**Om, Hari**
Principal, Sri Aurobindo College, University of Delhi.

**Rathore, Sherin**
Professor, Head, Department of Financial Studies, University of Delhi (South Campus), Delhi-110021.

**Saini, A.K.**
Faculty of Management Studies, University of Delhi, Delhi-110007.

**Sharma, J.P.**
Department of Commerce, Sri Aurobindo College, University of Delhi.

**Sharma, J.P.**
Reader, Department of Economics, Zakir Hussain College (Evening), University of Delhi.

**Singh, Harminder**
Senior Lecturer, SGGS College of Commerce, University of Delhi.

**Singh, Sanjay K.**
Senior Lecturer, Department of Commerce, Dayal Singh College (E), University of Delhi.

**Singh, Y.P.**
Professor, Head of Commerce Department and Dean of Faculty of Commerce and Business, University of Delhi, Delhi-110007.

**Tuteja, S.K.**
Reader, Faculty of Management Studies, Univeristy of Delhi, Delhi-110007.

# 1

# THE EURO AREA: PROSPECTS, CHALLENGES AND OPPORTUNITIES

*V.K. Bhalla*

On 1st January 1999, a unique event in the history of Europe occurred. The euro area, comprising the economies of 11 countries, introduced the new single European currency, the *euro*. The euro area has a population of 292 million, compared with 270 million of in the other single currency area, the USA. The GDP of the European Economic and Monetary Union (EMU) area comes to 5 trillion euros—about three quarters that of the USA, and nearly two thirds more than Japan. Add the four EU states that so far remain outside EMU —the UK, Sweden, Denmark and Greece—the EMU area GDP virtually matches that of the USA. The euro zone itself is already the largest trading partner in the world, with a 20% net share (excluding intra-euro trade), in global exports of goods and services for 1998, followed by the USA with 16% and comfortably exceeding Japanese 8%. Against this background, the new economic area easily bears comparison with any other in the world.

## THE EURO AREA ECONOMIC OUTLOOK

The economic activity in the euro area in 1999 was characterised by a progressive upturn in output growth, following the slowdown in 1998. In retrospect, the adverse effects of the crisis of emerging market economies on the growth of the activity to the euro area appear to have been rather brief and limited. Reflecting the improvement in the economic outlook for growth, Eurostat confirmed an increase in the real GDP by 2.3% in 1999, despite weak growth in the first half of the year. The strong dynamics in the second half of the last year are expected to continue in 2000.

**Balance of Payments of the Euro Area**

The current account surplus of the euro area declined slightly to approximately 0.75% of GDP in 1999 (€43.2 billion), from around 1% of GDP in 1998 (ECU 60.3 billion). The reason for this decline was a decrease in the surplus on trade in goods which, in turn, was mainly the result of a strong increase in import values in the course of the year, attributable to higher import prices, particularly energy, along with a low level of export values in the first half of the 1999 and, to a lesser extent, the deterioration in the services trade balance. By contrast, lower deficits were recorded for the current transfers and income accounts in 1999.

Over 1999 as a whole, the goods trade surplus of the euro area declined to €99.9 billion from ECU 118.8 billion in 1998. In the second half of last year, however, export values began to show stronger underlying growth, reflecting both rising foreign demand and improvements in price competitiveness. Despite the increase in exports during the course of the year, import values continued to grow faster than exports, which seems to be related to higher import prices, partly resulting from higher oil prices and the weakening of the euro, along with signs of increased activity in the euro area during the last six months of 1999.

The services balance also deteriorated in 1999, compared with 1998, reaching a deficit of €6.6 billion by the end of last year. Higher payments, combined with virtually zero growth in receipts, underlay the rise in the deficit in services. By contrast, the deficits on the current transfers and income accounts fell in 1999, declining by €3.0 billion and €4.6 billion respectively. The improvement in he income account was mostly a result of lower investment income payments in 1999, compared with the very high levels reached in 1998. (See Table 1).

In January 2000 the current account of the euro area recorded a deficit of €6.6 billion, compared with a deficit of €2.4 billion for the same month last year. A fall in the goods surplus (from €4.8 billion in January 1999 to €0.9 billion in January 2000) and a larger deficit for the income account, only partially offset by reductions in the deficits for services and current transfers, explain the deficit.

In 1999, the euro area residents increased foreign direct investment, while portfolio investment outflows declined. The direct and portfolio investment net outflows amounted to €168.5 billion, i.e. lower than the ECU 187.9 billion in the previous year. The major determinant of the outflows from the euro area were net direct investment outflows. The latter increased from ECU 102.6 billion in 1998 to €147.2 billion in 1999; in particular, euro area Presidents invested more abroad (€212.5 billion in 1999, compared with ECU 183 billion in 1998). At the same time foreign direct investment in the euro area remained subdued (€65.2 billion, compared with ECU 80.4 billion in 1998).

The increase in net direct investment outflows contrasted with a €64.0 billion decline in net portfolio investment outflows to €21.3 billion in 1999, compared with 1998. This was related to the swing in debt instruments from net outflows in 1998. This was related to the swing in debt instruments from net outflows in 1998 (ECU 84.8 billion) to net inflows in 1999 (€34.8 billion) Both lower investment on the part of euro area residents abroad and stronger demand on the part of foreign

**TABLE 1**

**Balance of Payments of the Euro area[1]**
(EUR billions: ECU billions for 1998 (not seasonally adjusted))

| | *1998 Jan.-Dec.* | *1999 Jan.* | *1999 Jan.-Dec.* | *1999 Nov.* | *1999 Dec.* | *2000 Jan.* |
|---|---|---|---|---|---|---|
| **Current account balance** | 43.3 | - 2.4 | 24.3 | 2.2 | 1.6 | - 6.6 |
| Credits | 1,264.0 | 95.4 | 1,291.5 | 112.9 | 118.3 | 110.8 |
| Debits | 1,220.6 | 97.7 | 1,267.2 | 110.7 | 116.7 | 117.4 |
| Goods balance | 118.8 | 4.8 | 99.9 | 8.3 | 8.4 | 0.9 |
| Exports | 772.4 | 53.5 | 791.3 | 73.6 | 73.4 | 63.7 |
| Imports | 653.6 | 48.7 | 691.4 | 65.2 | 65.0 | 82.8 |
| Services balance | - 0.9 | - 2.9 | - 6.6 | - 1.1 | - 0.7 | - 1.9 |
| Exports | 232.0 | 14.9 | 232.4 | 19.1 | 21.1 | 17.8 |
| Imports | 232.8 | 17.8 | 239.0 | 20.3 | 21.8 | 19.7 |
| Income balance[2] | - 28.8 | - 2.3 | - 26.2 | - 0.5 | - 1.3 | - 4.3 |
| Current transfers balance | - 45.8 | - 2.0 | - 42.8 | - 4.5 | - 4.8 | - 1.3 |
| **Capital account balance** | 12.7 | 2.7 | 12.8 | 0.8 | 2.6 | 1.4 |
| **Financial Account balance[3]** | - 69.1 | 0.4 | - 62.7 | - 0.6 | - 6.1 | 17.1 |
| Direct investment | - 102.6 | - 4.7 | - 147.2 | - 17.5 | - 26.6 | 20 |
| Abroad | - 183.0 | - 11.8 | - 212.5 | - 19.9 | - 33.8 | - 5.4 |
| In the euro area | 80.4 | 7.1 | 65.2 | 2.4 | 7.2 | 7.4 |
| Portfolio investment[3] | - 85.3 | 8.8 | - 21.3 | - 18.0 | 7.0 | - 17.5 |
| Assets | - 302.1 | - 19.1 | - 280.5 | - 31.1 | - 18.9 | - 25.1 |
| Liabilities | 216.8 | 27.9 | 259.2 | 49.1 | 25.9 | 7.6 |
| Financial derivatives[3] | - 8.2 | - 1.9 | 0- 0.8 | 1.6 | - 0.4 | - 1.3 |
| Other investment[3,4] | 118.5 | 0.3 | 93.2 | - 3.2 | 14.7 | 35.5 |
| Reverse assets[3] | 8.5 | - 2.1 | 13.4 | 0.6 | - 0.8 | - 1.6 |
| **Errors and omissions[3]** | 13.1 | - 0.7 | 25.5 | - 2.5 | 1.8 | - 11.9 |

1. Figures may not add up due to rounding.
2. Monthly figures for 1998-99 are not closely comparable with later observations.
3. Data before end-1-98 are not closely comparable with later observations.
4. Flows before January 1999 include estimates.

investors for euro area debt securities, in particular money market instruments, contributed to the turnaround. On the other hand, net equity outflows increased to €56.1 billion (from ECU 0.4 billion in 1998), mainly as a result of higher investment in foreign equities on the part of euro area residents (which rose to €150.0 billion, from ECU 98.7 billion in 1998).

In January 2000 the combined net direct and portfolio investment outflow declined to €15.5. billion, compared with €19.6 billion in December 1999. This was the result of a swing in direct investment from net outflows to net inflows, attributable mainly to lower direct investment abroad by euro area residents in January 2000 (€5.4 billion, compared with €33.8 billion in December 1999).

Net direct investment inflows contrasted with net portfolio investment outflows ( €17.5 billion in January 2000), owing to a strong increase in equity net outflows to €18.0 billion in January 2000 (from €3.6 billion in December 1999). In particular, equity investment in the euro area declined to €4.0 billion in January 2000, from €16.9 billion in December 1999. Foreign investors also reduced their new investment in euro area debt securities, mostly money market instruments, to €3.6 billion, from €9.0 billion in December 1999. Altogether, portfolio investment in euro area securities declined to €7.6 billion in January 2000, from €25.9 billion in December 1999.

Moreover, portfolio investment abroad by euro area residents increased to €25.1 billion in January 2000, from €18.9 billion in December 1999. This was accompanied by both an increase in the investment of Euro area residents in foreign equities and higher investment in foreign debt instruments.

The growing international integration of capital markets offer greater opportunities for a more efficient allocation of global resources. As recent experience has shown, however, it also carries risks of destabilisation, especially in countries where domestic financial systems are fragile or macroeconomic imbalances are still present. In such a situation, economic policy faces new and more complex challenges. It is important to stress, however, that the improved outlook for the global economy points to the possibility of addressing old problems and facing new challenges with the higher probability of success. This is particularly true for the euro area economy where the outlook for growth has recently improved, contributing to more optimistic prospects at the global level. The European Central Bank's (ECB's) stability- oriented monetary policy for the euro area is contributing to these developments by aiming, in fulfilment of its mandate, to maintain price stability, thereby fostering a favourable environment for business activity.

**The Euro and the Financial Markets**

Not only has EMU permanently altered the monetary framework within the common currency area, it has also provided a significant boost to the continent's financial markets, supporting their growth and promoting their deepening. However, the development and progress have not been even across the spectrum of financial markets and financial services. The start of *Stage Three* of EMU has acted as a catalyst for the development and integration of the euro area capital markets towards a pro-European capital markets. The euro's positive influence has been more immediate and clearly evident than in Europe's financial markets, especially the market for interbank deposits and the international corporate bond market. Both markets have grown rapidly and have been transformed into more efficient vehicles for the allocation of liquidity and savings. By contrast, other market segments, such as collateralised money markets and equity markets, have largely retained their national character and have so far not been able to capitalise on the enhanced potential for efficiency and liquidity offered by greater cross-border activity

*Money Markets*

The conduct of monetary policy in the framework of EMU requires an efficient mechanism for the allocation of central bank liquidity throughout the single currency zone. The interbank market in unsecured credit has provided this mechanism as it rapidly adapted to the new framework. In this role it has been supported by TARGET the large-value funds transfer system for the euro area, which quickly overcame minor initial operational problems to become the backbone of the euro area's payment system. The Governing Council of the ECB decided to raise the interest rate on the Eurosystem's main refinancing operations, which continue to be conducted as fixed rate tenders, by 25 basis points, to 3.5%, starting with the operation to be settled on 22 March 2000. The interest rates on the marginal lending facility and on the deposit facility were also increased by 25 basis points, to 4.50% and 2.50% respectively, both with effect from 17 March 2000. At the two subsequent meetings held on 30 March 2000 and 13 April 2000, the Governing Council decided to leave the ECB interest rates inchanged.[2]

The decision of 16 March 2000 to increase the ECB interest rats was taken in order to address the prevailing upward risks to price stability, as indicated by both pillars of the monetary policy strategy of the Eurosystem.[3] In particular, it was considered that the prolonged deviation of M3 growth from the reference value of 4½%, especially when seen in conjunction with the dynamic growth of credit to the private sector, pointed to the existence of ample liquidity in the euro area. In addition, in view of the strength of the upturn in economic activity, the potential spillover of the protracted increases in import and producer prices to consumer prices was seen as a factor affecting the outlook for prices in the medium term. Subsequently, monetary data showed the three-month average of annual M3 growth covering the period from December 1999 to February 2000, equal to 5.9%, compared with 5.8% in the three-month period from November 1999 to January 2000. M3 growth thus remained around 1½ percentage points above the reference value of 4½%. The higher three-month average of annual M3 growth reflected an increase in the annual rate of growth of M3 in February 2000 to 6.2%, from 5.2% in January 2000. This resulted from both strong seasonally adjusted growth of M3 in February 2000 and a strong base effect. The picture of ample liquidity in the euro area is also confirmed by the continue robust annual rate of growth of the loans to the private sector, which stood at 10.5% in February, 2000.

The early resolution of all uncertainty relating to the money market reference yield curve also contributed to this successful transition. During the first few weeks of 1999 the EONIA (euro overnight index average) rate, extended by the Euribor yield curve and supported by an active derivatives market, emerged as the clear choice of market participants. The establishment of a single money market in euros is clearly evidenced by the convergence of yields across the euro area, and its efficiency demonstrated by the continuing tightening of bid-ask spreads, which are currently about 40% lower than five years ago (Table-2).

The emergence of an efficient euro area money market has allowed the treasurers of many large companies to reduce costs by centralising their cash management operations. Banks have formed a two-tiered structure in which larger institutions with a pan-European presence handle the cross-border flow of liquidity and smaller institutions play a more restricted regional role. The significant increase in cross-border inter-bank activity between institutions in the euro area after the fourth quarter of 1998 is a direct consequence of this development.

**TABLE 2**

**Three-month money market rate bid-ask spreads[1]**

| | | *1996* | *1997* | *1998* | *1999* | *2000[2]* |
|---|---|---|---|---|---|---|
| Euro area[3] | average | 14.4 | 12.4 | 9.6 | 8.9 | 8.4 |
| | stand *dev.* | *3.0* | *3.5* | 1.8 | *3.1* | *3.1* |
| Germany | average | 16.5 | 15.1 | 8.2 | 9.2 | 8.5 |
| | *stand.dev.* | 6.3 | 7.6 | 2.9 | *4.1* | *3.1* |
| France | average | 14.1 | 11.2 | 11.3 | 8.7 | 8.5 |
| | *stand. dev* | 4.6 | 2.7 | *3.0* | 2.8 | *3.1* |
| Italy | average | 11.3 | 9.3 | 10.1 | 8.9 | 8.5 |
| | *stand. dev.* | 2.3 | 2.4 | 2.8 | 2.6 | *3.1* |
| United States | average | 12.5 | 11.3 | 8.8 | 9.0 | 9.3 |
| | *stand. dev.* | 2.9 | *5.3* | *4.0* | 2.9 | 2.8 |
| Japan | average | 12.0 | 9.8 | 11.5 | 10.5 | 10.4 |
| | stand. dev. | 2.0 | 3.8 | 3.6 | 5.9 | 1.1 |

1. Spreads in basis points of eurocurrency deposit rates, London close.
2. Upto mid-April.
3. Prior to 1999, weighted average of the rates of Germany. France and Italy weights according to the ECB capital key

Source: Standard & Poor's DRI.

In contrast to the unsecured deposit market, the repo market has failed to break out of the segmentation that characterised it prior to the introduction of the euro. Existing market rules and architecture that may have served participants' needs well at national level are not necessarily conducive to the development of a true pan-European general collateral market. Cross-border activity remains limited, keeping the market from achieving its frill liquidity potential and resulting in persistent pricing differentials and variations in market depth across segments. The slow pace of harmonisation of national market practices and conventions and the lack of a unified market infrastructure continue to present obstacles to further development Some of these obstacles, such as the cumbersome interface between delivery systems, settlement procedures and market practices, are technical and hence easier to overcome. Others, however, such as differences in documentation and tax treatment, as well as uncertainty regarding title to the underlying securities, relate directly tc deep-seated structural differences in national tax and legal systems. Achieving greater harmonisation across the euro area on this front requires more far-reaching intervention, and hence a significant commitment, by national authorities.

*Bond Markets*

Arguably the most impressive effect of EMU on the continent's financial structure has been the tremendous boost that the single currency has given to European fixed income markets. Issuance of euro-denominated bonds surged in 1999, with total funds raised increasing to multiples of their pre-EMU average. Both government and private borrowers have been attracted to the new currency. However, it is the intensified activity by the latter, especially European corporations, that has been the most significant development

At one stroke, the conversion of government debt denominated in the legacy currencies into euros created a market that currently surpasses in size its Japanese counterpart and stands second only to the US Treasury market. At end-December 1999, the stock of long-term euro-denominated debt issued by the euro area governments amounted to around 2.2 trillion or two thirds of the outstanding stock of US Treasury bonds. Over the medium term, the combination of budget deficits in most euro area countries and the ceilings on indebtedness imposed by the Maastricht Treaty are likely to maintain the market at its current size. In contrast, current and projected fiscal trends are pulling the US and Japanese markets in opposite directions, with the former expected to shrink and the latter to expand significantly.

The economic convergence process in the run-up to EMU went hand in hand with an impressive narrowing of interest rate differentials across the 11 participating economies. Current yield spreads are typically contained within 40 basis points or less at any point on the yield curve. Closer inspection suggests that a significant portion of these yield differentials reflects technical and liquidity considerations rather than economic risk. Yield differentials in the vicinity of 20 basis points for similarly rated borrowers, such as the German, French and Dutch governments, are too large to be justified by market perceptions of differential credit risk, especially in view of the fact that the spread between French and Dutch bonds and the lower-rated Italian and Belgian bonds is narrower. Moreover, differences in issuers' creditworthiness are unlikely to exhibit the required term structure to account for the fact that national yield curves often cross each other at different points on the maturity spectrum.[4]

Liquidity, security design and issuance policies are key in explaining the interchange between German and French bonds in the highest-priced position at different points along the maturity spectrum. German bonds enjoy benchmark status at the short end of the yield curve and then again in the 10-year maturity range, where they are complemented by the most heavily traded futures contract worldwide. Over the intermediate maturity range, the French Treasury has managed to carve a niche for its securities through an innovative, transparent and investor-friendly issuance policy.

Idiosyncratic national debt management policies and differences in market conventions are not without costs. No single government bond market is sufficiently large and deep to become the benchmark for the whole euro area, let alone challenge the US market in its leading role. Moreover, different structures and conventions in national bond issuance translate into inefficiencies in other market segments. One example is the repo market where development is hampered by imperfect harmonisation of conventions. The corporate bond market could also benefit from a well defined reference government yield curve off which it could be priced in a consistent way. Greater coordination among euro area treasuries with respect to the calendar of issuance, coupon, maturity and other more technical characteristics of the bonds issued could lead to greater fungibility and larger pools of bonds across the maturity spectrum which would be likely to carry a liquidity premium. Bonds issued by the governments of the smaller economies would arguably be the main beneficiaries of such a boost in prices.

Given the potential benefits in promoting market structure and reducing debt servicing costs, calls have been made for greater cooperation among EMU governments in this area. The issue, however, is much more complex than a harmonisation of market structure and conventions. It goes to the heart of the debate on how far national discretion could or should be surrendered in the name of achieving benefits that are unevenly distributed across the euro area. For some of the more formal proposed schemes, it is also a question of the extent to which cooperation would imply, or be perceived as implying, shared fiscal responsibilities, which are explicitly ruled out by the Maastricht Treaty. Any argument based on the economic benefits of greater coordination has to be carefully weighted against the further erosion of national independence. This debate *is familiar* from the process that led to Maastricht and it shows that closer economic intergration is likely to continue to raise similar issues.

The euro has been particularly attractive to private sector borrowers both within and outside the euro area. Between July 1998 and December 1999, euro 11 private sector borrowers issued 76% of their debt in euros, compared to an average of 50% in the predecessor currencies between January 1990 and

June 1998. Over the same period, private borrowers residing outside the euro area issued a fifth of their international debt in euros, nearly a twofold increase over the total share of the legacy currencies before July 1998.[5]

While it could be argued that low interest rats and a weakening currency may have played some role in stimulating borrowers' interest in the euro, structural factors have clearly also contributed to the increase in issuance. Chief among these factors has been a significant expansion of the investor base. The single currency has effectivley relaxed regulatory currency matching requirements for assets and liabilities imposed on many institutional investors that had led to a strong national bias in their portfolio allocation. Insurance companies and pension funds have thus been able to take advantage of the elimination of exchange rate risk while at the same time achieving a greater degree of portfolio diversification by investing across the single currency area. German investors, for instance, had already sharply increased their purchases of euro-denominated foreign assets ahead of the introduction of the new currency. These purchases actually intensified thereafter, with euro area assets accounting for roughly two thirds of the total gross outward portfolio investment from Germany in 1999.

The composition of borrowers that have tapped the euro bond market partly reflects the traditional structure of European finance, but partly also its changing profile. The largest issuers, in terms of both the number of issues and the volume of funds raised, have been European banks. German banks' sales of securitised assets in the form of Pfandbriefe account for a large part of this segment. Indeed, the success of the Pfandbrief market has prompted a number of European countries to introduce legislation that replicates its institutional features in an effort to facilitate the development of bank asset securitisation. Such recent innovations in France, Spain and Luxembourg have yet to mature and achieve the liquidity and investor acceptance enjoyed by their German counterpart. A smaller but growing share of bonds has been issued by non-financial corporations, which have capitalised on the increasing appetite for credit risk among European investors. Within this group, there is a high concentration of telecommunications companies that have made extensive use of bond markets to finance the flurry of merger and acquisition activity in this sector. Large-scale borrowers, such as supranational institutions and other US dollar-based agencies and finance companies, remain under-represented in the euro-denominated bond market, relative to their size and global presence. An often cited explanation for this phenomenon is the unfavourable conditions in the swap market, which raise the effective US dollar financing costs for these borrowers accustomed to sub-Libor rates.

The advent of the euro has rendered investment strategies based on cross-currency yield arbitrage and directional bets on national interest rates obsolete, encouraging investors to focus more closely on credit risk. European institutional portfolio managers have begun to educate themselves in the evaluation and management of credit risk, and have gradually developed an appetite for it. The progressive expansion of the market towards lower credits bears witness to this process. What used to be a market only for borrowers rated AA or higher has been able to accommodate a broadening array of credits. The sub-investment grade segment, while still much smaller and less diversified than its US dollar counterpart, has regained momentum after suffering a severe setback in the aftermath of the 1998 financial market turmoil.

The introduction of the single currency has played a critical role in increasing the contestability of the market for the provision of corporate financial services. Table-3 shows that historically the nationality of the underwriter of an international bond has been more closely associated with the currency in which the bond is issued than with the nationality of the borrower. This suggests that any established relationship between corporatons and their investment bankers is not as important a factor in the selection of underwriters as the ability of the latter to correctly price and place the issue in a market they know well. The advent of the euro has diminished any local advantage European bankers had derived by virtue of their familiarity with investors with a strong national currency bias. While the effect of this change has failed to alter the strength of the stylised facts, the fees for the euro-denominated segment of the market, however, have rapidly converged towards the level of its US dollar counterpart over the last two years. Together with the growing similarity in the average credit quality of the borrowers and the close relationship between issuance levels in the two segments, this convergence in fees is a clear indication of the progressive integration of the international bond market

The blossoming of the euro-denominated corporate bond market will have a lasting impact on the European financial structure, traditionally characterised by the predominance of bank-intermediated forms of finance. A broader and more receptive investor base is likely to encourage more classes of private borrowers to substitute debt securities for bank loans. At the same time, banking institutions are themselves likely to use the market as a source of funding that will support their portfolios of less liquid assets. Clearly such developments, by expanding the range of available funding channels, will also enhance the efficiency of the mechanism for the allocation of savings, thereby benefiting the entire European economy. However, by increasing the sensitivity of corporate and bank balance sheets to capital market conditions, this trend is also likely to pose new challenges for financial stability in the area.

**TABEL 3**

**Currency of issue versus business relationship in the choice of bond bookrunner**

| *Borrower's nationality* | | *Currency of issue* | | | |
|---|---|---|---|---|---|
| | | *Euro legacy currencies* | *Euro* | *US dollar* | *All currencies* |
| Market share of bookrunners whose nationality matches the issue currency (in %) | | | | | |
| Euro area | 1996-98 | 59.0 | 63.1 | 41.1 | 53.8 |
| | 1999-2000[2] | 56.3 | 60.0 | 39.6 | 55.1 |
| United States | 1996-98 | 34.6 | 28.6 | 81.7 | 71.9 |
| | 1999-2000[2] | — | 26.9 | 79.4 | 71.1 |
| All | 1996-98 | 53.2 | 58.2 | 64.2 | 57.8 |
| | 1999-2000[2] | 50.5 | 53.0 | 69.3 | 58.2 |
| Market share of bookrunners with the same nationality as the borrower (in %)[3] | | | | | |
| Euro area | 1996-98 | 39.7 | 35.4 | 19.2 | 28.1 |
| | 1999-2000[2] | 18.1 | 42.1 | 22.3 | 36.6 |
| United States | 1996-98 | 52.6 | 44.5 | 81.7 | 74.2 |
| | 1999-2000[2] | — | s3.s | 79.4 | 75.2 |
| All | 1996-98 | 28.2 | 27.7 | 38.6 | 32.1 |
| | 1999-2000[2] | 19.2 | 36.3 | 51.2 | 41.5 |

1. Percentage share of the volume of bonds issued by borrowers of a specific nationality (rows) won by booltrunners of the same nationality as the specified currency of issue (columns). For example. in 1996-98, US banks ran the books of 41.1% of all US dollar bond issues by euro area borrowers.
2. Up to mid-March.
3. Percentage share of the volume of bonds issued by borrowers of a specific nationality (rows) and denominated in the specified currency (columns) won by bookrunners of the same nationality as the borrower For example, in 1996-98. the books of 19.2% of all US dollar bond issues by euro area borrowers were run by banks from the same country as the borrower.

Sources: Capital DATAZ 815 calculations.

## *Equity Markets*

Two of the most significant developments in Europe's

equity markets during the past year are only tangentially linked to the introduction of the new currency: healthy issuance and further maturation of Europe's specialised exchanges for young and growing company stocks. Issuance has been supported by generally buoyant stock prices as well as by the continuing trend of government withdrawal from commercial activities. Gross issuance of international equity by euro area companies grew in 1999 by almost 70% over its average level for the previous two years.[6] Declining bond yields in much of the euro area, a result of the economic convergence, have contributed to intensified interest by retail investors in riskier but potentially more rewarding equity investments. In fact, record inflows into equity mutual funds have supported valuations across most of the area's equity markets.

A new, more capital market-friendly breed of European entrepreneurs has brought increasing numbers of small and medium-sized companies into the public equity markets. This trend has been underscored by the success of the network of "new markets", which have been created in many European countries with the objective of providing access to equity finance for small, dynamic companies with a high growth potential. After a period of strong growth in early 1999, the market was unsettled by an excess supply of new equity for much of last year. Conditions improved again in view of the global rally in "new economy" stocks. This time, strong initial public offering activity was met by a more diverse group of investors showing greater commitment to the sector.

The advent of the euro was widely expected to mark the beginning of a new paradigm in the valuation of equity for companies in the EMU area. The importance of diverging macroeconomic factors affecting share prices was expected to diminish because of the elimination of exchange rate risk, the fully unified monetary policy stance and the greater cohesion of fiscal policy across the EMU economies. In addition, the expansion of cross-border commercial activity, boosted by progress towards a single market in the European Union, was expected to increase the importance of sector-specific factors at the expense of country-specific factors in influencing individual company valuations. Evidence from company valuations so far, however, has failed to detect a major shift. Individual company stock continues to co-move more closely with that of other companies in the same country than with that of similar companies elsewhere in the euro area, an indication that prices continue to be driven principally by local investors with a considerable geographical portfolio bias.

One factor that is likely to have contributed to this segmentation of equity markets is the absence to date of an integrated trading infrastructure covering the entire EMU area. There have been many attempts to establish a unified platform that would allow investors from inside as well as outside the common currency zone to trade seamlessly in equities of European companies, through bilateral or multilateral agreements among the existing national bourses. The most ambitious such plan is for an alliance among six of the largest stock exchanges in the euro area, together with the London and Zurich exchanges, aimed at creating a pan-European market for the largest and most heavily traded stocks. The intention is to start with simple steps such as the harmonisation of opening hours and to progressively establish a common trading infrastructure, as well as uniform settlement and clearing facilities. By improving market liquidity and reducing trade processing costs, such a development would help the European equity markets to realise their full potential and grow to a size commensurate with the area's economy (Table-4). Progress in this project, however, has been slower than initially expected. Agreement on a common architecture has been hampered by the ambitions of individual alliance members and a reluctance to change established practices

**TABLE 4**

**Stock market indicators**

| | *Market capitalisation*[1] *in billions of US dollars* | | | *1999 in % of* | *Turnover*[2] *in billions of US dollars* | | | *Number of listed stocks*[1] | | |
|---|---|---|---|---|---|---|---|---|---|---|
| | *1990* | *1995* | *1999* | *GDP* | *1990* | *1995* | *1999* | *1990* | *1995* | *1999* |
| Euro area | 1.169 | 2.119 | 5.526 | *85* | 737 | 1.237 | 4,342 | 2,485 | 2.592 | 3.893 |
| Germany | 355 | 577 | 1,432 | 68 | 509 | 594 | 1.551 | 413 | 678 | 1.043 |
| France | 314 | 522 | 1,503 | *105* | 121 | 213 | 770 | 578 | 450 | 968 |
| Italy | 149 | 210 | 728 | 62 | 42 | 87 | 539 | 220 | 250 | 264 |
| Spain[3] | 111 | 198 | 432 | 72 | | 163 | 739 | 427 | 362 | 723 |
| Netherlands | 120 | 356 | 694 | *176* | 41 | 124 | 471 | 260 | 217 | 233 |
| Belgium | 65 | 105 | 184 | 74 | 9 | 18 | 59 | 182 | 143 | 159 |
| Austria | 11 | 33 | 33 | *16* | 11 | 13 | 13 | 97 | 109 | 97 |
| Portugal | 9 | 18 | 67 | *62* | ... | 4 | 40 | 181 | 169 | 125 |
| Finland | 23 | 44 | 349 | 272 | 4 | 19 | 110 | 73 | 73 | 147 |
| Ireland | | 26 | 69 | *75* | | ... | 48 | ... | 80 | 84 |
| Luxembourg | 10 | 30 | 34 | 192 | — | — | 1 | 54 | 61 | 50 |
| United States[4] | 3.059 | 6.858 | 16.773 | *181* | 1.778 | 5,481 | 19,412 | 6.599 | 7.671 | 7.297 |
| Japan[5] | 2,918 | 3.667 | 4.455 | 102 | 1,288 | 884 | 1,676 | 2.071 | 2,263 | 1,889 |
| United Kingdom | 849 | 1,408 | 2.955 | 206 | 543 | 1.153 | 3.399 | 1.701 | 2.078 | 2,292 |
| Canada[6] | 242 | 366 | 789 | *121* | 71 | 185 | 389 | 1.111 | 1.196 | 1.106 |
| Switzerland | 160 | 434 | 678 | 262 | 65 | 340 | 562 | 182 | 233 | 239 |

1. Listed domestic stocks.
2. Value of share trading; total domestic and foreign listed companies. Due to different reporting rules and calculation methods, turnover figures are not entirely comparable.
3. For turnover, Madrid Stock Exchange only; otherwise, also including the stock exchanges of Barcelona, Bilbao and Valencia.
4. For turnover. New York Stock Exchange and Nasdaq; otherwise, also including AMEX.
5. For turnover, Tokyo Stock Exchange only; otherwise, also including Osaka Stock Exchange.
6. Stock exchanges of Toronto, Montreal and Vancouver.

Sources: International Federation of Stock Exchanges (FIBV); International Finance Corporation; Swiss Exchange.

and rules. Disappointment with the lack of progress and increasing competitive pressure from a number of newly created electronic trading systems have prompted some exchanges to seek closer cooperation on a smaller scale. The most prominent examples are the announced mergers between the London Stock Exchange and Deutsche Borse, on the one hand and between the Paris, Amsterdam and Brussels exchanges, on the other. The first deal will create the second largest stock exchange in the world by market capitalisation, while the second will be a significant competitor within Europe. Other European exchanges are expected to join these two alliances at a later stage.

*CONSOLIDATION IN THE FINANCIAL SECTOR*

The euro has played a central role in reshaping financial intermediation in the EMU area and its periphery by reinforcing the factors that have been driving the consolidation process in the banking and non-bank intermediary sectors for some time. The euro lifted the economic barriers to the cross-border supply of financial services within the single currency area and thus expanded the scope for growth and diversification for the area's banks. Its influence has strengthened the trend towards larger institutions that would be able to reap the full benefits of greater economies of scale brought by technological progress.[7] At the same time, it has intensified competition, at least at the wholesale level, reinforcing the incentive to create institutions capable of competing effectively on a pan-European scale for corporate banking business.

The pace of financial sector consolidation in Europe accelerated in anticipation of the introduction of the new currency and has continued unabated. The merger wave has also spilled over to the periphery of the euro zone, partly in sympathy with the consolidation taking place within the area, and partly in anticipation of future EMU entry. However, while financial sector mergers and acquisitions often cross industry lines, they remain largely confined within national borders. Current cross-border activity mostly takes the form of strategic alliances, often reinforced by the acquisition of minority, non-controlling stakes.

**TABLE 5**

**Merger and acquisition activity in the euro area financial industry[1]**

| | *Same country* | | *Other euro country* | | *Other non-euro country* | | *Total* | | *As a percentage[2]* | |
|---|---|---|---|---|---|---|---|---|---|---|
| | *No.* | *Value[3]* | *No.* | *Value[3]* | *No.* | *Value[3]* | *No* | *Value[3]* | *No.* | *Value[3]* |
| Banks — banks | | | | | | | | | | |
| 1998 | 7 | 8.445 | 1 | 147 | 12 | 13,787 | 20 | 22.379 | *12.7* | *13.0* |
| 1999 | 9 | 41.242 | 4 | 9,465 | 15 | 7,495 | 28 | 58.202 | *15.9* | *34.2* |
| 2000[4] | 3 | 4.528 | 0 | 0 | 5 | 11.654 | 8 | 16,182 | 26.7 | *62.0* |
| **Banks — non-bank financial** | | | | | | | | | | |
| 1998 | 4 | 28,604 | 1 | 646 | 3 | 897 | 8 | 31,147 | 24.2 | *37.9* |
| 1999 | 3 | 20,816 | 1 | 800 | 12 | 4.130 | 16 | 25.746 | *20.8* | *56.4* |
| 2000[4] | 8 | 4,768 | 1 | 1,631 | 4 | 653 | 13 | 7.052 | *484* | *39.1* |
| **Non-bank financial — non-bank financial** | | | | | | | | | | |
| 1998 | 6 | 7,299 | 2 | *7.974* | 7 | 1.201 | 15 | 16.474 | 11.8 | 13.8 |
| 1999 | 11 | 15.508 | 4 | 378 | 19 | 21.888 | 34 | 37.774 | *15.7* | *40.7* |
| 2000[4] | 4 | 5,071 | 1 | 9 | 454 | 10 | 5,534 | 23.3 | 18.8 | |

1. Either acquirer or target company is resident in the euro area. Only completed or pending deals; announcement date volumes.
2. Of mergers and acquisitions in all countries.
3. In millions of US dollars.
4. 1 January to 10 April.

Source: Bloomberg.

There are several factors that might explain this preference for national transactions. One is that domestic mergers offer clearer opportunities for reducing costs by trimming overlapping branch networks and excess capacity. Another factor is that such transactions present, in principle, fewer complications in terms of conflicts of corporate and managerial cultures between the two merging organisations, one of the commonest reasons for lack of success. A third factor is that a strong domestic presence is seen as a prerequisite for successful cross-border alliances as it gives the institution a stronger bargaining position. Finally, there is evidence that economies of scale are more prevalent in the wholesale business, which is arguably easier to centralise, than in the retail sector, where a local presence is crucial. In this sense, what has been observed so far is likely to be only the first stage in this consolidation process, with later stages focusing more on the international dimension.

Developments in the competitive environment of financial services and the related structural developments in the banking sector are of relevance for the single monetary policy. In the past, banks in the euro area have been the main providers of financial services in rather fragmented and sheltered domestic markets. However, as barriers between various domestic or local market have been reduced, banks are facing more competition from one another as well as from other providers of financial services. These changes in the competitive environment have resulted in pressure for banks to become more efficient and have prompted initiatives to maintain competitive positions, one manifestation of which is the merger and acquisition activity, which has gathered pace significantly over the past few years. This pattern of restructuring and consolidation continued in 1999. In particular, the number of large institutions involved in banks mergers was relatively high throughout 1999.

The main driving forces behind this trend towards restructuring and consolidation in the euro area banking sector are technological developments, globalisation, deregulation and increased demand for sophisticated financial services, with the introduction of the euro appearing to have acted as a catalyst for these forces. Indeed, these driving forces are seen to be reshaping the market so that financial services should become more competitive and also more integrated both within the euro area and at the global level.

However, most of the merger and acquisition activity in the euro area banking sector has not so far taken place across national borders within the euro area. The focus on national mergers may be explained by an incentive to improve efficiency by removing overlapping operations as well as by defensive strategies. In addition, issues related to cultural proximity and expectations the mergers and acquisitions at the national level are more manageable than cross-border mergers also seem to play an important role. This national orientation towards mergers and acquisitions has given rise to some concerns about the increased market shares of the largest domestic institutions. However, while some adverse effects on competition at the local level cannot be rule out in the short term, the main picture emerging in respect of the financial services market seems to be one of increased competition and reduced fragmentation in the long term.

These changes in the competitive conditions in the banking market, as well as well as the possible effects on the financial strength of the banking sector, may be of relevance for the transmission mechanism of monetary policy. First, the speed of monetary policy transmission may be enhanced, as banks in more competitive markets tend to adjust their retail interest rates more rapidly in response to changes in market rates. Second, the relative importance of the credit channel of monetary policy may be altered as a result of changes in relationships between banks and their clients, which are particularly relevant for the financing of small businesses and households. Finally, increased competition in the euro area would tend to speed up the move towards a more integrated banking system across participating countries, which could reduce cross-country asymmetries in the transmission mechanism of monetary policy.

**TABLE 6**

**Cost structure in the banking sector**

| | *Number of branches per 1,000 inhabitants* | | | *Employment per $1,000 assets* | | |
|---|---|---|---|---|---|---|
| | *1990* | *1995* | *1998* | *1990* | *1995* | *1998* |
| United States | 0.29 | 0.28 | 029 | 0.40 | 0.32 | 0.29 |
| Japan[1] | 0.18 | 0.19 | 0.19 | 0.07 | 0.06 | 0.5 |
| Euro area[2] | 0.56 | 0.55 | 0.55 | 0.21 | 0.15 | 0.15[3] |

1. For the employment ratio, commercial banks only.
2 For the employment ratio. Germany. France. Italy, Belgium, the Netherlands and Spain only.
3. 1997.
Source: National data.

## Forex Markets Developments

The improvement in the euro area economic and financial outlook does not appear to be appropriately reflected in the recent developments in the external value of the euro. The exchange rate of the euro declined against the currencies of most trading partners of the euro area in 1999, in particular against the major currencies such as the US dollar, the Japanese yen and the pound sterling. In nominal effective terms, weighted against the currencies of the euro area's major trading partners, the euro weakened by around 8% from the first to the fourth quarter of 1999 and the average level of he nominal effective exchange rate index in 1999 was around 6% below the level in 1998. In early 2000 the euro's depreciation continued and the average level of the nominal effective exchange rate index in January and February 2000 was 2.6% below that in the fourth quarter of 1999 and 10.3% below that in the first quarter of 1999.

Throughout the first half of the 1999, the euro depreciated by around 12% against the US dollar. The most important factors that contributed to the strength of the dollar were the changes in the respective cyclical outlooks for the United States and the euro area and the better than expected performance of the US economy in the aftermath of the global financial crisis in the second half of 1998. There was a turnaround in mid-July, 1999 when positive readings of euro area economic indicators triggered a rebound of the euro, which was further fuelled by expectations of a slowdown in the US economy and risks of large corrections on US stock markets. However, subsequent developments diminished these fears, there were continuous strong growth and subdued inflationary pressures in the US economy. At end-1999 the euro was quoted at USD 1.005. The pattern of relative economic performance and related exchange rate movements continued into early 2000, when the euro continued to depreciate against the US dollar. On 7 March 2000 the euro was quoted at USD 0.959.

Among the major currencies the Japanese yen experienced the most significant appreciation in 1999, *albeit* amid high volatility. From the beginning to the end of 1999, the Japanese yen rose by 30% against the euro and by 11% against the US dollar. This strengthening occurred mainly against the background of significant current account surpluses and in parallel with a turn around of the economy, which started to record slightly more positive growth after the relatively deep recession of 1998. In line with this improvement in growth, long-term nominal interest rates in Japan recovered from the troughs of below 1% which they had reached in the second half of 1998 to around 1.8% at the end the year. At end-1999 the euro was quoted at JPY 102.73. The Japanese yen continued to be relatively volatile in early 2000 and displayed no strong overall trend. On 7 March 2000 the euro was quoted at JPY 103.00.[8]

**Price and Cost Developments in the Euro Area**

The recent rises in the inflation rate in the euro area, as

measured by the Harmonised Index of Consumer Prices (HICP), stem, to a large extent, from the combined effects of both oil price and exchange rate developments. The rate of euro area inflation, as measured by the year-on-year increase in the overall Harmonised Index of Consumer Prices (HICP), rose to 2.0% in February, up from a revised 1.9% in January, 2000. The annual rate of increase in total producer prices also rose in February, 2000 to 5.7%, from 5.1% in January 2000, mainly as a result of the developments in intermediate goods prices, which, in turn, were significantly affected by oil price developments. In this context, the annual rate of increase in capital and consumer good prices has slowly begun to rise in recent months. This might be an indication that the rise in intermediate goods prices is gradually feeding through the production chain.

The year-on-year increase in energy prices rose from 12.0% in January to 13.5% in February, 2000 (see Table-7). This rise was partly due to a base effect arising from the decline in the energy index from January to February 1999, the upward contribution from basis effects to the annual rate of increase in the energy component has not come to an end. In the short run, the rise in the oil rice to €28.4 per barrel in March 2000, up up from €27.6 per barrel in February, is likely to continue to exert upward pressure on the HICP energy component. However, in the light of the recent agreement by the Organisation of the Petroleum Exporting Countries (OPEC) to increase oil production, oil prices have declined since mid-March 2000. The annual rate of increase in the HICP energy component is expected to slow in the course of 2000.

Movements in 12-month HICP inflation rates this year should not be overemphasised, however, as they will be substantially influenced by base effects related to the strong growth in oil prices which has been having an upward effect on the energy price component of the HICP since March

**TABLE 7**

**Price and Cost Developments in the Euro Area**
(annual percentage changes, unless otherwise indicated)

| | 1997 | 1998 | 1999 | 1999 Q2 | 1999 Q3 | 1999 Q4 | 2000 Q1 | 1999 Oct. | 1999 Nov. | 1999 Dec. | 1999 Jan. | 2000 Feb. | 2000 Mar. |
|---|---|---|---|---|---|---|---|---|---|---|---|---|---|
| **Harmonised Index of Consumer Price (HICP) and its components** | | | | | | | | | | | | | |
| Overall index | 1.6 | 1.1 | 1.1 | 1.0 | 1.1 | 1.5 | — | 1.4 | 1.5 | .17 | 1.9 | 2.0 | — |
| *of which:* | | | | | | | | | | | | | |
| Goods | 1.2 | 0.6 | 0.8 | 0.6 | 0.9 | 1.5 | — | 1.4 | 1.5 | 1.7 | 1.9 | 2.0 | — |
| Foods | 1.4 | 1.6 | 0.5 | 0.6 | -0.2 | 0.4 | — | 03 | 0.4 | 0.5 | 0.4 | 0.6 | — |
| Processed food | 1.4 | 1.4 | 0.9 | 0.8 | 0.6 | 0.9 | — | 0.8 | 0.9 | 1.0 | 1.0 | 1.0 | — |
| Unprocessed food | 1.4 | 1.9 | 0.0 | 0.3 | — | -0.4 | -0.3 | -0.2 | -0.5 | -0.1 | — | | |
| Industrial goods | 1.0 | 0.1 | 1.0 | 0.6 | 1.5 | 2.1 | — | 1.8 | 2.0 | 2.6 | 3.2 | 3.3 | — |
| Non-energy industrial goods | 0.5 | 0.9 | 0.7 | 0.7 | 0.6 | 0.6 | — | 0.5 | 0.6 | 0.6 | 0.8 | 0.5 | — |
| Energy | 2.8 | -2.6 | 2.2 | 0.5 | 4.6 | 7.8 | — | 6.3 | 7.1 | 10.0 | 12.0 | 13.5 | — |
| Services | 2.3 | 1.9 | 1.6 | 1.6 | 1.5 | 1.5 | — | 1.4 | 1.5 | 1.6 | 1.7 | 1.7 | — |

| | 1997 | 1998 | 1999 | 1999 Q2 | 1999 Q3 | 1999 Q4 | 2000 Q1 | 1999 Oct. | 1999 Nov. | 1999 Dec. | 1999 Jan. | 2000 Feb. | 2000 Mar. |
|---|---|---|---|---|---|---|---|---|---|---|---|---|---|
| **Other price and cost indicators** | | | | | | | | | | | | | |
| Industrial producer prices[1] | 1.1 | -0.8 | 0.0 | -1.3 | 0.7 | 3.2 | — | 2.2 | 3.1 | 4.1 | 5.1 | 5.7 | — |
| Unit labour costs[2] | 0.7 | 0.0 | — | 1.5 | 0.7 | — | — | — | — | — | — | — | — |
| Labour productivity[4] | 0.8 | 1.5 | — | 0.5 | 1.1 | — | — | — | — | — | — | — | — |
| Compensation per employees[2] | 2.4 | 1.5 | — | 2.0 | 1.7 | — | — | — | — | — | — | — | — |
| Total hourly labour costs[3] | 2.5 | 1.7 | 2.1 | 1.9 | 2.2 | 2.2 | — | — | — | — | — | — | — |
| Oil prices (EUR per barrel)[4] | 17.1 | 12.0 | 17.1 | 15.0 | 19.7 | 23.0 | 27.1 | 20.8 | 23.5 | 24.8 | 24.9 | 27.6 | 28.4 |
| Commodity prices[5] | 12.9 | -12.5 | -3.1 | -8.2 | 1.1 | 14.0 | 19.9 | 10.7 | 11.9 | 19.3 | 19.4 | 20.2 | 20.2 |

Source: Eurostat, national data, International Petroleum Exchange, HWWA—Institut fur Wirtschaftsforschung (Hamburg) and ECB calculations.

1. Excluding construction.
2. Whole economy.
3. Whole economy (excluding agriculture, public adminstration, education, health and other services).
4. Brent Blend (for one-month forward delivery). In ECU up to December 1998.
5. Excluding energy. In euro: in ECU up to December 1998.

1999. What matters for monetary policy are the trends underlying the outlook, for price stability in the medium term. In this respect, monetary and credit developments confirm that liquidity in the euro area is still ample. The exchange rate of the euro also remains a cause for concern with regard to future price stability. In the context of the favourable prospects for strong economic growth, the impact of these developments on inflationary pressures will need to be monitored closely.

Against the background, monetary policy must remain vigilant in assessing upside risks to price stability and take appropriate action if and when required. Monetary policy has to be forward-looking, since responding to risks to price stability before they materialise will avoid the need for a costly process of disinflation at a large. Such a forward-looking approach is clearly also the best contribution monetary policy can make to ensuring the sustainability of economic growth.

**Emerging Trends in the Labour Markets**

Gradual reduction in unemployment continued at the beginning of 2000. In February 2000 the standardised rate of unemployment in the euro area stood at 9.5%, unchanged from the previous month, and 0.8 percentage point below the rate recorded a year earlier. Although it is not evident, owing to rounding effects, the slightly downward trend in the unemployment rate continued in February, 2000. Indeed, in January and February 2000 the rate of unemployment declined at the same pace on average, as in 1999, thus confirming the continuation of the pattern of a gradual reduction in unemployment.

With regard to age groups, the unemployment rate fell slightly in February, 2000 for both those under 25 years of age and those aged over 25 (see Table-8). For the former group, the rate of unemployment stood at 17.9%, i.e. 0.1 percentage point below the rate recorded a month earlier. The decline at the beginning of 2000 was, therefore, less pronounced than in the latter part of 1999, during which a particularly strong decline in youth unemployment was recorded. By contrast, for those over 25 years of age, the recent decline in the unemployment rate, to 8.3% in February 2000, compares favourably with the pattern of unchanged rates at the end of 1999. At the national level, the general pattern of a downward trend in the unemployment rate continued in February, 2000.

In short, the pace of net job creation is likely to gain momentum during the course of 2000, in line with the strengthening of economic activity and, accordingly, unemployment should benefit from this favourbale scenario. At the same time, in addition to the improvement in the labour market brought about by cyclical effects, further advances in structural reforms would help to consolidate gains in employments and to strengthen the reduction in unemployment.

This phase of economic growth in the euro area provides a great opportunity to make further progress in bringing down the high level of uemployment in the euro area. An important means of achieving this will be continued wage moderation, which, in turn, will also help to contain inflationary pressures. This notwithstanding, the key to achieving a sustainable reduction in the level of unemployment is structural reform in the euro area. Only when labour markets are more flexible and competitive pressures are high will it be possible to prevent bottlenecks on the supply side from triggering upward pressures on prices at a relatively early stage of an economic recovery.

Fiscal policy has to play its part in this context. The favourbale economic prospects will lead to higher tax revenues. In line with the Stability and Growth Pact, it is not opportune to use these extra revenues for higher spending. Now is the

**TABLE 8**

**Unemployment in the Euro Area**
(as a percentage of the labour force; seasonally adjusted)

| | 1997 | 1998 | 1999 | 1999 Q1 | 1999 Q2 | 1999 Q3 | 1999 Q4 | 1999 Sep. | 1999 Oct. | 1999 Nov. | 1999 Dec. | 2000 Jan. | 2000 Feb. |
|---|---|---|---|---|---|---|---|---|---|---|---|---|---|
| Total | 11.5 | 10.9 | 10.0 | 10.3 | 10.0 | 9.9 | 9.7 | 9.8 | 9.7 | 9.7 | 9.6 | 09.5 | 9.5 |
| Under 15 years[1] | 23.2 | 21.3 | 19.0 | 20.0 | 19.2 | 18.8 | 18,1 | 18.6 | 18.3 | 18.2 | 18.0 | 18.0 | 17.9 |
| 25 years and over[2] | 9.9 | 9.4 | 8.7 | 8.9 | 8.8 | 8.7 | 8.5 | 8.6 | 8.5 | 8.5 | 8.4 | 8.5 | 8.3 |

Source: Eurostat.

Note: According to ILO recommendations.

1. In 1999 this category represented 23.1% of total unemployment.

2. In 1999 this category represented 76.9% of total employments.

time to step up fiscal consolidation in order to help to reduce further the debt-to-GDP ratios in the euro area and to approach more quickly fiscal budgetary positions in surplus or balance.

**Fiscal Developments in the Euro Area**

The current phase of strong growth in the Euro area provides a good opportunity to make progress in reducing and restructuring fiscal expenditure and reforming pension arrangements. At the end of 1999 and in the early 2000 most euro area countries submitted updated stability programmes covering the period up to 2002-03 to the European Commission in accordance with the Stability and Growth Pact. According to the Stability and Growth Pact, all EU Members States are committed *to adhere to the medium-term objective of budgetary positions close to balance or in surplus.* This objective is considered appropriate in order *to allow Member States to deal with normal cyclical fluctuations while keeping the government deficit within the 3% of GDP reference value.* In addition, the safety margin implied by the *close to balance or in surplus* requirement should also cover other burdens on public finances. These include unexpected tax shortfalls and expenditure overruns, the need to ensure a fast decline in debt ratios in those countries in which they still stand above 60% and the necessity of coping with an increase in expenditure relating to the ageing of the population in the future. Moreover, the Broad Economic Policy Guidelines for 1999 urged Member States, *provided the economic outlook unfolds better than expected in their stability or convergence programmes, to frontload the budgetary adjustment efforts envisaged in their programmes as of the year 2000 and, where programmes target minimum adjustment to aspire to more ambitious objectives and update stability/convergence programmes accordingly.*

According to the updated stability programmes, economic growth assumptions for 2000 and the next few years were often revised slightly upwards as compared with the original programmes (see Table-9). In this environment governments aim to further consolidate general government budgetary positions in the medium term and partly also to exceed previous consolidation targets. In this sense, some of the updated stability programmes clearly represent a step forwards compared with the original programmes, while others could be more ambitious. All in all, government plans would imply a further improvement in the average euro area deficit and debt-to-GDP ratio in 2000 and beyond.

A few countries already appear to comply fully with the requirements of the Stability and Growth Pact and are expected to do so throughout the forecasting horizon. Most countries are expected to achieve deficits of below 0.5% of GDP or fiscal surpluses and debt levels of below 60% of GDP by 2002-03. According to current plans, all euro area Member States are expected to be able to cope with normal cyclical fluctuations by that time. However, some governments envisage only very modest deficit cuts in 2000, while stronger efforts are planned for later years. Such a strategy implies that unforeseen developments might put fiscal targets at risk.

**International Role of the Euro**

The introduction of the euro on 1 January 1999 was a major event with important implications not only inside but also outside the euro area. The euro is the second most widely used currency at the international level, as a result of both the legacy of the former national currencies replaced by the euro and the economic weight of the euro area in the world economy. The development of the euro as an international currency will mainly be a market-driven process. In particular, the use of the euro by private agents as an investment and financing currency, as well as a payment and vehicle currency, will play a prominent role. The decisions of private sector agents will be influenced to a large extent by the degree of integration, liquidity and diversification of financial markets and by the cross-border relationships of the euro area. Moreover, the

**TABLE 9**

**Member States' 1998-99 stability programmes and their 1999-2000 updates**

| | *Real GDP growth rate (%)* | | | | *Budget balance ratio (% of GDP)* | | | | *Debt ratio (% of GDP)* | | | |
|---|---|---|---|---|---|---|---|---|---|---|---|---|
| | *2000* | *2001* | *2002* | *2003* | *2000* | *2001* | *2002* | *2003* | *2000* | *2001* | *2002* | *2003* |
| **Belgium** | | | | | | | | | | | | |
| Stability programme | 2.3 | 2.3 | 2.3 | . | -1.0 | -0.7 | -0.3 | . | 112.2 | 109.6 | 106.8 | |
| Updated Programme | 2.5 | 2.5 | 2.3 | 2.3 | -1.0 | -0.5 | 0.0 | 0.2 | 112.4 | 108.8 | 105.0 | 101.3 |
| **Germany** | | | | | | | | | | | | |
| Stability programme | | 2½ | — | . | -2 | 1½ | -1 | — | 61 | 60½ | 59½ | . |
| Updated Programme | 2½ | | 2 | | -1¼ | -1 | -1 | - | ½61 | 60½ | 59½ | 58½ |
| addendum to the Updated programme | 2½ | | 2½ | . | -1 | -1½ | -1 | -½ | 61 | 60½ | 59½5 | 8½ |
| **Spain** | | | | | | | | | | | | |
| Stability programme | | 3.3 | | . | -1.0 | -0.4 | 0.1 | . | 64.3 | 61.9 | 59.3 | . |
| Updated Programme | 3.7 | | 3.3 | | -0.8 | -0.4 | 0.1 | 0.2 | 62.8 | 60.6 | 58.1 | 55.8 |
| **France** | | | | | | | | | | | | |
| Stability programme | | 3.0 | | . | - | - | -0.8 | . | . | . | 57.1 | . |
| Updated Programme | 3.0 | | 3 | | -1.7 | -1.3 | -0.9 | -0.3 | 59.4 | 59.0 | 58.1 | 57.2 |
| **Ireland** | | | | | | | | | | | | |
| Stability programme | 6.4 | 5.8 | . | . | 1.4 | 1.6 | . | . | 47.0 | 43.0 | . | . |
| Updated Programme | 7.4 | 6.5 | 5.7 | . | 1.2 | 2.5 | 2.6 | . | 46.0 | 40.0 | 36.0 | . |

| | | | | | | | | | | | | |
|---|---|---|---|---|---|---|---|---|---|---|---|---|
| **Italy** | | | | | | | | | | | | |
| Stability programme | 2.8 | 2.9 | . | . | 1.5 | -1.0 | . | . | 110.9 | 107.0 | . | . |
| Updated Programme | 2.2 | 2.6 | 2.8 | 2.9 | -1.5 | -1.0 | -0.6 | -0.1 | 111.7 | 108.5 | 104.3 | 100.0 |
| **Luxembourg** | | | | | | | | | | | | |
| Stability programme | | 3.7 | | . | 1.2 | 1.3 | 1.7 | . | . | . | . | . |
| Updated Programme | 4.3 | 4.4 | 4.5 | 4.6 | 2.5 | 2.6 | 2.9 | 3.1 | *. | *. | *. | *. |
| **The Netherlands** | | | | | | | | | | | | |
| Stability programme | | 2¼ | | . | . | . | -1.1 | . | . | . | 64.5 | . |
| Updated Programme | 2.5 | 2.0 | 2.0 | . | -0.6 | -1.3 | -1.1 | - | 62.3 | 61.8 | 61.0 | . |
| **Austria** | | | | | | | | | | | | |
| Stability programme | 2.6 | 2.1 | 2.2 | . | -1.7 | -1.5 | -1.4 | . | 62.2 | 61.2 | 60.0 | . |
| Updated Programme | - | - | - | — | - | - | - | - | - | - | - | - |
| **Portugal** | | | | | | | | | | | | |
| Stability programme | 3.2 | 3.2 | 3.3 | . | -1.5 | -1.2 | -0.8 | . | 55.8 | 54.7 | 53.2 | . |
| Updated Programme | 3.3 | 3.6 | 3.6 | 3.5 | -1.5 | -1.1 | -0.7 | -0.3 | 57.1 | 55.2 | 53.3 | 51.0 |
| **Finland** | | | | | | | | | | | | |
| Stability programme | 2.7 | 2.6 | 2.6 | . | 2.2 | 2.1 | 2.3 | . | 46.4 | 44.8 | 43.2 | . |
| Updated Programme | 3.9 | 3.0 | 2.6 | 2.6 | 4.7 | 4.2 | 4.6 | 4.7 | 42.9 | 40.7 | 38.0 | 35.2 |

* *According to Luxembourg's updated stability programme general government debt, which in total represented 4.3% of GDP in 1999, will remain relatively stable in the forecasting period.*

international role of the euro will be affected by the economic conditions in the euro area. Thereby highlighting the contribution of all economic policies to a sound and stable currency.

Since the internationalisation of the euro, as such, is not a policy objective, it will be neither fostered nor hindered by the Eurosystem. The orientation of the Eurosystem's monetary policy towards price stability will remain a major factor behind investors' confidence in the euro. Conversely, the Eurosystem is aware of potential implications for the conduct of its monetary policy of the internationalisation of the euro. These potential implications should not be allowed to impair its ability to maintain price stability.

The emergence of the euro area — with characteristics similar to those of the two other major economic regions, the United States and Japan, in terms of large size and low trade openness — and the expected increase of the euro's international use also have implications for international co-operation. Given its economic weight in the world (more than one-fifth in terms of GDP), the euro area is generally expected to play an important role in the process of international co-operation. Fewer players at the global level and more balanced relationship among them should, in principle, facilitate international co-operation, while at the same time strengthening the awareness of each layer of the need to assume his respective responsibility. This process is assisted by regular exchanges of views and consultations among major economic areas. In addition to adequate representation arrangements, a more efficient international co-operation process and a smaller risk of policy inconsistencies require the euro area to take a single position whenever appropriate. This is also supportive of the euro area exerting an international influence commensurate with its economic weight and further limits the risk for the Eurosystem of being pressed to pursue inappropriate short-term-oriented policy measures, which would undermine longer-term domestic and thereby external stability.

## THE EURO AREA: *THE TASK AHEAD*

EMU's foreign relations with other states elicit a great variety of hopes, but also uncertainties and fears. These are by no means limited to speculation and conjecture as to the Euro's future role in the world monetary system. In part, they go far beyond this and extend to questions of the influence and power of the European Union in international politics. While some aspire to and expect greater weight for Europe on the world political stage, even to the extent of parity with the USA, others see dramatic consequences looming for transatlantic relations. Harvard professor Martin Feldstein even prophesies—completely contrary to the foundation-stone theory, according to which the launch of the euro (somehow) coincides with the laying of the foundations for further political unification of Europe—a destabilisation of the political cohesiveness of Europe itself, and certainly a straining, if not a disruption of relations with the USA: potential powder kegs that could unnecessarily expose the prospects of transatlantic relations to enormous tensions in the years to come.

Robert Mundell, Professor of Economics at Columbia University and the Johns Hopkins Bologna Center, takes his chain of arguments welcoming the Euro's introduction in the diametrically opposite direction: He does see a fundamental political weakness in the euro due to the lack of a political unit contiguous with the EMU area. Also, the euro has no fallback in a medium of stable value as we know it from the periods of fixed exchange parities under the Gold Standard and of effective gold-dollar parities under Bretton Woods. These diagnosed weaknesses of EMU and the euro are mitigated, however, by the transatlantic partnership in NATO; in any case, the western convictions and defence community has not only now provided a guarantee of security for half a century, it has guaranteed the very economic and political stability of western Europe. It has been helped in this by the substantial gold and currency reserves of the EU member states.[10]

Slightly exaggerated, the controversy boils down to whether the euro—the intended milestone of European integration—will be not only Europe's downfall, but a risk factor for transatlantic relations as well, or, conversely, whether the common currency will not only smooth and propel European integration, but also help improve relations on this and the far side of the Atlantic. With a view to monetary policy, are the conditions for more stable exchange rates already in place? And if so, is it true that what's good for Europe is good for the United States? Neither question—as to the cohesion of the European states among themselves and as to their capacity for good, stable cooperation with the USA (and the rest of the world)—can yet be conclusively answered; the European institutions, and above all the member states themselves, have yet to lay down key elements in both respects, and are approaching the task more with hesitation than with resolve.

If in adopting the common currency, the EMU member states have indeed converged upon a trajectory of steady growth, then this ought to be in the interests of their trading partners, who should likewise profit from rising employment and higher incomes in Europe by way of open markets. As regards free movement of goods, however, transatlantic relations are currently far from tranquil. In trade policy especially, the conflicts now lie manifestly and painfully bare. A further hardening of the fronts, it seems, cannot be ruled out. The dispute between America and Europe could then exert a heavy strain on the WTO. The EU, and particularly the traditional exporting nations (Belgium, the Netherlands, the Scandinavian countries and Germany), must not pass up the opportunities offered by rapid, continued development of the open trade system—not least in view of the protectionist mood now spreading in the American public, and also the latent instability of European trade policy, which only turned in favour of free trade following the entry of Austria, Finland and Sweden in 1995. The new record attained by the American growth performance as well as its trade deficit will give only temporary relief

The European Union must in no circumstances respond to the fixed internal exchange rates delivered by the euro by retreating into itself in the mistaken belief that its own market is big enough. The spectre, invoked by its trading partners and some of its own member states, of a *Fortress Europe* beset by structural sclerosis and long-term unemployment—a uniform single market encompassing the agricultural sector and guarded at its periphery by high and effective common barriers—can only be exorcised by decisive and credible action. This is the only course befitting of a world reserve currency. The safest approach to begin with would be a clear declaration of commitment to the WTO by finally accepting the decisions of the arbitration process, as is expected as a matter of course from all other parties including the USA. Further groundwork for intensive cooperation in the economic and political spheres has already been laid by the New Transatlantic Agenda, developed between the European Union and the US administration as early as 1995, and the Transatlantic Partnership on Political Cooperation of 1998. Among other things, these propose a transatlantic free-trade zone, though this vision must not be allowed to distort the further development of free world markets in general. Even so, there is much here that can and should be implemented to secure and spur the economy, innovation, growth and employment, chiefly on this, but to an decisive extent also on the other side of the Atlantic.

Some also hope to see greater stability in the exchange rate between the euro and the US-dollar, or at least, more than used to obtain between the American currency and the D-Mark, other member currencies of the European Monetary System, and even the yen. But does swapping eleven national currencies for supranational money and a larger currency area combined with mere political ambition automatically mean more stable exchange rates? In view of the Euro's brief history, any assessment would be premature, but developments so far appear to suggest that it doesn't. From the beginning of the year, the Euro's dollar exchange rate—to the surprise of markets and politicians alike—slid continuously downwards until the new currency had lost a total of 14 per cent of its initial value; the subsequent, moderate corrective rise shows the cause to have been the diverging growth prospects and hence monetary-policy perspectives of the two economic zones.[11] Going by the more recent economic indicators and survey data published since mid-July, the two economies have now at least begun to converge. In other words, the euro is back on drier land. Neither reason for a renewed Europhoria nor of a Europhobia.

To be sure, the downward pressure on the euro since its launch is not solely a result of dashed hopes in the supposedly automatic growth and business-stimulating effects—whose non-appearance, of course, had causes of its own—of economic and monetary union. There were also a number of stress factors relating to integration policy in Europe, above all the still manifest lack of real political support at national level for the new currency's stability after the final selection of participants in May 1998 and its successful launch at the beginning of 1999. At first, a belief appeared to spread among the national governments that once the ESCB and ECB had been established, monetary stability was thenceforth the responsibility of those institutions alone—and that, having successfully undergone the preparatory process of convergence, which also entailed lasting consolidation of their state finances, the issue was no longer current. This belief must be energetically opposed, as must the idea that the fiscal convergence criteria of the Maastricht Treaty are less important now that EMU is in place. In fact, the opposite is true: a common currency that lacks nationhood—a state, a people and a respectable central budget—requires that most of the work of finding an optimum policy mix must come from the member states themselves. No-one else can do this for them, not least because the problems of unemployment and the tasks of reforming taxes, contributions and welfare provision in conjunction with the labour market must be addressed at national level.

Healthy and lastingly reformed state finances are not just a minimum requirement for securing overall economic stability under monetary union, but a key condition of continuous and job-creating growth. It is here that the argument comes full circle. Past experience has shown that excessive debt ratios (like the implicit borrowing entailed by welfare provision in an ageing society) deeply shake confidence in the economic outlook and, in conjunction with large budget deficits, severely narrow the scope and thus, critically, the stabilising potential of fiscal policy—almost to the point of eliminating it underglobalised financial markets and free flow of capital. In such conditions, long-term interest rates are higher than elsewhere and also (as they contain a risk premium) higher than necessary, and private investment is withheld. This stunts the growth of productive potential; income, employment and consumption prospects deteriorate in the long term; and state finances and the welfare budget deteriorate yet further.

The hard work and perseverance needed to break out of this economically and politically debilitating vicious circle has been well demonstrated by Belgian fiscal policy over a period of many years. Its present objective, of maintaining the primary surplus (as in 1997 and 1998) at 6% of GDP for the foreseeable future indeed demands enormous effort. Nonetheless, the policymakers should continue the consolidatory course followed since 1993, and keep on their endeavours to reduce the debt ratio from its still unusually high level of 117% (as it stood at the end of 1998). The next stage entails implementing the Belgian stability programme, which stipulates a gradual reduction of new borrowing from 1.3% of GDP last year to 0.3% in 2002. Barring economic setbacks, this should even mean aiming for a balanced budget.

Regrettably, the fiscal policy efforts of other EMU participants have been far less ambitious, as the ECB has repeatedly pointed out.[12] The alarming fact here in terms of stability and integration policy is that, in the foreseeable future, the majority of the EMU member states will probably not even attain the pact's medium-term objective of running an approximately balanced budget in times of normal economic activity—let alone a surplus when their economies boom. And there are yet other serious signs that some governments, including those of the largest EMU members— Italy and France, and until recently also Germany as the so far leading protagonist of monetary stability and fiscal solidity and sustainability—are not honestly and lastingly facing up to the rules of the EMU game. This does not bode well for the resilience of the pact. In Germany, however, there may be a change around the corner. Here Mr. Eichel has been pushing through with an austerity-programme that brings about spending cuts in the forthcoming budgets up to 75 billion euros within the next four years. This *Zukunftsprogramm* is to be seen as a first step to put in order the public balance sheet in Germany thereby regaining room for fiscal manoeuvre.

Indeed it is now, in the decisive phase of confidence-building in the euro and its establishment as a new international currency, that governments ought to be discharging the obligations they adopted earlier and be energetically pursuing necessary structural reforms that they should have carried out before the launch. No doubt, at present with by and large very low interest rates, be it in the short run or the long run, the lack of fiscal consolidation and sustainability has been nicified by the fair weather conditions of price stability, a good deal of which imported by very favourable terms of trade now coming to an end, which may not last. The critical test is still ahead and nobody should think that raising money rates would be welcome then. The promises of governments will not keep themselves either, especially with growth weak and employment faltering. This is all compounded by a dramatic shift in the age structure of the population—as the average life expectancy lengthens by 5 whole years for every 25 that pass, combined with a dramatical fall in the birth-rate—and its inevitable consequences for pensions and their funding, factors which only serve to make the reform jam even worse. Thus, the reforms cannot wait any longer, on no count.

The situation is all the more urgent in view of Europe's most intransigent problem: unacceptably high unemployment. Research by international institutions (the IMF and the OECD) unanimously concludes that more than 80% of unemployment in the three largest economies of the euro- zone—generating about 75% of its GDP—can be traced to structural causes that can be neither eliminated nor circumvented by monetary policy, state spending programmes or international cooperation and integration. Nor is it possible to deny that the "Washington Consensus", which led IMF, World Bank and US government policies towards heavily indebted (developing) countries to focus upon macroeconomic stability throughout the 1980s, is no longer sufficient its task.[13] Until the Asian crisis 1997, the objectives of this corset of macroeconomic surveillance and conditioning were as follows: free trade, full capital convertibility (including full freedom of movement for short term capital), stable but adaptable exchange rates, budget consolidation, stability- promoting monetary policy, growth-promoting tax reforms combined with the unquestioning guarantee of ownership rights, and privatisation and deregulation of the state sector and industry. It has since become apparent—in part from the reform process in former socialist planned economies—that what is required is a complementary, more comprehensive policy approach giving greater and more systematic consideration to structural and above all microeconomic needs, to endogenous growth factors and, crucially, to safeguarding the credibility and trustworthiness of the monetary, regulatory and economic order. The legal framework, enforcement of justice, auditing and supervision in the private banking sector, education and training, and infrastructure building and transformation are especially important here.

Today, this need to supplement the macroeconomic essentials, including the imperative of stable money, with others of a microeconomic nature is fed by the financial market revolution, itself a product of the prevailing order of freely flowing capital, securitisation, disintermediation, and the increasing professionalism and computerisation of market participants. The universal trend of internationalisation and globalisation, tearing down the barriers between economies in its wake, is also driven by the headlong development of information and communication technologies with their ability to overcome or even annual geographical distance. This ongoing erosion of economic boundaries exposes not only companies to global competition, but also the "sovereign" economic, financial, fiscal and social policies of nation states, which now find themselves subjected to a rigorous process of international benchmarking. As a result, centres of economic activity are faced with rapidly mounting pressure to adapt and an increasing need to innovate.[14]

Both of these result from the globalisation of markets and

the growing locational freedom of choice enjoyed by free enterprise. They hit "old", cost-sensitive sectors of industry the hardest, and are not in the least held back by apparently ingrained, culturally and linguistically inspired national traditions and differences. They necessitate the independent nurturing of regional development potential, preferably in the form of an unmistakable investment profile backed by public- private partnerships, modern infrastructure, and training for a dedicated and motivated workforce.

There can be no doubt that the shifts in the global competitive arena raise serious questions as to the possible responses of government. *Is national economic policy powerless in the face of global market forces? Have the regions already been reduced to the much-feared "rat-race to the bottom", complete with social dumping and the gradual dismantling of the welfare state? Is "prostitution" by way of increasingly generous subsidies, taxes, land grants, infrastructure costs and the rest all that remains?* We all know that economics teaches that globalisation has great overall benefits for all economies and societies. Each nation can make better use of its comparative advantage. But this requires continuous adaptation, structural change, renewal and resolve—all the more since the launch of monetary union and the common currency, with its combination of vast opportunities, not inconsiderable risks and as yet undischarged obligations resulting from inadequate preparation.

The euro, long regarded by many as a kind of secret weapon against high unemployment, scant investment and faltering growth in Europe, in no way obviates the need for restructuring within. On the contrary! Precisely because monetary union further heightens competition (chiefly through increased price transparency, with the elimination of boundaries between national economies already far advanced in the single internal market and the open world-trade system), the log jam of reform must be cleared as fast as possible, and structural change pursued throughout the single currency area with yet greater resolve.

This relates first of all to wage policy, or the wage structure and the cost of labour. As nominal exchange rates are no longer there to serve as a corrective within the euro currency zone, and interest rates throughout it are under the strong equalising pressure of the common currency and of opportunities for arbitrage in merging financial markets, the remaining nominal (and real) factors—wages, contributions and taxes—must adapt all the faster and more enduringly to prevailing sectoral and regional conditions, at the risk, if they fail to do so, of perpetuating and entrenching unemployment. This no doubt will aggravate regional inequalities and hence "passive restructuring" in the form of brain drain. It is also beyond question that in the course of accelerated structural change, existing differences in development levels and regional divergencies in relative wage and productivity growth—let alone exogenous shocks—will affect regions yet more directly and rapidly than they have in the past; after all, a key instrument of prior policy is now lacking for good.

The elimination of geographical borders through European integration and globalisation not only means unions and employers must develop a new awareness focused more sharply on the regions; it places demands upon all areas of economic, fiscal, financial, labour market, skills and technology policy. These must be more strongly directed towards regionalisation, the promotion of growth and innovation, and fostering new enterprise. Hence there can be no question that the still pending completion of the Single Market, especially as regards indirect and direct taxes and energy, transport and environmental policy, necessitates an enormous amount of work to ensure not only that market participants always meet with a level playing field allowing fair and efficient competition, but also that sufficient concessions are made to the state in its own fields of equal opportunities and social justice.

The fact that it is now increasingly the regions that compete directly for investment, entrepreneurial managers, creative minds and mobile international capital is only one sign of their new part in an increasingly globalised world economy and world society combined with a reduced role for the nation state. The regions thus increasingly face economic and infrastructural responsibilities that national policy is no longer able to deal with in full. Yet this signals not general national impotence and the end of political power, but the need and opportunity for a new politics, which, though its outlines have yet to be defined within the nation state's democratic federal system, must be approached with resolve, moderation and reason.[15]

Today's nation states must consciously face up to all this so as to create, strengthen and continuously promote active regions—regions that draw upon their own endogenous potential. This is where centralisation, arbitrary apportionment of opportunities and indiscriminate subsidies meet their limits. The regions, then, with their task to generate trust for all the economic agents now provide the best leverage points for growth, investment and jobs. The key resources are enterprise, academic qualification and scientific creativity, readiness to cooperate across disciplines, and international reach. Today's knowledge-based society attaches far greater value to high quality schooling and vocational training, to colleges, universities and industrial research, and in fact to the entire system of knowledge and technology transfer, including developments such as the emerging academic infrastructure of networked databases. Without a doubt, this will result in a gradual marginalisation of the nation state, for example in education and training or even in welfare provision. There is an enormous need for deepening and widening reform here, for example in public investment, education and science.[16] Other changes must be actively pursued by the regions themselves. These include converting and extending former industrial regions into high-performance, broadly based service centres, including information and communications functions and attractive cultural offerings.

Upgrading Europe's regional policies to meet the challenges of the European single market, the single currency and increasing global integration requires that the regions and their public corporations be granted greater autonomy to revenue and spending, while firmly embedding their conduct in the confines of the European stability and growth pact as well as the rules of competition policy on market distortions. There is also substantial need for reform at the European level. The common European currency imposes a clearer division (i.e. assumption) of responsibilities in European, national and regional fiscal policy. The chances for effective economic growth must be improved throughout the regions. EMU must not be allowed to degenerate into a "transfer union" with increasing mass transfers to compensate for uneven development between member states. Because in EMU, only monetary policy has been surrendered to supranational control, and economic, fiscal, structural and social policies remain almost entirely in national hands—such rudimentary plans for common policy-making as do exist tending to fall foul of individual member's right of veto—strict application of the European stability and growth pact as well as competition policy is imperative, not least to ensure that the fruits of expansionary regional and national spending can be harvested where they were sown.

The elements of a European financial constitution that are incorporated in the EC Treaty, however, represent only the first building block of a European order governed by the principle of subsidiarity. They make an indispensable contribution towards EMU's lasting success, but they do represent more of a minima moralia than a vision of the future of Europe. Supreme efforts are still required before the

European Union—particularly an extended Union encompassing successful reforming states in central and eastern Europe—can become an enduring political structure, before it really can speak with one voice, and before it can take up its due position on the world political and economic stage so that its international partners and the financial markets believe and trust in it—and so that the common currency is given the lasting perspective of stability and solidity that is vital for an international transaction, investment and reserve currency with an anchoring function extending beyond European borders. Not least for the sake of the supranational currency, the European Union must prove itself, together with all its member states, as reliable, predictable, integrating, stability-conscious, open and fair partner in trade and politics.

## NOTES & REFERENCES

1. Although the value of exports of goods again grew strongly in January 2000, compared with the same month a year earlier, the goods surplus continued to diminish as imports grew even more rapidly, following the 20% rise in import prices in the 12-month period up to December 1999. Preliminary estimates suggest that around half of the rise in import prices resulted from the sharp increase in the dollar price of all, with the decline in the euro accounting for most of the remainder.
2. The analysis of developments in short-term interest rates was complicated, however, particularly in the last part of 1999, by the effective of market concerns about the impact that the transition to the year 2000 might have no money market interest rates. The associated risk premium led to a pronounced change in market rates as soon as they spanned the end of the year. This leap was most pronounced for rates at the short end of the money market curve. However, after the successful transition to the year 2000, the risk premium in money market rates quickly disappeared.
3. In 1999 the ECB managed to steer short-term money market rates by means of he interest rate which was applied to the main refinancing operations. The overnight interest rate, as measured by the EONIA (the "euro overnight index average"), was generally very close to the rate applied to the main refinancing

operations, the average spread between the two rates being equal to 3 basis points in 1999. The volatility of the EONIA rate was relatively low. Somewhat larger fluctuations were normally only recorded towards the end of the reserve maintenance periods, which is when the minimum reserve constraint on the banking system becomes binding. In view of the steady pattern of the EONIA rate, the ECB saw no need to conduct fine-tuning open market operations in the course of 1999. Other money market rates were equally stable, apart from episodes when market participants anticipated a move in ECB interest rates or, towards the end of the year, when short-term interest rates rose on account of market concerns related to the transition to the year 2000.

4. In order to assess how various underlying factors may have influenced nominal long-term bond yields in the euro area in 1999, it is useful to remember that, broadly speaking, the nominal yield on a government bond with a specified time to maturity can be broken down into three elements. These are the real interest rate required by investors for holding the bond until it matures, compensation for the average expected inflation rate during the life of the bond, and a component associated with term or risk premia linked to, inter alia, uncertainty about future rates of inflation. The yield on index-linked bonds can assist in producing this breakdown. The differential between a long-term bond yield and the real yield available on an index-linked bond of the same maturity is generally known as the "break-even" inflation rate. This is because with this rate of inflation, the expected return to an investor will be the same regardless of whether the investment is made in a fixed nominal income or an index-linked bond. However, the break-even inflation rate is not a direct measure of inflation expectations because it does not take into account the role of various risk premia. On the one hand, the break-even rate tends to overestimate expected inflation since the yield on the nominal bond usually contains an inflation risk premium. On the other hand, the lower level of liquidity that usually characterises index-linked bond markets implies that the real yield on index-linked bonds may incorporate a liquidity premium. The only index-linked bonds that exist in the euro area were issued by the French Treasury with 10-year and 30-year maturities. The break-even inflation rate of these bonds refers to a specific measure of the French Consumer Price Index (CPI, namely the CPI excluding tobacco, and does not refer to the euro area HICP. These properties illustrate the limitations of this indicator of evaluating developments in the euro area.

5. The largest private issuers of debt securities in 1999 were banks, which accounted for the bulk of total private sector issuance volume, followed respectively by non-financial corporations, other financing companies and utility companies. Taking a global prespective, the growth of net issuance of euro-denominated debt securities during 1999 was particularly strong when compared with US dollar denominated debt securities issuance. Yen-denominated issuance also experienced a strong recovery in 1999 when compared with 1998.

6. Stock prices in the euro area remained relatively subdued in the first few months of 1999, reflecting the sluggish pace of economic recovery in the euro area. Later on, as expectations regarding the pace of future activity began to improve, stock prices in the euro area started to edge upwards. The resilience of this increase to the parallel increases in long-term bond yields in the euro area was notable and appeared to indicate strong underlying expectations for corporate profitability and dividend growth in the euro area. The improvement in stock prices was initially more apparent for those firms with a higher degree of exposure to the external economic environment than in the stock prices of firms with a more domestic orientation. To the extent that larger firms tend to have a higher degree of exposure to the external economic environment, this was indicated by the stronger performance of the Dow Jones EURO STOXX 50 index, which is compared with that of the broad Dow Jones EURO STOXX index.

   In the second half of 1999, as market participants became more optimistic with regard to the prospects for domestic demand growth in parallel with improvements in business and consumer confidence, stock price increases became more broadly based across the different sectors of the economy. Towards the end of the year, particularly after mid-October, relatively sharp stock price increases were seen in the technology and telecommunications sectors. In these sectors, by the end of 1999, stock prices had increased by 134% and 105% respectively compared with the end of 1998, which contributed significantly to aggregate euro area stock price increases. Increases in the technology and telecommunications sectors seemed to be partly linked to favourable profit growth expectations following corporate restructuring and mergers and acquisitions activity in these sectors and significant expansion of the internet business.

7. Euro area companies involved in merger and acquisition activities and operations such as leveraged buyouts—in which the takeover of a company is financed through the issuance of high-yield

bonds—financed these deals, to a significant extent, with large euro-denominated debt securities issues, which often served to repay bridging facilities (mainly syndicated loans). This led to some very large issues, unprecedented in the history of European capital markets.

8. In nominal effective terms, the euro declined by 2.2% in March 2000, driven by its weakening—in order of relative importance—against the Japanese yen, the pound sterling and the US dollar. The real effective exchange rate of the euro — a proxy for the euro area's price and cost competitiveness—exhibits a pattern similar to that of the nominal exchange rate, given that, since the launch of the euro, inflation differentials between the euro area and its main trading partners have been negligible.
9. The HICP is the measure of price used by the Governing Council for the purpose of assessing price stability. In order to fulfill the treaty requirement for CPI contented on a comparable basis, taking into account differences in natural definition, the HICP was developed by the European Commission (Eurostat) in close liaison with the national statistical institutes and the European Monetary Institutes and later the ECB.
10. "The euro has two weaknesses: it is not backed by a central state, and it has no fallback value. In an unstable world, these weaknesses would be fatal. But the present environment is far from unstable. ... If ... NATO survives in a post-euro world, the stability of the next decades should be as assured as die past four decades. Coupled with very substantial EU gold and currency reserves, which could be centralised or earmarked for the ECB if the need arises, membership in Nato suffices to mitigate the weakness of the EU central government". Robert Mundell. The Euro and International Monetary Reform, in: Entgrenzung ala Erkenntnis- und Gestaltungsaufgabe, Fesischrift fur Reimut Jochimsen. Berlin 1998, p. 337.
11. Changes in interest rate expectations between dollar and euro-denominated futures have mirrored this differing assessment of the two economies' vigour and monetary policy itineraries, doubtless influenced to a large extent by the strength of the dollar. In October 1998, the six-to-nine-month dollar forward rate was still 1% higher than the interest rate on comparable euro con- nets. By the beginning of July 1999, the spread had widened to nearly 3 percentage points. Soon afterwards, on 12 July this year, the euro reached its historical low of 1.0124 dollars, having lost 14% of its value since the start of the year (1.1789 dollars). It comes as no surprise that in the meantime

the euro has gained in value against the dollar following the incipient convergence of growth and interest rate expectations.

12. Scc Thc implementation of the Stability and Growth Pact, ECB Monthly Bulletin, May 1999.
13. See Joseph B. Stiglitz, More Instruments and Broader Gait buying toward the Post-Washington Consensus, WIDER Annual Lectures 2, Mind by UNU World Institute for Development Economics Research (UNU/WIDER). The United Nations University. Helsinki, January 1998.
14. See Reimut Jochimsen, Perspektiven der rcgionalen Slandortpolitik— Herausforderungen fUr Deutschland aufder Schwelle mm 21. Jahrhundert, RWI-Mitteilungen...zeitschnft fUr Wirtscbaftsforschung, Volume 50 (1999), No. 112, p. 1-12. No. 64: 28. September 1999
15. For a detailed analysis, see Reimut Jochimsen, Was bleibt von den Lehren der Nationaiolconornie in einer globalisierten Wirtschaft? In Franz Lehner (Ed.), Wertschopfung — MaBstibe einer neuen Okonomie, Schriftenreihe des IAT, Vol. 12. Munich 1999, p.49-81.
16. Germany, for example, has now fallen behind in terms of investment in education and training: with public and private expenditure on education and training at 5.8% of GDP, it now lies just below the OECD average (5.9%). Source: Bericht zur technologischen Leistungsrahigkeit der Bundesrepublik, January 1999.

# 2

# GLOBALISATION AND THE CHANGING ROLE OF COST MANAGEMENT

*Sherin Rathore*

For the past so many years since independence cost management was but a subliminal concern for corporate India. It was confined to the bottom of the driving force that can propel a corporation on the path to competitiveness. The reasons are not far to seek. A protected economy, a widely accepted cost plus pricing system and absence of customer power were enough reason to foster complacency with regards to cost management. In the initial years liberalisation further added fuel to the fire, for it ushered in a buying boom and companies concentrated only on meeting customer demand. Assured of an exploding market-keeping costs down was farthest from their concern. When, however, the first post liberalisation recession was ushered, the corporate India was jolted. Companies discovered to their horror that although sales have melted overnight the costs that they had indifferently allowed to settle round their midruffs was not easy to shed. The result the inevitable-unable to cut costs in proportion to dropping sales, company after company were knocked out. Business world's analysis of Indian companies by market capitalisation-considered to be a good indicator of performance that captures past achievements and future expectations, makes startling revelations.

In the past eight years (1990-98) India Inc. has been transformed beyond recognition. Many once mighty names do not make it to the Top 100 anymore. The spectacular drop outs include:

| *Sl. No* | *Rank 1990* | *Company* | *Sl. No.* | *Rank 1990* | *Company* |
|---|---|---|---|---|---|
| 1. | 11 | Century Enka | 6. | 35 | Hindustan Development |
| 2. | 22 | Oswal Agro Mills | 7. | 36 | J. K. Synthetics |
| 3. | 23 | SKF Bearing | 8. | 41 | Bombay Dying |
| 4. | 24 | Ballarpur Industries | 9. | 44 | Crompton Greaves |
| 5. | 25 | GNFC | 10. | 46 | SPIC |

Change your cost is the new mantra-this is also borne out by the B-T-Gallup MBA study 1998. Cost has become corporate India's worst enemy, its narrowest operational bottleneck and the single most important cause for its strategic myopia. However, a significant development has been a change in the perception towards cost reduction. Cost management is being resorted to not only by those organisations who have difficulty in surviving, but even market leaders are pursuing it as a strategic imperative. Infact, there has been a change in the perception of cost management itself, and this is a worldwide phenomenom. As Cyrus Khora of Price Water House Coopers observes, "worldwide the conventional approaches to cost reduction were characterised by across the board approaches, that had no focus and were arbitrary. It failed to improve structures and processes. The savings achieved were unsustainable in long run, cost resurfaced at various levels of the organisation sooner or later." Today cost management is part of a strategy for long term growth in both market share and profitability. The targets for cost reduction are market driven and reductions are sustained on an on going basis, so that the company improves its competitive position regularly. Used thus cost management effortlessly transcends the daily drudge of numbers, oriented cost cutting and launches the corporation into an orbit of global competitiveness. A company manages its cost as a holistic entity. Since it covers all functions, encompasses strategy as well as operations and subsumes everything and every one, it is also termed as Total Cost Management

## FROM COST ACCOUNTING TO TOTAL COST MANAGEMENT—*THE SHIFT*

In todays complex, dynamic and uncertain environment is not enough to play the cautious game of improvement. What is required in a habitat that is changing faster than its inhabitants, is adopting novel approaches not used before to source, manufacture, distribute and market a product in simple words to strategise. Michael E. Porter simplified the choices before firms by charting two routes for them: Cost leadership or differentiation. A firm can either be the lowest cost producer in its industry. Or it can demand a premium for adding more value to the product than its competitor the shift is reflected in:

### Cost Management Starts with Strategy

In a total cost, corporation cost management begins with strategy. Just as cost can be the determinant of strategy, so too does strategy become the determinant of cost. For every strategic choice a company makes, be it a new product, a new market etc. must be validated by its cost implications. Nor is the cost outcome of a strategic move a static decision making tool. On the contrary if a company finds a particular strategic position irresistible it must then find ways to minimise the cost impact

### Maximise Profits by Paring Down Costs to a Minimum

Total Cost Management (TCM) translates itself into the universal set of attempts to improve operational efficiencies in a way that lowers the costs of those operations. And in the process it yokes operations to strategy, ensuring that the former delivers the results that the latter has established.

**Scope of Cost Management Extends to Entire Value Chain**

In today's competitive environment it is no longer a company competing against another, but it is a value chain that competes against a value chain. There must therefore be complete cost control along the entire value chain not just one individual activity. Thus whether a company occupies just one slot in this chain or straddles several the inexorable logic of cost management a lies to it. Besides every single attempt to lower the cost of an activity is accompanied by an examination of its cost implications on upstream and downstream activities, both within and without the company. Total Cost Management thus revolves round 4 pivots.

1. Total Cost Consciousness
2. Total Cost Measurement
3. Total Cost Responsibility
4. Total Cost Improvement

A total cost corporation therefore links its battle against costs with its strategies. However, the relationship is not one way, costs also dictate strategy For instance the wisdom of a strategic move can be pre-audited in terms of the costs that it will entail. These costs are, however viewed from a strategic perspective e.g. the conventional cost accounting of a new contract would be measured in terms of the cost of the additional resources needed for it. And the margins from the venture would be considered in taking a go-no-go decision. A total Cost Corporation on the other hand will examine the impact of the move on costs elsewhere in totality the last dimension of total cost management is time. On the temporal scale too, cost management stretches all the way into the future. The company has to continuously pave its costs- instead of effecting a one-time improvement. Corporation must realise that it is only through total cost management. They would be able to achieve global cost competitiveness.

## REFERENCES

1. Hansen, Stephen C., Cost analysis, cost reduction and competition. *Journal of Management Accounting Research*, vol. 10. MAS, American Accounting Association, Florida, USA.
2. Foster, George, and S. Mark Young, 'Frontiers of Management Accounting research,' *Journal of Management Accounting Research*, vol. 9, MAS, American Accounting Association, Florida, USA.
3. Knocked out, *Business World*, September 1998.
4. Schonberger, Richard J., World Class Performance management, *Performance Exceller in Manufacturing and Service Organisaitons*, American Account Association, Florida, USA.
5. Copeland, T.T. Koller, and J. Murrin, Valuatran: Measruing and Managing the value of companies. 2nd edition, New York, NY: John Wiley & Sons, 1995.
6. Bonner, S.E. and N. Penningıon, *Judgement and Decision Making in Accounting*, Englewood Cliffs. NJ: Prentice Hall, 1999.

# 3

# EMERGING STOCK MARKETS, ECONOMIC DEVELOPMENT AND GROWTH

*Y.P. Singh*

World stock markets are booming, and emerging markets compose a disproportionately large amount of this boom. Over the past fifteen years, world stock market capitalisation rose by more than six times from $ 4.7 trillion and emerging market capitalisation jumped from less than 4 to 15 percent of total world capitalisation. Furthermore, emerging markets have become more integrated with world capital markets. Recent correlated movements in stock markets Of America, Europe and Asia bear testimony to this effects. International investors have noticed and participated in this rapid development of emerging stock markets. The investments have flowed to emerging markets in the form of direct and portfolio investments. Notably, portfolio flows of equity investment to emerging markets soared to $39 billions in 1995 from a mere $0.1 billion in 1985.

The rapid development of emerging stock markets has also attracted the attention of academia and policymakers. Recent research has focused on the benefits for investors of holding a globally diversified portfolio and the benefits for countries of removing barriers to international capital flows. On the policy front, many countries have reformed their laws and regulations and removed capital controls and other barriers to attract foreign capital flows. Earlier, direct foreign investment was being sought, but in the recent past even the portfolio flows are being welcomed. While analysts have studied emerging stock markets, economists need to acquire more information to understand the linkages between the functioning of stock markets and economic development and growth.

This paper focuses on four important issues: *First,* it defines the concept of stock market development. Here we try to compare liquidity, concentration, volatility, institutional development, and international integration across industrial and developing countries. Besides identifying general characteristic of these measures and defining stock market development, this will indicate the area of further research into the relationship between stock market development and financial intermediaries, corporate finance decisions, and economic growth. These measures, can be used for intercountry comparisons of the level of stock market development. *Second,* with With new data emerging from various economies, the relationships between stock markets and financial intermediaries can be established. However bankers in many countries may be worried that stock markets will steal business. The evidence in the literature points to the contrary. Countries with better-developed stock markets also have better-developed banks and nonbank financial intermediaries — such as finance companies, mutual funds, investment companies, brokerage houses, and pension funds — and countries with weak stock market tend to have weak financial intermediaries. Thus, stock market development goes hand-in-hand with other aspects of financial development. *Third,* this paper analyses the relationship between stock market development and long-run economic growth. New theoretical work shows how stock markets might boost long-run economic growth, and new empirical evidence supports this view. Specifically, the level of stock market development does a good job of predicting future economic growth. Therefore in developing countries capital market reforms should be high on the reform agenda. *Fourth,* in addition to above three apects, the paper tries to analyse the ties between stock market development and financing choices of firms. This important issue has never been previously investigated. It has been found that in many countries, improvement in the functioning of the stock market produces a higher debt- equity ratio in firms. While stock market development naturally inlays greater use of equity markets in raising capital, it also stimulates greater use of bank finance, so corporate debt-to-equity ratios actually rise in the initial phases of equity market development. Thus, for these countries, stock market and banks are not substitute sources of corporate finance; stock market development actually tends to increase the quantity of bank loans. Current research has already complemented these findings, the paper also builds a theoretical framework for understanding the interactions among banks, equity markets, and corporate decisions.

## STOCK MARKETS AND ECONOMIC DEVELOPMENT

This section introduces the analysis of the role of stock markets in corporate financing decisions and economic development, and presents new information on the co-development of financial intermediaries and stock markets. Early observations by Gurley and Shaw (1955, 1960) and Goldsmith (1969) indicate that as economies develop self financed capital investment first gives way to banks under mediated debt finance and later to the emergence of equity markets as an additional instrument for raising external funds. Financial structure — the mix of financial intermediaries and markets — changes as countries develop, as reflected by the differences in financial structure across countries and across time for individual countries.

The financial structure of economies varies with their income. Moving from poorer to richer economies, commercial banks and nonbank financial institutions grow in importance, while the role of the central bank diminishes. Furthermore, the financial system allocates more credit to the private sector as a share of GDP in richer countries; and richer countries tend to have larger overall financial systems and stock markets as percentages of GDP than poorer countries.

The financial structure evolves over time to persue the goals of economic growth. Gurely and Shaw state that at initial levels of development commercial banks are the dominant financial institutions. As economies grow, however, specialised financial intermediaries and equity markets develop and prosper. Initially the low-income economies had virtually no stock market activity or non bank institutions. But by 1990, however, both nonbanks and stock markets began to develop. The financial systems in middle - and high income economies have evolved in to a similar pattern. The middle- and high income economies are simply ahead of the low - income group.

Countries follow a financial development path that is not without its anomalies. Many differences in financial structure exist across countries at similar stages of economic development. For example, in the United Kingdom, the assets of commercial banks composed 65 percent of financial system assets in 1990, but this figure was almost 80 percent in Germany. Similarly, the assets of nonbanks were 15 percent of the financial system assets in Germany, but they were over 30 percent in the United Kingdom. These anomalies apply to developing countries also. Although there is a general trend involving financial structure and the level of GDP per capita, there are exceptions and differences within the categories exist.

## FINANCIAL INTERMEDIARIES AND ECONOMIC DEVELOPMENT

The financial structure evolved with economic development, and the stock market development is a part of this evolution. Research on the ties between financial development and economic growth revolves around almost exclusively on financial intermediaries. It is seen that central and commercial banks compose the vast majority of the financial systems of developing countries. Thus, development economists have focused on the ties between banks and economic growth. Moreover, statistics on central and commercial banks are readily available, until recently, but there were few data on stock markets in developing countries.

Theoretical reasons also underlie the profession's focus on financial intermediaries (see Gertler 1988; Levine 1996a, 1996b; and Stiglitz 1994). As argued by Diamond (1984), Stiglitz and Weiss (1981), and others, banks and other financial intermediators have important advantages over securities markets in reducing the information asymmetries that produce adverse selection problem and in ameliorating the inefficiencies created by information differences. For example, information asymmetries may create an adverse selection problem in securities markets (Akerlof 1970; Greenwadls, Stiglitz, and Weiss 1984; and Myers and Maijluf 1984). If potential investors cannot distinguish high-quality from low-quality firms, then outside purchasers of securities will only pay a price that reflects the average price which may be attractive to low-quality firms but unattractive to high-quality firms. In these circumstances the good quality firms will not want to issue securities at going prices, Thus, some theories emphasise the importance of financial intermediaries and the weakness of security markets in effectively allocating capital.

Goldsmith (1969) after using the data on thirty five countries found that: (a) the size of financial intermediaries as a share of GDP tends to rise with per capita income, and (b) when a country grows faster than the normal, the ratio of financial system assets to GDP also tends to experience above-average growth.

McKinnon (1973) argued that appropriate financial sector reforms expedite growth-inducing financial development. More recently, King and Levine (1993a, 1993 b) have examined the empirical ties between financial intermediation and long-run economic growth. The major findings from this research are that, after controlling for many other factors associated with long run growth, the level of financial intermediary development is strongly linked to long-run growth and finance does not simply follow economic growths. The predetermined component of financial development is a good predictor of future economic growth. They also showed a strong link between financial developments and the rate of long-run economic growth and asserted that it does not merely reflect contemporaneous shocks that affect both financial development and economic growth.

Existing evidence suggests that well-developed financial intermediaries assist economic development, but there is little evidence on the role of stock markets in economic growth. Thus to have a comprehensive view of the ties between financial and economic development, we must conceptually and empirically explore the relationship between the functioning of equity market and economic growth. This is where the new research should focus on.

## STOCK MARKETS AND ECONOMIC GROWTH

Stock market development is a common feature of financial and economic development. Many analysts view stock markets in developing countries as "casinos" that have little positive — and potentially a large negative— impact on economic growth. Other analysts argue that, because not much corporate investment is financed through the issuance of equity (Mayer 1988), stock markets are unimportant for economic growth. Various conceptual arguments emphasise the potentially positive neutral, or even negative implications of stock market development for economic growth.

Levine (1991) has shown that, stock markets may affect economic activity through the creation of liquidity. Many profitable investments require a long-term commitment of capital, but investors are often reluctant to relinquish control of their savings for long periods. Equity markets are liquid therefore these liquid equity markets make investment less risky and more attractive because they allow savers to acquire an asset—equity—and to sell it quickly and cheaply if they need access to their savings or want to alter their portfolios. At the same time, companies enjoy permanent access to capital raised through equity issues. By facilitating longer-term, more profitable investments, for long-term economic growth, by making investment less risky and more profitable, stock market liquidity can also lead to more savings and investment. Investors will come to the stock market if they can leave it whenever they want.

The crucial role of financial market liquidity in affecting the efficiency of physical production, enjoys historical support. According to Hicks (1969), new technological inventions did not ignite the industrial revolution in England in the eighteenth century. Most of the innovations that characterized the early phases of the industrial revolution had been invented much earlier. Rather, more liquid financial markets made it possible to develop projects that required large capital injections for long periods before the projects ultimately yielded profits. Without liquid capital markets, savers would have been less willing to invest in the large, long-term projects that characterised the industrial revolution; "the industrial revolution therefore had to wait for the financial revolution,".

The alternative views about the effect of liquidity on long-term economic growth, are as follows:

Increased liquidity can deter growth through at least three channels.

(a) By increasing the returns to investment, it makes greater investments to flow to secondary markets for immediate gains, leading to a fall in savings and investment in the real sectors of the economy. If saving rates fall enough and if there is an externality attached to capital accumulation, greater stock market liquidity could slow economic growth.

(b) By reducing the uncertainty associated with investment, greater stock market liquidity may reduce saving rates because of the ambiguous effects of uncertainty on savings. Less uncertainty makes an investment more attractive to risk-averse agents, less uncertainty also lowers demand for precautionary savings. Therefore the ultimate impact of lower uncertainly is lowering of the saving rate thereby affecting adversely the economic growth.

(c) Stock market liquidity may adversely affects corporate governance. Very liquid markets may adversely affect corporate governance. Highly liquid markets may encourage investor myopia. Because more liquid markets make it easy for dissatisfied investors to sell quickly and be out of the market. Liquid markets may weaken investors' commitment and reduce investors' incentives to exert corporate control. This view that emphasis enhanced stock market liquidity may actually hurt economic growth rather than promote it.

The economic growth can also be affected by risk diversification through internationally integrated stock markets. Since high-return projects also tend to be comparatively risky, stock markets that facilitate risk diversification encourage a shift to higher-return projects (Obstfeld 1994). Thus, better-functioning, and more internationally integrated stock markets boost economic growth by shifting society's savings into higher return investments, everything else being equal.

However every thing else is not always equal. As noted above, greater risk sharing — a reduction in uncertainty — can reduce the need for precautionary savings, reduce saving rates, and thereby retard economic growth. As a result, the theory is ambiuguous about the ultimate effects of greater risk sharing through internationally integrated stock markets on economic growth.

Moreover stock markets also affect incentives for investors to acquire information about firms. Therefore larger and more liquid markets make it easier for an investors who has obtained information about a firm to trade at posted prices. Thus, the investor can make money before the information becomes widely available and prices change (Kyle 1984). If investors can profit from obtaining information, they will be more likely to research on information and monitor firms, so that any information can be drawn to encash on. To the extent that larger, more liquid stock markets increase incentives to research firms, the improved information will improve resource allocation and accelerate economic growth. Stiglitz (1985, 1994) argues that developed stock markets are more efficient therefore incorporate the information in its prices immediately which are revealed in stock markets though price movements. This quick public revelation creates a free-rider problem; it reduces incentives for investors to expend lots of resources in obtaining information about firms because investors can get this information by observing prices.

Finally, stock markets may influence economic growth through changes in incentives for corporate control. We have already said that greater stock market liquidity may generate investor myopia and diffuse ownership that reduce incentives for investors to monitor carefully (Shleifer and Vishny 1995). A countervailing arguments is that stock markets that accurately value firms improve the efficacy of tying manager compensation to stock: if stock prices rise, both the managers, and the owners benefit, so that managers will have incentives to maximise firm's value (Jensen and Murphy 1990). Thus, well- developed stock markets can help align the interests of owners and managers and thereby spur efficient resource allocation and economic growth.

## STOCK MARKETS AND FINANCIAL INTERMEDIATRIES

How should we define stock market development? How can stock market development be empirically measured? Theory does not provide a unique concept of stock market development to guide empirical research. Existing models suggest the stock market development is a multifaceted concept, involving issues of market size, market liquidity, and integration with world capital markets.

A good body of literature exist on market integration of stock markets and lot of testing has been done to examine whether emerging stock markets are integrated into the world markets (Errunza and Losq 1989; Bekaert 1995; Buckberg 1995; Harvey 1995; and Tesar and Werner 1995). To test whether integration is important for economic development, requires country-specific measures of the degree of integration. If markets are financially integrated, capital should flow across borders to equalise the price of risk. Perhaps, if the markets are not integrated, possibly because of capital controls or other barriers, then the price of risk may differ across markets. Recently tests have been conducted on International Arbitrate

Pricing Model (IAPM). The studies point out that market segmentation is larger for emerging markets than developed markets. Various studies have shown that the market segmentation is larger for emerging markets than developed markets and that market segmentation decreases over time for many countries, suggesting a reduction in the barriers to capital flows.

Korajczyk's (1996) has given the measure of market integration, as well as measures of stock market size, liquidity, volatility, concentration, and institutional development for forty-four developed and emerging markets from 1986 to 1993. After using these measures Demirguc-Kunt and Levine (1996) find that:

(i) Large markets tend to be less volatile, more liquid, and less concentrated in a few stock than smaller markets,

(ii) Internationally integrated markets tend to be less volatile, Institutioanlly integrated markets tend to be less volatile,

(iii) Institutionally developed markets with strong information disclosure, laws, international accounting standards, and unrestricted capital flows have larger, more liquid markets, and

(iv) That Indonesia, Turkey, Portugal, and Venezuela have experienced explosive stock market development. The fact that all four countries liberalised restrictions on portfolio and dividend flows hints at the importance of policy in affecting stock market development

Levine and Zervos (1995), for example, show that countries which liberalised restrictions on capital and dividend flows showed a marked improvement in the functioning of their stock exchanges. They also explored the effects of liberalisation of capital controls of fourteen countries namely, Argentina, Brazil, Chile, Colombia, India, Jordan, Republic of Korea,

Malaysia, Pakistan, Philippines, Portgal, Thailand, Turkey, Venezuela that significantly reduced barriers to international capital and dividend flows in the 1980s, and showed that these countries enjoyed rapid improvements in the functioning of their stock markets. Their study suggested that stock return volatility rises immediately following capital control liberalisation. The analysis by Demirguc-Kunt and Levine implies that, in the long run, stock return volatility is lower in countries with more open capital markets.

Demirguc-Kung and Levine also examine the interaction between stock market development and financial intermediaries. They found that as countries grow and reach middle income (about $2,000 per capita in 1990), stock markets and nonbank financial intermediaries develop rapidly. They asserted that the stock markets and nonbanks grow as stock markets and nonbanks prosper.

Demirguc-Kunt also find that level to stock market development is positively corrrelated with the development of financial intermediaries. Thus, stock markets and financial institutions are generally complementary.

## STOCK MARKET AND LONG-RUN ECONOMIC GROWTH

Levine and Zervos (1990) examine the empirical relationship between measures of stock market development and long-run growth rates. They construct aggregate indices of overall stock market development that combine information on stock market size, liquidity, and international integration. Levine and Zervos use instrumental variables procedures and control for many other variables associated with economic growth to assess the strength of the empirical relationship between economic growth and stock market development (see also Levine and Renelt 1992). Assuring the initial level of GDP per capita, initial investment in human capital, political stability, the level of banking development, and measures of monetary, fiscal, and exchange rate policy, the predetermined component of stock market development remains positively and significantly correlated with long-run economic growth.

The strong correlation between overall stock market development and long run economic growth seems economically important. They found that the countries having the same level of stock market development might differ in economic growth but these countries enjoyed a slower growth rates. This suggests a potentially a strong economic relation ship between stock market development and economic growth. However a lot of work remains to be done, but the results are consistent with theories and historical analyses that imply a positive relationship between stock market development and economic performance. Haver (1991), documents the] positive impact of capital market development and capital market reform on competition and industrialisation using evidence from Brazil, Mexico, and the United States during the nineteenth and early twentieth centuries.

## FINANCING DECISIONS OF FIRMS AND THE STOCK MARKETS

Finance theory suggests that firms decide to issue — debts or equity securities on the basis of taxes and others market imperfections (see Harries and Raviv 1991 and Damirgtic-Kunt 1992 for a review of the literature). Although Rajan and Zirigales (1994) and Demirguc-Kunt and Maksimovic (1994) study international differences in capital structures, they analyse the impact of firm characteristics on financing choices of firms within individuals countries. However, differences among firms can explain only part of the great cross- country variation in firm debt-equity ratios. The existing literature overlooks the level of the stock market development as decerminants of financing choice. Demirguc-Kunt and Makismovic (1996) empirically explored the effect of financial markets development., particularly stock market development, on financing choices of firms. Looking at a sample of thirty industrial and developing economies, they observe that the effect of stock market development on firm debt-equity ratios depend on the initial level of stock market development. Firms in countries with underdeveloped stock markets first increase their debt equity ratios as their stock markets develop. They found that net only do they issue new equity, but they also borrow more. This relationship changes as stock markets develop. Finns in countries with relatively developed stock markets substitute equity for debt as stock markets develop further. These findings are consistent with the view that at early stages of market development, improvement in stock market functioning tends to improve information quality, monitoring, and corporate control, such that these improvements induce creditors to lend more.

Boyd and Smith (1996) develop a theoretical framework that helps in explaining important aspects of the Demirguc-Kunt and Makeismovic findings on corporate finance and financial market development. Boyd and Smith construct a model in which firms finance capital needs externally through a combination of debt and equity, and in which the level of development debt and equity markets interacts with physical capital investment decisions. The model given by Boyd and Smith predicts that:

(i) as an economy moves along its growth path, the use of more specialised and complex Lechnologies will become more common, this will lead to a rise in the relative cost of monitoring, so that firms will reduce their investments in projects with high returns and high monitoring cost,

(ii) richer countries tend to use more equity and less debt finance,

(iii) at low levels of economic development, agents do not use equity markets.

However, savers and firms begin to use stock markets once the economy attains a critical level of real per capita income. Furthermore, the Boyd and Smith model suggests that stock markets and banks may act as complementary rather than as substitute sources of capital.

## *CONCLUSION AND POLICY IMPLICATIONS*

The above analysis show that financial services are important for economic development, therefore countries must devote efforts towards (a) improving the financial systems of countries to stimulate economic development and (b) coping with financial crises that threaten economic prosperity. Through out the period of 1985-1995, the World Bank mostly focused on the reforms of banking systems — removing interest rate controls, reducing government involvement in credit allocation, minimising taxation of financial intermediaries, managing bank insolvencies, and training bank managers and supervisors. More recently, World Bank programs have stressed the development of capital markets in general and stock markets in particular. A lot of literature has flowed to substaintiate the relationship between stock market and economic development.

Some economists are of the opinion that the extent to which developing countries should rely on the highly liquid investment that stock markets typically attract. However the recent events in Mexico should not cause countries to adopt more restrictive policies towards international capital flows. As noted above, Levine and Zervos (1995) show that countries which reduce barriers to international capital flows enjoy rapid improvements in the functioning of their stock markets. Although stocks return volatility may rise in the short run following capital control liberalisation, countries that are more open to international capital flows tend to have less volatile markets in the long run than those with tighter capital controls, as shown by Demirguc-Kunt and Levine.

Current researches have shown that there is a definite relationship between stock markets and economic development A big body of literature exist on individual countries which has established this relationship see El-Erian and Kumar (1995), Claessens (1995), and Morgenstren (1995). For comparisons of market wading and information systems in developing countries, see Glen (1995).

It is not clear that every country needs its own active stock market. Theory and evidence suggest that countries benefits from easy access to well functioning stock markets. However, the geographical location of the market is not necessarily important. Future research can examine the effects of the cross-listing and cross-trading of shares.

Finally, the research also does not suggest that policymakers should push stock market development. The available information suggests that policymakers should remove impediment to stock markets, such as tax, legal, and regulatory barriers. But no strong evidence supports interventionist policies, such as tax incentives, that artificially boost stock market size and activity. Future research could focus more on the policies that facilitiate healthy stock market development.

## REFERENCES

Akerlof, George, (1970). "The Market for Lemons Quality Uncertainty and the Market Mechanism". Quarterly Journal of Economics 84: 488-500.

Bekaert, Greer, (1995). "Market Integration and Investment Barriers in Emerging Equity Markets." The World Bank Economic Review 9(1): 75-107.

Bencivenga, Valerie R., Bruce D. Smith, and Ross M. Starr. (1996). "Equity Markets, Transactions Costs, and Capital Accumulation An Illustration." The World Bank Economic Review 10(2) 241-65.

Boyd, John, and Bruce Smith, (1996) "The Revolution of the Real and Financial Sectors in the Growth Process." The World Bank Economic Review 10 (2) 37 1-96.

Buckberg, Elaine, (1995). "Emerging Stock Markets and International Assets Pricing." The World Bank Economic Review 9 (1): 51-74.

Claessens, Stijin, (1995). " Corporate Governance and Equity Prices: Evidence from Czech and Solvak Republics." World Bank, ECA/MNA Regions Technical Department, Washington, D.C.

Demirguc-Kunt, Asli (1992), "Developing Country Capital Structures and Emerging Stock Markets," WPS 933. World Bank, Policy Research Department, Washington, D.C.

Demirguc-Kunt, Asli, and Ross Levine, (1996). "Stock Market Development and Financial Intermediaries: Stylized Facts." The World Bank Economic Review 10 (2) 291-32 1.

Demirguc-Kunt, Asli are Ross Levine, (1996). "Stock Markets, Corporate Finance, and Economic Growth An Overview", World Bank Economic Review, 10(2) 223-239.

Demirguc-Kunt, Asli, and Vojislav Maksimovic, (1994). "Capital Structures in Developing Countries: Evidence from Ten Countries." WPS 1320. World bank, Policy Research Department, Washington, D.C.

——, (1996). "Stock Market Development and Financing Choices of Firms. "The World Bank Economic Review 10(2): 34 1-369.

Diamond, Dougals, (1984). "Financial Intemediation and Delegated Monitoring." Review of Economic Studies 5 1(3, July) 34 1-369.

El-Erian, Mohammed A., and Manmohan Kumar, (1995). "Emerging Equity Markets in the Middle Eastern Countries." International Monetary Funds, Middle Eastern and Research Departments, Washington, D.C.

Errunza, Vihang, and Etienne Losq, (1989). "Capital Flow Controls, International Asset Pricing and Investors' Welfare: A Multi-Country Framework." Journal of Finance 44(4):1025-38.

Gertler, Mark, (1988), "Financial Structure and Aggregate Economic Activity An Overview." Journal of Money, Credit and Banking 20(3, August, Pt. 2): 5 59-88.

Glen, Jack. (1995), "An Introduction to the Microstructure of Emerging Markets." IFC Discussion Paper 24. Washington, D.C.: International Finance Corporation.

Goldsmith, Raymond, W. (1969), "Financial Structure and Development. New Haven, Conn.: Yale University Press.

Greenwald, Burce, Jospech E. Stiglitz, and Andrew Weiss, (1984), "Information Imperfections in the Capital Market and Macroeconomic Fluctuation," American Economic Review 74(2, May): 194-200.

Gurley, John G., and Edward S. Shaw, (1955). "Financial Aspects of Economic Development." American Economic Review 45:515-38.

——, (1960). Money in a Theory of Finance, Washington, D.C.: Brookings Institution. Haber, Stephen H., (1991). "Industrial Concentration and Capital Markets: A Comparative Study of Brazil, Mexico, and the United States, 1830-1930." Journal of Economic History 51 (September): 559-80.

Harris, Milton, and Arthur Raviv, (1991). "The Theory of Capital Structure." Journal of Finance 46:297-356.

Harvey, Campbell R, (1995). "The Risk Exposure of Emerging Equity Markets." The World Bank Economic Review 9(1):1950.

Hicks John A., (1969). A theory of Economic History. Oxford, U.K.: Clarendon Press.

Jensen, Michael, and Kevin Murphy, (1990). "Performance Pay and Top Management Incentives." Journal of Political Economy 98: 225-63.

King, Roved G., and Ross Levine, (1993a). "Finance, Entrepreneurship and Growth: Theory and Evidence." Journal of Monetary Economics 35:5 13-42

——., (1993b). "Finance and Growth: Schumpeter Might Be Right." Quarterly Journal of Economics 108 (3):717-38.

Korajczyk, Robert A., (1996). "A Measure of Stock Market Integration." The World Bank Economic Review (10(2):267-89.

Kyle, Albert S., (1984). "Market Structure, Information, Futures Markets, and Price Formation." In Gray O. Storey, Andrew Schmitz, and Alexander H. Sarris, eds., International Agricultural Trade: Advanced Readings in Price Formation, Market Structure, and Price Instability. Boulder, Cob.: Westivew.

Levine, Ross, (1991), "Stock Markets, Growths, and Tax Policy." Journal of Finance 46(4, September): 1445-65.

——., (1996a). "Financial Development and Economic Growth: Views and Agenda." World Bank, Policy Research Department, Washington, D.C.

——.,(1996b). "Financial Sector Policies: Analytical Framework and Research Agenda." In Niels Hermes and Robed Lensink, eds., Financial Development and Economic Growth,: Theory and Experiences from Developing Countries," London: Rolutledge.

Levine, Ross, and David Renelt, (1992). "A Sensitivity Analysis of Cross- Country Growth Regressions," American Economic Review 82(4, September) 942-63.

Levine, Ross, and Sara Zervos, (1995). "Capital Control Liberalisation and Stock Market Development." World Bank, Policy Research Department, Washington, D.C.

——., (1996) "Stock market Development and Economic Growth." The World Bank Economic Review 19(2):323-39.

Mayer, Cohn, (1988). "New Issues in Corporate Finance". European Economic Review 32:1167-88.

McKinnon, Ronal I., (1973). "Money and Capital in Economic Development." Washington, D.C.: Brookings Institution.

Mishkin, Frederic S. (1996), "Understanding Financial Crisis: A Developing Country Perspective." In Annual World Bank Conference on Development Economics 1996. Washington, D.C.: World Bank.

Moregenstern, Claudia J., (1995). "Capital Markets in Russia." International Finance Corporation, Capital Markets Department, Washington, D.C.

Myers, Stewart C., and N.S. Majluf, (1984). "Corporate Financing and Investment Decisions, When Firms Have Information That Investors Do Not Have." Journal of Financial Economics 13 (2, June):187-221.

Obstfeld, Maurice, (1994). "Risk-Taking, Global Diversification, and Growth," American Economic Review 84 (5, December) 1310-29.

Rajan, Raghuram, and Luigi Zingales, (1994). "Is There an Optimal Capital Structure? Evidence from International Data." University of Chicago, Graduate Schools of Business, Chicago.

Shlefier, Adnrei, and Robert XV. Vishny, (1995). "A Survey of Corporate Finance." Harvard Institute of Economic Research Discussion Paper 1741. Harvard University, Cambridge, Mass.

Stiglitz, Joseph E., (1985). "Credit Markets and the Control of Capital." Journal of Money, Credit and banking 17(2, Many): 133-52.

——; (1994). "The Role of the State in Financial Markets." In Proceedings of the World Bank Annual Conference on Development Economics 1993. Washington, D.C.: World Bank.

Stighitz, Joseph E., and Andrew Weiss, (1981). "Credit Rationing in Markets with Imperfect Information." American Economic Review 71(3, June) 393-410.

Tesar, Linda, and Ingrid Werner, (1995). "U.S. Equity Investment in Emerging Stock Markets." The World Bank Economic Review 9(1): 109-30.

# 4

# LEGISLATIVE REFORMS IN INDIA: THE POST LIBERALISATION SCENARIO

*S.P. Narang*

Legislative reform is the index of maturity of any developing economy. Beginning July 1991 the Government of India initiated the process of standardisation, harmonisation and modernisation of laws as part of economic reforms process with a view to align them with the national regulatory and administrative environment conducive for the successful implementation of market oriented reform policies.

In this paper an attempt has been made to discuss legislative reforms initiated so far since July 1991, particularly in the area of Company Law, Securities Laws, Intellectual Property Laws and Laws relating to Foreign Exchange, Money Laundering, Competition, Alternative Dispute Resolution and Information Technology.

## THE COMPANIES ACT, 1956

The Companies Act, 1956 was enacted with a view to consolidate and amend the law relating to companies and certain other associations. Since its inception, the Act has been amended on various occasions to keep pace with the changing business and economic scenario, emergence of professionalism and spread of portfolio awareness etc. Full and fair disclosure of various matters in prospectus; detailed information of the financial affairs of the companies to be disclosed in annual reports, provision for intervention and investigation by the Government into the affairs of a company, regulation of appointment and remuneration of managerial personnel, enforcement of proper performance of their duties by company management and protection of minority shareholders, are some of the features of the Companies Act, 1956. It includes provisions protecting the interests of investors by providing for Company Law Board's intervention against non-payment of public deposits and compulsory redemption of preference shares in certain cases. The Act also provides for compulsory listing of all public issues.

In the early 1990s, a need was felt to harmonise the Companies Act with the developments taking place the world over to ensure a conducive regulatory framework for the growth of Indian Corporate sector, and this was reflected in the Companies Bill, 1993. However, in August 1996, a working Group was constituted which submitted its report in 1997. On the basis of this report the Companies Bill, 1997 was introduced in the Parliament which has been referred to the Standing Committee.

**The Companies Bill, 1997**

The main features of the Bill were :

(i) Classify public companies as listed and unlisted companies.

(ii) Self-regulation without Government control.

(iii) Allow SEBI to have administration and supervision (including powers to prosecute) of work relating to issue of securities and other related matters in case of listed public companies.

(iv) Permit companies to make inter corporate loans/ investments without the approval of the Central

Government. [Allowed by Companies (Amendment) Act, 1999].

(v) Prescribe minimum paid-up capital requirement for public and private companies.

(vi) Constitution of a Company Law Tribunal replacing the existing Company Law Board.

(vii) Provide nomination facility [Allowed by Companies (Amendment) Act, 1999].

(viii) Make it mandatory in all listed companies and unlisted companies with a paid-up capital of Rs.1 crore to appoint a Company Secretary.

(ix) Make it mandatory for every company not required to employ a whole-time secretary and having a paid-up capital of Rs.10 lakhs or more to attach with the Board's report a certificate from a secretary in whole-time practice.

(x) Permit buy-back of securities [Allowed by Companies (Amendment) Act, 1999].

**The Companies (Amendment) Act, 1996**

The main amendments which were effected in the Companies Act, 1956 by the Companies (Amendment) Act, 1996 are as under :

(i) Companies can amend object clause of the Memorandum of Association by passing a special resolution. No need to get confirmation of Company Law Board. The copy of Resolution to be filed with ROC within one month (Sections 17 and 18).

(ii) Companies cannot accept deposits from public if they are in default in repayment of any deposit and interest thereon (Section 58A).

(iii) Companies cannot issue preference shares which are irredeemable or are redeemable after the expiry of a period of twenty years from the date of issue (Section 80).

(iv) Companies which have defaulted in repayment of deposits cannot make inter corporate loans/ investments and or provide guarantees (Sections 370 and 372).

(v) Admissibility of micro films, facsimile copies of documents, computer print outs and documents and computer media as documents and as evidence (Section 610A).

**The Companies (Amendment) Act, 1999**

Taking the reforms process a step further, the Companies (Amendment) Act of 1999 was passed providing inter-alia for buy back of shares and issue of Sweat shares. This has been done primarily to boost morale of national business houses and also to encourage foreign institutional investors as well as foreign direct investment in the country.

The main amendments were as under:

(i) Infrastructure Development Finance Company Ltd. included in the list of public financial institutions.

(ii) Nomination facility allowed in shares, debentures and deposits (Sections 58A, 109A and 109B).

(iii) Buy-back of shares allowed – new Sections 77A, 77AA and 77B inserted.

(iv) Issue of Sweat Equity Shares allowed.

(v) Establishment of Investor Education and Protection Fund.

(vi) Constitution of National Advisory Committee on Accounting Standards – Section 210A.

(vii) Sections 370 and 372 superseded by insertion of Section 372A. The limit of inter corporate loans and investments increased upto 60% of the paid up share capital and free reserves or 100% of free reserves whichever is more.

**The Companies (Second Amendment) Bill, 1999**

The Companies (Second Amendment) Bill, 1999 was introduced in Lok Sabha (Lower House of Indian Parliament) on 23rd December, 1999. This Bill aims at introducing essential elements of corporate governance in the functioning of corporates through introduction of measures like small shareholders' representation on Board of Directors and Director's Responsibility statement.

The Bill contains 224 clauses. The main amendments proposed in the Bill are—

(a) Minimum paid-up capital requirement for Private and Public Company.

(b) SEBI to be entrusted with powers with regard to all matters relating to public issues, transfer of securities, payment of dividend etc. relating to listed public companies.

(c) Certain measures have been proposed for protecting small shareholders/deposit holders.

(d) Provision for voting through postal ballot for important items.

(e) The period for disbursing dividend to be reduced to 30 days from the date of declaration of dividend.

(f) Board of directors' report to include a director's responsibility statement.

(g) Private companies to be excluded in reckoning the number of companies which an auditor can audit.

(h) Compulsory appointment of at least one director elected by small shareholders.

(i) No person can hold office of director in more than 15 companies at a time.

(j) Constitution of Audit Committee by companies having paid-up capital of not less than Rs.5 crores.

(k) Obtaining of Compliance Certificate from a Company Secretary in whole-time practice by Companies having paid-up capital of Rs.10 lakhs or more and which are not required to employ a whole-time secretary.

## CAPITAL MARKET AND SECURITIES LAWS

The earliest legislation remotely touching the stock market was introduced in 1865 by the Government of Bombay to deal with the situation arising out of the Share Mania of 1860-65. Subsequently, Atlay Stock Exchange Enquiry Committee was appointed in September, 1923 which stressed and emphasised the need for the stock exchange to frame and maintain systematic and settled rules and regulations in the interest of general investing public and the trade. Pursuant to these recommendations, the Government of Bombay offered charter to Bombay Stock Exchange (BSE) in July, 1925 and the Government assumed authority to control the rule making power of the exchange and granted BSE monopoly to organise trading in securities but the exchange turned down the offer. Subsequently, a special legislation namely, Bombay Securities Contracts Act, 1925 for controlling stock exchange came into force w.e.f. January 1, 1926.

Today, the legislative framework dealing with securities markets comprises of Securities Contracts (Regulation) Act, 1956, Depositories Act, 1996, Securities and Exchange Board of India Act, 1992 and various regulations and guidelines issued by Securities and Exchange Board of India (SEBI) including listing agreement of the Stock Exchanges.

**Securities Contracts (Regulation) Act, 1956**

SCRA was enacted in 1956 with a view to regulate the transactions in securities and to check speculative transaction in the securities. These transactions were sought to be regulated through a system of control over the establishment of stock exchanges and their management including the members. Establishment of stock exchanges without prior approval of the Government was prohibited. By providing for the prior approval, the Government sought to have effective control on transactions in securities and also inculcate certain degree of discipline and regulation on such transactions.

**Securities and Exchange Board of India Act, 1992**

Capital Issues (Control) Act, 1947. This control was exercised through the Office of the Controller of Capital Issues. These controls have since been removed by repeal of the Capital Issues (Control) Act, 1947 on May 29, 1992 by the Securities and Exchange Board of India Act, 1992 providing for the establishment of the Securities and Exchange Board of India to protect the interests of the investors in securities and to promote the development of and to regulate the securities market and matters connected therewith. SEBI has issued rules and procedures for registering and regulating the various market participants and intermediaries.

***Securities and Exchange Board of India (SEBI)***

The setting up of the Securities and Exchange Board of India (SEBI) on April 12, 1988 initially as a non statutory body, its statutory empowerment thereafter on April 4, 1992 and further strengthening of its powers through the Securities Law (Amendment) Acts of 1995 and 1998 mark the process of installation of a regulatory edifice for Indian Securities Markets.

To enable SEBI to effectively carry out its function of investor protection, it has been empowered to file complaints against certain violations of the Companies Act. These cover issues pertaining to primary market such as listing of securities, refund of excess application money, delay in issue of shares and despatch of dividend warrants. SEBI has the authority to levy monetary penalties for a range of violations such as failure to redress investor grievances or observe rules and regulations by mutual funds, asset management companies, failure to disclose the aggregate of shareholding in a company, or to make public announcement for acquisition of share in the context of the takeover code.

SEBI has recently issued a compendium containing consolidated Guidelines, Circulars, instructions relating to issue of capital effective from January 27, 2000. The compendium titled SEBI (Disclosure and Investor Protection) Guidelines, 2000 has replaced the original Guidelines issued in June 1992 and clarifications thereon. It also consolidates the Issue related RMB General Instructions (Gr) Series Circulars and other guidelines relating to preferential issues, advertisement, book-building etc. Certain changes have been made in the guidelines relating to entry norms, lock-in-period and promoter's contribution as part of the consolidation exercise in order to streamline the current procedures and smoothen out the aberrations in IPOs market.

A new era of corporate governance has also emerged with SEBI accepting the recommendations of the Kumar Mangalam Birla Committee on Corporate Governance. SEBI in this context has directed all Stock Exchanges in India to insert in their Listing Agreement a new clause 49 on Corporate Governance.

### Depositories Act, 1996

In India the need for depository system was realised for the healthy growth of primary market, reducing the time gap between the allotment of shares and transfer of entitlements arising out of each allotment. Thus, the idea of setting up a depository and the introduction of scripless trading and settlement was conceived for improving the efficiency of the markets and eliminating the various problems associated with dealing in physical certificates. With a view to give this idea a legal force, the Depositories Act, 1996 was passed by the Parliament.

The Depositories Act 1996, lays down the legislative framework for facilitating the dematerialisation and book entry transfer of securities in a depository. The Act provides that a depository, which is required to be a company under the Companies Act, 1956, and depository participants need to be registered with SEBI. The depository carries out the dematerialisation of securities and the transfer of beneficial ownership through electronic book entry. The investors, however, have the option to hold securities in physical or dematerialised form, or to rematerialise securities previously held in dematerialised form. SEBI issued regulations in May 1996, which inter-alia, cover the norms for registration of depositories and participants, the eligibility criteria for admission of securities to a depository, the specific rights and obligations of depositories, participants and issuers and inspections by SEBI. The Depositories Act was amended in 1997 to enable units of mutual funds and Unit Trust of India, securities of statutory corporations and public corporations to be dealt through depositories

## INTELLECTUAL PROPERTY LAWS

The law relating to intellectual property in India is contained in Patents Act, 1970, Trade and Merchandise Marks Act, 1958, Copyright Act 1957 and Designs Act 1911. However, in view of advances in technology and to meet the obligations under TRIPs agreement, Government of India has enacted/ introduced following new legislations in the field of Intellectual Property.

**Trade Marks Act, 1999**

The Trade and Merchandise Marks Act, 1958 had virtually lost its utility due to strides made in business and practices. Therefore the trade marks law has been comprehensively reviewed keeping in view developments in trading and commercial practices, increasing globalisation of trade and industry, the need to encourage investment flows and transfer of technology, simplification and harmonisation of trade mark management systems and to give effect to important judicial decisions through resulting in the enactment of Trade Marks Act, 1999 repealing the 1958 Act. .

Trade Marks Act, 1999 provides for registration of trade mark for services, in addition to goods; prohibition to the registration of trade marks, which are imitation of well known trade marks, besides enlarging the grounds for refusal of registration. The provisions for defensive registration of trade marks have been omitted and a single register with simplified procedure for registration and with equal rights have been prescribed. The procedure for registration of registered user have been simplified and the scope of permitted use is enlarged and registration of "Collective Marks" owned by associations, etc. have been permitted. The Act also provides for establishment of an Appellate Board for speedy disposal of appeals and rectification applications which at present lie before High Court. The Act transfers the final authority relating to registration of certification of trade marks to the Registrar instead of the Central Government and provides for enhanced punishment for the offences relating to trade marks. The Act also prohibits the sale of spurious goods; use of some one else's trade marks as part of corporate names, or name of business concern. The Act provides for increasing the period of registration and renewal from 7 to 10 years; makes trade mark offences cognizable, enlarge the jurisdiction of courts to bring the law in this respect on par with the copyright law, amplify the powers of the court to grant ex parte injunction in certain cases.

**The Geographical Indications of Goods (Registration and Protection) Act, 1999**

Until recently, Geographical indications were not registrable in India and in the absence of statutory protection, Indian geographical indications had been misused by persons outside India to indicate goods not originating from the named locality in India. Therefore, with a view to prevent misuse of Indian geographical indications and to extend protection to goods imported from other countries which provide for such protection, the Geographical Indications of Goods (Registration and Protection) Act, 1999 has been passed by both the Houses of Parliament and placed on the Statute Book as the Geographical Indications of Goods (Registration and Protection) Act, 1999, after receiving assent of the President of India.

The new legislation aims at providing for the establishment of Geographical Indications registry; maintenance of a Register of Geographical Indication in Part A and Part B containing all registered geographical indications, and particulars of registered authorised users, respectively; registration of geographical indications of goods in specified classes; prohibition of registration of certain geographical indications; compulsory advertisement of all accepted applications; registration of authorised user and providing for infringement action; renewal, rectification and restoration of geographical indications and authorised user; higher level of protection for notified goods; prohibition of assignment and its registration as trademark; effect of registration and rights conferred by registration; offences and penalties; and provision for reciprocity, powers of Registrar, maintenance of Index.

**The Copyright (Amendment) Act, 1999**

The Copyright Act, 1957 has been amended to give effect

to the provisions of Article 14 of the TRIPs agreement providing term of protection to performers rights at least until the end of a period of fifty years computed from the end of the calendar year in which the performance took place. The Amendment Act also inserted new section 40A empowering the Central Government to extend the provisions of the Copyright Act to broadcasts and performances made in other countries subject to the condition however that such countries extend similar protection to broadcasts and performances made in India. Another new section 42 empowers the Central Government to restrict rights of foreign broadcasting organisations and performers.

### The Semiconductor Integrated Circuits Lay-out Design Bill, 1999

Realising the importance of protection of Intellectual Property Rights (IPR) embedded in the layout designs to encourage continued investments in R & D to result in technological advancements in the field of microelectronics and in view of requiremrent of TRIPs agreement for setting up of standards concerning availability, scope and use of Intellectual Property Rights, Geograpliical Indications, Layout-Design of Integrated Circuits etc., the Government introduced in Parliament, the Semiconductor Integrated Circuit Layout-Design Bill 1999 providing for protection of Semiconductor Integrated Circuits Layout-Designs by process of registration providing mechanism for distinguishing Layout-Designs which can be protected. The Bill also proposes to prescribe rules to prohibit registration of Layout-Designs which are not original and/or which have been commercially exploited, The Bill also provides for specified period for protection, provision with regard to infringement, payment of royalty for registered Layout-Design, provisions for dealing with willful infringement by way of punishment, appointing a Registrar for registering the layout designs and mechanism of Appellate Board.

**The Designs Bill, 1999**

The law relating to designs is contained in the Designs Act, 1911. However, in view of considerable progress made in the field of science and technology requiring the legal system for the protection of industrial designs to be more efficient in order to ensure effective protection registered designs, the Designs Bill 1999 has been placed before the Parliament to promote design activity and to ensure that the law does not unnecessarily extend protection beyond what is necessary to create the required incentive for design activity while removing impediments to the free use of available designs.

In view of the above, the Bill enlarges the scope of definition of "article" and "design" and introduces definition of "original"; amplifies the scope of 'prior publication'; incorporates the provisions for delegation of powers of the Controller to other officers and duties of Examiners; contains provision for identification of non-registrable designs; provision for substitution of application before registration of a design and introduces internationally followed system of classification in the place of Indian classification.

The Bill also contains provision for maintaining the Register of design on computer; for restoration of lapsed designs; and provides for appeal against order of the Controller before the High Court instead of Central Government as provided in the existing Designs Act, 1911. The Bill revokes the period of secrecy of two years of a registered design and provides for compulsory registration of any document for transfer of right in the registered design. The Bill also proposes to introduce additional grounds in cancellation proceedings and makes provision for initiating the cancellation proceedings before the Controller in place of High Court and enhance the quantum of penalty imposed for infringement of registered design.

Bill proposes to enhance initial period of registration from 5 to 10 years, to be followed by a further extension of a period of five years; and allows priority to other convention countries and countries belonging to the group of countries or inter-governmental organizations apart from United Kingdom and other Commonwealth countries.

**The Protection of Plant Varieties and Farmers Rights Bill, 1999**

The issue of enacting a law relating to Plant Varieties Protection and Farmers' Rights in India has become important particularly in view of the requirements of Agreement on Trade Related Aspects of Intellectual Property Rights (TRIPs) which obliges members to provide for the protection of plant varieties whether by patenting or by an effective sui generis system or by any combination thereof. With a view to meet the obligations under TRIPs agreement the Protection of Plant Varieties and Farmers' Rights Bill, 1999 was introduced in Parliament.

The proposed legislation aims at achieving the following objectives:

- (i) to stimulate investments for research and development both in the public and the private sector for the development of new plant varieties by ensuring appropriate returns on such investments;
- (ii) to facilitate the growth of the seed industry in the country through domestic and foreign investment which will ensure the availability of high quality seeds and planting material to Indian farmers; and
- (iii) to recognise the role of farmers as cultivators and conservors and the contribution of traditional, rural

and tribal communities to the country's agro-biodiversity by rewarding them for their contribution through benefit sharing and protecting the traditional rights of the farmers.

While providing for an effective system of protection of plant breeders' rights, the proposed legislation seeks to safeguard farmers' and researchers' rights. It also contains provisions for safeguarding the larger public interest. The farmer's rights include his traditional rights to save, use, share or sell his farm produce of a variety protected under this Act provided the sale is not for the purpose of reproduction under a commercial marketing arrangement. The proposed legislation also contains provisions to facilitate equitable sharing of benefits arising out of the use of plant genetic resources, that may accrue to a breeder from the sale, disposal etc. of seeds/planting material of a protected variety. The village and farming community proposed to be compensated in case their traditional or local varieties is used for the development of new varieties.

The Bill proposes to establish a National Gene Fund to promote activities aimed at conservation and sustainable use of genetic resources of agro-biodiversity. The proposed legislation will extend to all categories of plants but will not include micro-organisms. In order to be eligible for protection, a variety must be distinct, uniform and stable. The period of protection shall be eighteen years for trees and vines and fifteen years for other plants. Breeders' rights envisage that the breeder's authorisation will be required for production and commercial sale of the productive or propagating material of a protected variety.

The Bill proposes to establish Protection of Plant Varieties and Farmer's Rights Authority with the necessary powers to perform all functions relating to the protection of plant varieties.

**The Patents (Second Amendment) Bill, 1999**

The law relating to patents is contained in the Patents Act, 1970 which was last amended in March, 1999 to meet India's obligations under the Agreement on Trade Related Aspects of Intellectual Property Rights (TRIPS) forming part of the Agreement establishing the World Trade Organisation (WTO).

However, to modify the Act into a modem, harmonised and user-friendly legislation and to adequately protect national and public interests while simultaneously meeting India's international obligations, a Bill to further amend the Patents act, 1970 was placed before the Parliament on December 20, 1999 to make the law not only TRIPS compliant but also to provide therein necessary and adequate safeguards for protection of public interest, national security, bio-diversity, traditional knowledge, etc. Opportunity is also proposed to be availed of for harmonising the procedure for grant of patents in accordance with international practices and to make the system more user friendly.

## LAW RELATING TO FOREIGN EXCHANGE: THE MOVE FROM REGULATION TO MANAGEMENT

Immediately after the outburst of the Second World War, Exchange Control was introduced in India on 3rd September, 1939. Control was administered under the emergency powers derived from Defence of India Rules. The emergency powers were later on placed on a statutory pedestal through enactment of the Foreign Exchange Regulation Act, 1947 which came into force on 25th March, 1947. The Foreign Exchange Regulation Act, 1973 (FERA) was subsequently enacted to consolidate and amend the law in several respects, encompassing the experience gained over two decades of implementation of control through the earlier enactment of 1947, and considering the report of the Study Team on the question of leakage of foreign exchange through invoice manipulation and the Law Commission report on the Trial and Punishment of Social and Economic Offices.

Experience gained over the years in the administration of the Foreign Exchange Regulation Act, 1973 had shown that certain provisions, meant to deal with emergencies of different kinds, are no longer relevant and are required to be removed for improving the climate for foreign investment in India. Hence, the Foreign Exchange Regulation Act, 1973 was reviewed in 1993 and several amendments were enacted as part of the on-going process of economic liberalisation relating to foreign investment and foreign trade for closer interaction with the world economy.

In view of the significant developments that have taken place since 1993 such as substantial increase in foreign exchange reserves, growth in foreign trade, rationalisation of tariffs, current account convertibility, liberalisation of Indian investments abroad, increased access to external commercial borrowings by Indian corporates and participation of foreign institutional investors in stock markets in India, a Bill to repeal and replace the Foreign Exchange Regulation Act, 1973 was introduced in Lok Sabha on 4th August, 1998. The said Bill was referred to the Standing Committee on Finance, which submitted its report to the Parliament on 23rd December, 1998 with certain modifications and suggestions. After incorporating certain modifications and suggestions of the Standing Committee on Finance, Foreign Exchange Management Act 1999 was enacted and made effective from June 1, 2000.

There is clearly a departure from the previous Act, i.e. FERA, 1973 which aimed at regulating certain payments, dealings in foreign exchange and securities, transactions indirectly affecting foreign exchange and the import and export of currency for conservation of the foreign exchange resources of the country and proper utilisation thereof in the interests of the economic development of the country. FEMA contains provisions relating to Current Account Transactions, Capital Account Transactions and determination of residential status on the basis of physical stay in the country. Therefore, it may be said that the present law is an attempt to move from control regime to flexible management approach and regulation by the guidelines issued by the RBI and the Central Government from time to time.

*Prima facie,* FEMA has put in place a framework to suit management of foreign exchange transactions in the liberalised environment. As far as permission of RBI is concerned, the Role of the RBI has been recognised and the emphasis has been laid on framing regulations, than granting permission on case to case basis, except in circumstances provided under section 3, which include dealing in and transfer of any foreign exchange or foreign security to any person other than the authorised person; making any payment to or for the credit of any person resident outside India, receiving any payment by order or on behalf of any person resident outside India, through a person other than authorised person; and entering into any financial transaction in India as consideration for or in association with acquisition or creation or transfer of a right to acquire, any asset outside India by any person.

The restrictions on drawal of exchange for purposes of Current Account Transactions have been removed. However, an enabling provision empowers the Central Government to impose reasonable restrictions for Current Account Transactions, in public interest. The Central Government, before imposing any reasonable restriction, has to take the RBI into confidence.

FEMA contains important provisions relating to Capital Account Transactions. The Act defines Capital Account

Transactions to mean a transaction which alters the asset or liabilities, including contingent liabilities, outside India of persons resident in India or asset or liabilities in India of persons resident outside India and includes transactions referred to in section 6(3) which empowers the RBI to regulate, prohibit or restrict through regulations, certain transactions.

Government has also recently notified the Rules and the Reserve Bank of India has issued various Regulations to carry out the provisions of FEMA.

## PREVENTION OF MONEY LAUNDERING

Today, the financial markets are growing exponentially in size and sophistication as never before. The quantum rise in demand for financial products, new and innovative means of financing, automated trading and settlement systems across the border as well as within the country have all contributed to a remarkably rapid development of the financial markets. Although the process of exploitation of these markets is legitimate business yet there is need to preserve their financial and operational integrity by curbing money laundering activities.

The genesis of legal measures to tackle money laundering can be traced back to the G-7 Summit in 1989 which established Financial Action Task Force (FATP) to tackle the problem of money laundering. At the same time there have been a series of international and regional instruments. Adoption of United Nations resolution in its Special Session on countering World Drug Problem on 8th to 10th June, 1998 makes it incumbent on the countries signatory to this declaration to combat the money laundering activities. All these instruments have in common an emphasis on States adopting certain basic standards.

In view of an urgent need for the enactment of a

comprehensive legislation for preventing money-laundering and connected activities, confiscation of proceeds of crime, setting up of agencies and mechanisms for co-ordinating measures for combating money laundering etc., the Prevention of Money-laundering Bill 1998 was introduced in the Parliament on the 4th August, 1998. The Bill was referred to the Standing Committee on Finance, which presented its report on the 4th March, 1999 to the Lok Sabha. After incorporating the recommendations of the Standing Committee, the Government introduced the Prevention of Money Laundering Bill 1999 in the Parliament on October 29, 1999.

Recommendations of the Standing Committee accepted by the Central Government were as follows :

(a) inclusion of definition of expressions "banking company" and "person";

(b) banking companies, financial institutions and intermediaries are required to furnish information of transaction to the Director instead of Commissioner of Income-tax;

(c) banking companies have also been brought within the ambit of the obligations of financial institutions and intermediaries;

(d) a definite time-limit of 24 hours has been provided for producing a person about to be searched or arrested before the Gazetted Officer or Magistrate;

(e) the appellant before the Appellate Tribunal have been authorised to engage any authorised representative as defined under Section 288 of the Income-tax act, 1961;

(f) punishment for vexatious search and for false information may be enhanced from three months' to two years of imprisonment, or fine of rupees ten thousand to rupees fifty thousand, or both;

In addition to the above recommendations of the Standing Committee, the Bill proposes to-

(a) relax the conditions prescribed for grant of bail so that the Court may grant bail to a person who is below sixteen years of age, or woman or sick or infirm;
(b) levy of fine for default of non-compliance of the issue of summons' etc.;
(c) make provisions for having reciprocal arrangement for assistance in certain matters and procedure for attachment and confiscation of property so as to facilitate transfer of funds involved in money-laundering kept outside the country and extradition of the accused persons from abroad.

The violations regarding the Narcotic Drugs and Psychotropic Substances Act, 1985 constitute most serious offence under the Bill and in this respect, the Director is empowered to attach the laundered property soon after a case is sent by the police officer or a complaint is filed with the Court for taking cognizance of the offence. In all other case, however, no attachment of properties can be made before a report, based on the investigations, is forwarded to competent magistrate. However, in any case, Director or any other officer who provisionally attaches any property is under obligation to file a complaint before the Adjudicating Authority, within thirty days from the date of such attachment.

The Bill contains a provision relating to the obligations of banking companies, financial institutions and intermediaries to maintain records and furnish information of all such transactions as specified by the Government. Failure to comply with this provision, however, attracts levy of fine of not less than Rs.10,000 and not more than one lakh rupees. The Bill also provides for immunity to the officers, from civil/criminal liability arising out of disclosure of information.

The Bill provides for appointment of Adjudicating Authority having powers of a Civil Court, and the proceedings before the Adjudicating Authority to be deemed as judicial in nature under Indian Penal Code. The Bill also provides for the establishment of Appellate Tribunal to hear appeals against the orders of the Adjudicating Authority and authorities as prescribed under the Bill. The Bill entitles the Director or any person aggrieved to appeal within 45 days to Appellate Tribunal against order of adjudication, levying of fine and retention of valuables and books. The Tribunal has been empowered to entertain appeal beyond the prescribed period of 45 days, for good and sufficient reasons. The Bill also provides for the establishment of designated Special Courts for trial of offences punishable with imprisonment ranging from 3 to 7 years and fine upto 5 lakhs for money laundering including offences specified under the Narcotic Drugs and Psychotropic Substances Act, 1985, which attracts imprisonment upto 10 years and fine upto Rs.5 lakhs.

## COMPETITION LAW

Legal framework dealing with competition in India is spread over various legislations. Besides the Monopolies and Restrictive Trade Practices Act, 1969 (MRTP Act) which is the principal legislation dealing with Monopolistic and Unfair Trade Practices since 1969, other legislations include Consumer Protection Act, 1986, Prevention of Food Adulteration Act, 1954, Standards of Weights & Measures Act, 1976, Packaged Commodities Rules, 1977, Patents Act, 1970, the Customs Tariff (Amendment) Act, 1995 and SEBI (Substantial Acquisition of Shares and Takeover) Regulations, 1997.

### Monopolies and Restrictive Trade Practices Act, 1969

The principal legislation dealing with competitive activities in India is the MRTP Act 1969. The main objectives sought to be achieved through the MRTP Act were prevention of concentration of economic power to the common detriment; control of monopolies and prohibition of monopolistic and restrictive trade practices. This was achieved through making it compulsory for seeking prior approval of any project being set up or in relation to mergers and takeovers by the companies or undertakings coming under the purview of the MRTP Act, compulsory registration of all such monopoly and dominant undertakings and registrations of restrictive trade agreements.

However, with the growing complexity of industrial structure and the need for achieving economies of scale for ensuring higher productivity and competitive advantage in the international market, and a shift in the thrust of the industrial policy to control and regulate the monopolistic, restrictive and unfair trade practices rather than making it necessary for certain undertakings to obtain prior approval of the Central Government for expansion, establishment of new undertakings, merger, amalgamation, take over and appointment of directors, the MRTP Act was amended in 1991 omitting the provisions of sections 20 to 26 and transfer the provisions contained in Chapter III A regarding restrictions on acquisition and transfer of shares to the Companies Act, 1956.

A Committee constituted by the Government of India to examine the provisions of the MRTP Act, in the light of international economic development relating to competition law to suit Indian conditions and to propose a modern competition law suitable to the needs of the country, has recently submitted its Report which has been adopted by the Department of Company Affairs. The Committee recommended the repeal of MRTP Act and enactment of new Indian Competition Law and establishment of a Competition Commission of India to implement the new Act and to take up the Monopolistic and Restrictive Trade Practices cases presently pending before the MRTP Commission. Committee also recommended the abolistion of MRTP Commission and suggested transfer of cases of Unfair Trade Practices to the concerned consumer Courts.

## ALTERNATIVE DISPUTE RESOLUTION

Like various other countries the justice dispensing system in India has also been at the receiving end for various reasons, including among others, mounting arrears of cases, inordinate delays in the administration of justice and exorbitant cost of litigation. With a view to make the legal process effective and capable of responding to the changing socio-economic conditions taking place in the wake of new policy measures adopted by the Government to integrate domestic economy with that of global economy, and also for furthering the process of judicial reforms, the Parliament enacted on August 16, 1996, Arbitration and Conciliation Act, 1996. The new legislation is conceived as a pace setter for introducing quicker and more efficient modes of resolution of commercial disputes.

An Arbitration Agreement under the Act, has to be defined to be necessarily in writing, which may be included in the main contract as a clause or a separate agreement may be entered into by the parties. An agreement shall be deemed to be in writing when it is signed by the parties, including exchange of letters, telex, telegram and other means of telecommunication. This also includes exchange of statements of claim and defence in which the existence of the agreement is alleged by one party and not denied by the other party.

The Act also recognises the role of institutions in the process of arbitration and authorises parties to request the institutions to determine the issue and arranging for administrative support in conducting the arbitration proceedings. One of the major element of new legislation is the provision relating to the appointment of arbitrators by the Chief Justice, where the parties are not agreeable to the procedure to be followed for the appointment of arbitrators. Chief Justice has however been empowered to designate any person or institution to take the necessary steps for the appointment of arbitrators. As far as the rules of procedure are concerned, it has been left to the parties concerned to agree on the procedure to be followed in arbitral proceedings. However, the arbitral tribunal has been allowed conduct the proceedings in an appropriate manner, where the parties are undecided as to the procedure for conduct of proceedings.

The Act also allows arbitral tribunal to resort to mediation, conciliation or other procedure for settlement of the disputes, during the arbitration proceedings.

The Act clearly enumerates the grounds on which the court can entertain the application for setting aside an award. These include, invalidity of arbitration agreement, violation of principles of natural justice and exceeding of terms of reference by arbitrator

The Act also contains provisions regarding international commercial arbitration . The arbitral tribunal is obliged to apply the rules of law as designated by the parties as applicable to the substance of the dispute. And in the absence of any agreement as to the applicable law between the parties, the tribunal can apply rules of law, it considers appropriate. However, the tribunal can in no case decide the applicable Law unless authorised by the parties.

The Act also contains provisions regarding enforcement of certain foreign awards, namely awards under New York Convention on the Recognition and Enforcement of Foreign Arbitral Awards (1958), and awards under Geneva Convention on the Execution of Foreign Arbitral Awards

## CYBER LAWS

New communication systems and digital technology have made dramatic changes in lifestyle and conduct of business. Businesses and consumers are increasingly using computers to create, transmit and store information in the electronic form instead of traditional paper documents. Information stored in electronic form is cheaper, easier to store, retrieve and speedier to communicate. Although people are aware of these advantages they are reluctant to conduct business or conclude any transaction in the electronic form due to lack of appropriate legal framework. Two principal hurdles which stand in the way of facilitating electronic commerce and electronic governance are the requirements as to writing and signature for legal recognition.

In this backdrop, the Information Technology Act, 2000 has been enacted providing for legal recognition of electronic records and digital signatures, to enable the conclusion of contracts and the creation of rights and obligations through the electronic medium. The Act also provides for a regulatory regime to supervise the Certifying Authorities issuing Digital Signature Certificates and to create civil and criminal liabilities for contravention of the provisions of the proposed legislation with a view to prevent possible misuse arising out of transactions and other dealings concluded over the electronic medium.

With a view to facilitate Electronic Governance, the Act provides for the use and acceptance of electronic records and digital signatures in the Government offices and its agencies. Consequential amendments have also been proposed in the Indian Penal Code and the Indian Evidence Act to provide for necessary changes in the various provisions which deal with offences relating to documents and paper based transactions. Similarly, the Act amended the Reserve Bank of

India Act to facilitate electronic fund transfers between the financial institutions and banks and the Bankers' Books Evidence Act to give legal sanctity for books of account maintained in the electronic form by the banks.

## CONCLUSION

Legal modernisation is required when development in science and industry coupled with policy reforms greatly accelerate the pace of change. Accordingly, the legislative reform process was initiated in India to make the legal framework compatible with global standards. Moreover, with the initiation of second generation reforms process a number of legislations have been enacted/introduced in Parliament and it is hoped that an entirely new regulatory environment conducive to the economic growth of the country will be in place in times to come.

## REFERENCES

1. The Companies Act, 1956
2. The Companies Bill, 1997
3. The Companies (Second Amendment) Bill, 1999
4. The Companies (Amendment) Act, 1996
5. 'The Companies (Amendment) Act, 1999
6. Securities Contract (Regulation) Act, 1956
7. Securities and Exchange Board of India Act, 1992
8. Depositories Act, 1996
9. Trade Marks Act, 1999
10. The Geographical Indications of Goods (Registration and Protection) Act, 1999.
11. The Copyright (Amendment) Act 1999
12. The Semiconductor Integrated Circuits Lay-out Designs Bill 1999
13. The Designs Bill 1999
14. The Protection of Plant Varieties and Farmers Rights Bill 1999
15. The Patents (Second Amendment) Bill 1999

16. Foreign Exchange Management Act, 1999
17. Foreign Exchange Regulation Act, 1973
18. The Prevention of Money Laundering Bill 1999
19. Monopolies and Restrictive Trade Practices Act, 1969
20. Arbitration and Conciliation Act 1996
21. The Information Technology Act, 2000
22. Annual Report(1995-96),The Securities & Exchange Board of India
23. Isher Judge Ahluwalia, Rakesh Mohan, Onkar Goswami and Charles Oman(Ed.), Policy Reforms in India (1996) OECD Publication
24. A Ramaiya,The Companies Act, 1956
25. S M Dugar,MRTP Law & Practice(1991)
26. R. Swaminathan, Law & Practice of FERA(1996)
27. H V Mirchandani & V K Sharma Guide to New Arbitration Law(1996)
28. Deleep Goswami,"SEBI's Newely acquired power to prosecute companies neglecting Investor Protection" Chartered Secretary p.205(1994)
29. Rajendra P. Chitale, "Regulatory Framework for Securities Market, Chartered Secretary"p.942(1995)
30. Background Papers for workshop on Depositories Ordinance 1996, organised by the ICSI at New Delhi on February 28, 1996.
31. Background Papers for Seminar on ADR organised by ICADR at New Delhi on October 7, 1995.

# 5

# WILL DISINVESTMENT BAIL OUT THE GOVERNMENT?

*B.N. Asthana*

The public sector in India was a setup to achieve the commanding heights in the economy. The Industrial Policy Resolution adopted in 1948 assigned a distinct place to it. The Directive Principles of State Policy as enshrined in the Constitution gave constitutional support to mixed economy. In the background of all this the public sector in India has been playing an important role in Indian economy. During the years following Independence the public sector grew in size and significance. Its records of performance is quite impressive. However, it is characterised by certain features which have effected the functioning of this vital sector of Indian economy adversely. Its working has not been on commercial lines. Its administration is top-heavy. The Boards of public sector companies have been functioning under a distorted notion of accountability. The members have been inducted not from the profession but come from a class of bureaucrats and politicians of all shapes and hue who have no idea of running a business enterprise. There is complete absence of autonomy, R&D activity and technology upgradation. Consequently the thrust on performance improvement is missing.

A time has come when the government has to initiate

structural reforms. In developing economies the need for such reforms is a continuous process. Of the various reform measures, disinvestment in public enterprises is one. This need not disturb the votaries of the public sector; for it is a world-wide phenomenon. It is being looked upon as a panacea for all evils attending the public sector. Even in some of the most advanced socialistic countries like the USSR there is a growing inclination towards privatisation in some form. This remedy is being viewed as a measure designed to reduce strain upon the public exchequer and to enhance efficiency and competition. This change in approach to the public sector has not been easy. Decades of brain-washing as to exploitative nature of the private sector has made its social acceptance very difficult.

It is in the context of these developments and in the context of the recent announcement of the Finance Minister while presenting the budget for 1999-2000, that he proposes to raise Rs. 10,000 crores. from disinvestment to reduce fiscal deficit, that the question of disinvestment has become quite important. However, it may be helpful at this stage to bring out the distinction between privatisation and disinvestment. *Privatisation involves a complete change in ownership and management. In disinvestment, the government may retain the ownership; the extent of which would depend upon the scaling down of the government's share in equity.*

It would be useful to briefly go into the evolution process adopted by the government of India. The steps taken by the Government would go well into the 21st century. The strategy emanating from these steps would determine the pattern of disinvestment which the Government of India would be following. The Government would need to step up the process of disinvestment to enhance the efficiency of the PSUs; *and* would *also* need to bail it out of the financial distress from time to time; the twin objectives with which disinvestment is usually resorted to. Disinvestment changes the work-culture of the public enterprises to a material extent. The practices, procedures and the system in vogue are completely transformed by bringing about a change in the philosophy of the enterprise and makes the employees responsive to the needs, aspirations and expectations of the customers.

Sporadic efforts to disinvest have been made from time to time. However, the efforts were put on a planned footing by the Indian Government by the setting up of a Disinvestment Commission in August, 1996, with wide terms of reference. It was to advise the Government of *all* matters pertaining to disinvestment in PSUs. The Commission expressed itself in favour of planned disinvestment, spread over a long period of time. This would help the Government in bargaining on more favourable terms. The strategy initially suggested by the Commission is to classify PSUs into 'Core' and 'non-Core' classes, setting disinvestment limits for the two. The core group would consist of 20 PSUs with disinvestment limit of 49 per cent. The non-Core sector would include 15 PSUs.

The Disinvestment Commission made the following other recommendations for the smooth working of the disinvestment process:-

1. Creation of Disinvestment Fund to which all proceeds from disinvestment would be credited. The National Renewal fund should be merged with this fund. The objectives of this fund would be to; (i) enable the PSUs to tide over temporary crunches; (ii) strengthen marginally loss making units; and (iii) assist the labour force rendered surplus in the process of restructuring.
2. The PSU Boards to the granted greater autonomy commensurate with their performance.

3. The PSU shares should have access to capital market. Shares should also be offered to employees with a ceiling of the 200 shares, and to small investors at a discount of 10 per cent.

The recommendation to establish a Disinvestment Fund was designed to ensure that the disinvestment proceeds are kept apart from the non-debt receipts of the Government. It has been a long standing complaint of the PSU, that they are not autonomous. Several decision-making areas have been denied to them. The number of shareholders in most PSUs is small. In order to broad-base the holdings and empowering the employees, offer of shares to the common man and the employees is a good idea.

The working of the disinvestment process is marked by lapses from the beginning. There is apprehension that it would continue to be so. The Government took unduly long time to take action on the report. It was expected that the Government would appoint a Committee of experts to suggest guidelines to implement the recommendations. The Disinvestment Commission has observed at the outset that the process of disinvestment would be a long drawn out one. A standing committee of the Government of India should have been appointed to lay down the process in minutest details and to continue to monitor the working. It appears that the government did not want to appoint a body of experts to lay down the investment process and a control process to take care of the national interests. In the absence of such a mechanism, the functionaries of the government who were least equipped to deal with sensitive and delicate financial matters were entrusted with the task. In the result, the Government of India in the MoF and the DoPEs rushed with the task of disinvestment through Mutual Funds. In the process the twin object of access to capital market and broad-basing the share holdings was frustrated. It is alleged that the selling price of shares was fixed without any economic basis, and at a level which was extremely unfavourable to the PSUs. The whole matter of the upset price for selling the shares was a closely guarded secret between the MoF and the DoPEs. At no stage an effort was made to involve the financial experts from the capital and money markets and the stock exchanges having a knowledge of share price movements. The MoF entered into an agreement with the MFs in one go in a deal which was a hush-hush affairs. The entire deal smacks of an unholy alliance between the powers that be and is characterised by lack of transparency. All norms of financial propriety were thrown to the winds. It appears that the MoF and the DoPEs had become a law unto themselves, going about ordering the MFs to buy PE shares—a practice which cannot be justified by any ethical norms. The recommendation of the Disinvestment Commission that the shares should be offered to the small investors and the employees was treated with contempt. The shares were sold in haste at very low prices. The fact that the price was initially fixed at Rs. 15-20 had to be readjusted to Rs. 30, is a proof enough of the unseemly haste and disregard of public interest. The NAV of the holdings of most of the MFs suffered tremendous erosion later, leading the investors to a state of penury and misery. The fact of undue haste was admitted by a member of the Planning Commission and Chairman of the Committee for Disinvestment.

There is no denying the fact that the disinvestment is the need of the hour. It is capable of bailing out the PSUs and the Government, provided the intentions and the capacity of the Government is good. Measures such as disinvestment are serious measures. They should be preceded by wide publicity and creation of suitable climate for sale of PE shares, the essential features of which are wide publicity, education of public opinion, adequate linkage between the PEs and the Capital Market, and listing of shares on the stock exchange. A permanent independent committee of experts for disinvestment outside the MoF and free from government influence should have been appointed.

The government has taken some bold steps to ensure success of their disinvestment programme. The strategy is to disinvest simultaneously in domestic and foreign markets where most favourable prices are available. As a part of this strategy the Government have reduced their shareholding in CONCOR, TAII, and VSNL through GDR. The planned reduction of their stake in IOC had to be postponed in early March, 1999, for the fiscal 1999-2000, to await better prices. The decision to download in BALCO, Modern Foods, Kudermukh and ITDC has been taken. For BALCO and Modern Foods, the Government is looking for strategic partners to bid. For the rest, global advisers have been appointed as a search committee, to find strategic partners. The process may take well over a couple of years. By the time we will be in the 21st century.

The change in strategy is expected to pay off, notwithstanding the dismal past record of the Government. In 1996-97 the FM had fixed a target of Rs. 5,000 crores of disinvestment, but could manage only about Rs. 500 crores. In 1997-98 the target was initially Rs. 4,800 crores, later stepped up to Rs. 7,000 crs and ended up with a realisation of barely Rs. 900 crores. More than the financial features, the success of a state policy depends upon the credibility of the Government. This has taken a severe beating at the hands of the people, even in the limited sphere of disinvestment.

From all available accounts it is clear that the Government is going ahead with the disinvestment programme. The current debate is on whether the stake should be reduced below 51 per cent. Public opiion is in favour of the 51 per cent figure. However, Financial Secretary Vijay Kelkar is advocating for 49 per cent. His opiion will effect profoundly the next step of the Government. Put simply, Kelkar's view is that with 49 per cent of holdings, PE would become private and would become more competitive.

The modus operandi offered by Kelkar is simple. He advocates the setting up of a new corporate body called as Special Purpose Vehicle (SPV). The Government will be offering shares to the investors through the SPV. For some unknown reason Kelkar believes that this will for greater transparency to disinvestment process, minimise delays and bring about efficiency. However, the common investor, having burnt his fingers with the MFs when the latter were compelled to buy disinvested shares, is no taker of the efficiency and transparency argument. The route Kelker proposes to take should be cleared of governmental interference and vested interests who made millions at the expense of the small investors in the past decade. The intentions of the Government are under a grave doubt. The course of events needs to be looked into. The UF Government was reduced to a care-taker status on Nov. 28, 1997. It was no moral right of such a government to take decision on a vital nature, asking the DoPEs to issue a brief order divesting the powers of the Disinvestment Commission and reducing it to the status of a mere advisory body. This meant that the Commission could no longer monitor the progress and supervise the implementaiton of its recommednations. This move of the Government met with violent reaction in the monetary world.

There is no doubt that disinvestment is the need of the hour. As Prof. V.V. Ramanadham pointed out long back, the concept of comparative advantage requires that when a public enterprise loses its dignity, it is preferable to privatise it. However, disinvestment should not be resorted to in the closing weeks of a financial year; it should be evenly spaced throughout the year, so as not to give the impression of the distress disinvestment. Disinvestment has so far failed in India; but it must succeed.

## REFERENCES


1. Assisi, C. and P. Mahesh: The Pain of Letting go, *Investment Week,* April 14, 1997.
2. How Vital is Disinvestment of PSU's, *Southern Economist,* May 1, 1998.
3. Krishna, Y.: Disinvestment the Indian Way, *The Journal of Institute of Public Enterprises,* 1996, pp. 166-69.
4. Leelavathy, D.S., New Vistas in PSU disinvestment, *Southern Economist,* Oct., 1999, pp. 11-14.
5. Nigam, Raj K. (ed.): *Management of Public Sector in India,* Vora & Co., Bombay, 1969.
6. Pathak, Rakesh Hari: PSU Disinvestment: Need for Strategic Planning, *PTI Economic Service,* 21(8), May 15, 1997.
7. Prasad, A.G.: PSU Disinvestment: Beyond Micro Privatisation, *Business Line,* May 30, 1997

# 6

# PROCURING FUNDS ON INTERNET-ACCOUNITNG AND CONTROL ISSUES

*Muneesh Kumar*

So far the emphasis of e-commerce effort has been the marketing and advertising The e-commerce offers unique advantages mainly in case of products that are information based, can be easily dematerialised (digitised) and where is markets for products are geographically scattered. Since most of the products that are being traded on Internet do not have all these characteristics, revenues from e-commerce are not coming in the proportions in which they were originally envisaged. The revenues from most of the e-commerce projects are yet to reach the critical mass level. On the other hand, cost of e-commerce infrastructure is increasing. The competition on Internet is hotting-up necessitating higher spendings on e-commerce projects in order to derive benefits from them. High rate of obsolescence in e-commerce infrastructure is reducing the time frame within which the investment must be recovered back. So the pay-back periods for e-commerce projects have to be pretty small.

It has become imperative for any e-commerce project to add a number of high value added applications. This will not only help in improving the utilisation factor of the e-commerce resources but also prepare the entire enterprise for the new e-economy. Procurement of resources is perhaps one such application that is likely to gain greater popularity. Procurement of resources, so far, has been restricted mainly to the raw-materials, though some of the sites have also started providing for procurement of human resources. Perhaps, one of the resources that deserves attention of planners of the e-commerce projects is the procurement of finances.

The primary objective of this paper to identify the accounting and control issues associated with procurement of funds and to make a modest attempt to identify the response of accountants in this regard. Though. the paper addresses the issues in the context of Indian business environment, it may find similar situations in many other developing nations of Asia.

## INTERNET AND CHANGING FINANCIAL MARKETS

Financial markets are perhaps the most dynamic markets world over. They have witnessed a phase of expansion, innovation and structural reorganisation in later half of eighties and early nineties. With the globalisation of developing economies, these markets are becoming more and more vulnerable to changes in far away financial markets. The improved communication facilities and convergence of computers and telecommunications have resulted in international boundaries becoming more and more blurred particularly in relation to financial markets. International financial developments influence the domestic financial markets quickly and decisively. Competition is becoming fierce in these markets. There are, now, more players in the financial markets offering a large variety of financial products to lure potential investments in financial products[1]. The Asian melt down and general decline in the confidence of investors in emerging markets has added to the challenge of luring investors to financial markets in these countries. Today, the two critical success factors in public offerings of financial products are: cost effectiveness and investor friendliness. However, the positive development in the last few years is the emergence of Internet as a facilitator of international financial flows. Internet is being considered as an important channel for marketing of financial products[2] not only because of its global reach but also due to other features. The present paper identifies the critical elements of the strategy for Internet facilitated marketing of financial products and the emerging accounting and control issues associated with such offerings. The paper highlights the need to address these issues in order to maximise both national and international financial flows.

## INTERNET AS A CHANNEL FOR PROCUREMENT OF FINANCE

Internet offers opportunities for accessing a large market for financial products, particularly for the emerging market economies. It permits the fund-raisers to market their financial products to investors located far and wide on the globe. Internet offers features that can provide a competitive edge to the finance manager in marketing the financial instruments. It is a relatively inexpensive[3] communication medium. The advantage with this medium is that it offers a unique environment which is interactive as well as private[4], global reach with facilities to update the broadcast any moment. By appealing directly to potential investors through Internet, companies can raise funds without spending a fortune on public issue expenses. The relatively low cost of offering also helps the companies to stagger the fund mobilisation over a longer period of time thereby reducing the total cost of funds. Moreover, Internet can be used as cost effective and investor –oriented channel for marketing of financial products. Internet based trading of financial products also offers unique environment for product innovation and developing niche markets.

It is evident that the advantages of public offering of financial products on the web are compelling. They can prove to be a boon for small companies proposing to raise funds that cannot justify the cost of public issue using the traditional media for advertising. Even bigger financial services companies such as Kothari Mutual Fund found it advantageous to use web site for its inviting subscription to its recent mutual fund scheme[5].

## ACCOUNTING AND CONTROL ISSUES

Public offering on Internet face the technical, legal and marketing problems that other e-commerce transactions are facing. In addition, these transactions of this nature give rise to some important accounting and control issues that need to be addressed properly before cyberspace becomes the darling of issue managers.

### *a. Accounting Standards and Disclosure Norms*

Perhaps, one of the paradigm shifts that Internet is likely to bring about in public offerings of financial products is that they shall attract investors from all over the globe, instead of targeting only the local investors. The investors abroad will have to depend primarily on the information contained in the financial statements and issue documents. Unfortunately, the accounting standards followed in different countries still are different. These differences regarding treatment of various items in the accounts make the process of evaluation based on financial statements more inconvenient. In the absence of understanding of these differences, the investor carries risk of errors in judgement. Such a risk results in loss of interest in the offering among the small investors who are not quite familiar with the accounting standards in the country of the issue. Recent efforts by the Institute of Chartered Accountants of India (ICAI) in the direction of matching Indian Accounting Standards with the International Accounting Standards are steps in the right direction. Perhaps, similar efforts, at much larger scale with greater commitment, are needed in other countries as well.

***b. Disclosure in Offer Document and Investor Protection:***

The differing investor protection laws and disclosure norms for offer documents in different countries are also likely to keep potential investors away from most public issues on Internet. It is desirable to develop model disclosure norms to be placed for consideration of relevant regulatory bodies. The recent craze for shares of dot.com companies has changed the yardstick for fair valuation of a company from 'earnings' to revenue[6]. With valuation of such companies being done as a multiple of revenue, a minor increase in the reported sales revenue can translate into significant increase in their market capitalisation. This gives enough incentive to corporate executives to indulge in inflating revenues figures using 'creating accounting'. Never before has the way the company recognises its revenue mattered so for an investor. Now investor's concern is shifting from 'quality of profit figure' to 'quality of revenue figure'. What concerns the accountants is the accounting techniques for revenue recognition being followed by even the most respected dotcom companies. Among the questionable techniques treating the entire amount paid by customer recognised as revenues, although a small percentage of this amount is kept by the company. For example, some travel sites are showing the entire sales price of airline tickets revenue. Some of the portals are including the price of barter advertisements booked in their revenue. The desire to shop for finances from abroad may also result in voluntary compliance by the issuing companies with the model techniques for revenue recognition and adhering to disclosure norms.

Another aspect of disclosure on Internet is the authentication of offer document. The contents of the web page for the public issues need careful scrutiny to avoid possibility of misstatement to solicit subscription. With issuer and subscribers located at such a far distance, it is not possible for the investor to distinguish between a good and bad management and company. As the changes in the content of web site can be effected almost instantaneously, there is a possibility of issuer making frequent changes to misguide the potential investor regarding the financial product and company profile. Any misleading statement made for a selected period of time in a day on the web page may not be easily noticed and even if noticed by a few, it may not be easy to establish in the court of law. The regulatory bodies in developing countries are yet to wake up such abuse of Internet publishing. Such changes can be noticed and controlled effectively if better mechanism for vetting the contents of web-site is developed and adopted. The vetting of the offer document on Internet may be done with the help of digital signatures and/or by denying the edit permission to the company with regard to the offer document. The possibility of alteration in offer document at different intervals can also be avoided by making it obligatory for the issuing company to place the vetted offer document of the web-site that is regulated by regulatory authorities like Securities and Exchange Board of India (SEBI). Such regulatory authorities already have access to the authentic copy of the offer document. Such a regulated web-site can also serve as an important and authentic source of information for investors regarding the available opportunities of investment in financial products.

In the absence of suitable changes in the investor protection law and practices, the situation is likely to be exploited and a few frauds by unscrupulous businessmen may shy away the investors[7] from Internet public offerings.

### *c. Electronic Payment Systems*

Electronic payment systems are becoming very important to e-commerce. The current online payment systems in most of the Asian countries are perhaps most primitive of the e-commerce technologies. Credit card system, which is most commonly used for online payment, was original developed for face to face transaction. As a result , they are full of security weaknesses. The recent rampant misuse of Global Credit Cards to pay registration fee for Unique Resource Locators (URLs) has not only put the Bank into trouble but also adversely affected the trust of customers in electronic payment systems. Perhaps setting up of Secure Payment Gateways[8] and guarantees by industry councils can help a lot in providing secure and trustworthy payment environment.

More secure electronic payment systems are yet to achieve the critical mass. The proliferation of different e-money systems and standards has hampered the growth of universally acceptable e-money.

Enormous currency fluctuations in international finance pose another serious currency translation problem in accounting, particularly in case of payments for financial products that could be substantial in value. Accountants shall have to develop methods for assessing the credit risks associated with the e-money so that business managers can frame strategies for managing such risk.

***d. Internal Control Systems***

Internet based offerings of financial products are subject to inherent and control risks. Most of these risks are there due to the lack of original source documents in paper form establishing the identity of the investor and other particulars of the transaction. Such a document may be created by printing the details from the original electronic form. However, the electronic form may be subjected to errors and frauds much before the hard copy is actually taken or at the time of taking a hard copy. As the electronic signatures do not find much meaning on the hard copy, authentication of the hard copy is also an important issue that deserves attention in this regard. In the absence of adequate accounting and access controls, fraudulent alteration of investor records may be difficult to avoid and detect.

Another operational risk is the risk of incomplete/duplicate recording of information regarding the investment order received from the investor. Inspite of the advancements in communication technology, communication failures and faulty deliveries of messages is not uncommon. As a consequence, the investor may send the investment order twice to doubly sure of delivery at the end of issuer of financial product. Better techniques of data validation and verification need to be developed to ensure correct recording of the details regarding the transaction.

**Accountants' Respnose**

The accounting and control challenges posed by the e-financial environment are really daunting but not unsurpassable. In fact, the most serious challenge before the fund-raisers to gain the trust of the investor in this alternative medium for communication for seeking and availing of investment opportunities. Accountant have for centuries been playing a crucial role in building up mutual trust between the investors and fund seeking business enterprises.

Use of Internet for soliciting funds from other countries is likely to gain more popularity among investors if the International Accounting Standards find universal acceptability. Accounting bodies like Asia-Pacific Conference on International Accounting Issues, American Accounting Association, etc. have a role to play in promoting international interaction in this regard and focus the attention on the need to minimise, if not eliminate, the differences in the accounting standards followed in different countries.

The problems relating to Maintaining a log of transmission between investor and the issuer of financial product needs to be maintained to deter frauds, trace causes of errors, facilitate backup and recovery and monitor actions on the part of staff of the company. It will also help in minimising the possibility of repudiation by the investors of contents of the investment order. Such a log may also the serve as audit trail for auditing purposes.

## CONCLUDING OBSERVATIONS

Internet public offerings of financial products are offering a host of opportunities for small companies whose funding requirements are too small to be of interest to investment bankers and brokers. Even for the bigger companies requiring smaller amount at different stages of implementation of their expansion projects, Internet offering is likely to be an attractive option. However, there are certain security, investor protection and accounting issues that are to be addressed fully to ensure that the potential investors do not shy away from this market. It is essential to ensure that necessary steps are taken both at the macro level and company level to ensure that the trust of the investors in E-Commerce infrastructure not adversely affected. In fact, the system must be put in place well before a glut of problems hit at the door of E-Commerce environment. Formation of Small Business Capital Acquisition Association in California[9], that guarantees the integrity of companies that list their shares on WWW is one of the examples of how solutions emerge as the need arises. SEBI must also equip itself to handle web-based offer documents. It must establish a regulated web-site which is used exclusively for hosting the offer documents and place the authentic copies of such documents on it. It must develop better practices and processes to keep an online watch on the content of the web-sites of the issuing companies and for handling of investors' grievances at the speed of Internet. Cyber-laws need to incorporate relevant provisions to ensure fair trading environment for investor and the issuer of the financial products.

Internet facilitated offerings also pose a number of challenges before the accounting profession. Developing better accounting control systems for paperless electronic records would require giving a fresh look at source documents for accounting. Accountants will have to spread a control-consciousness among all in and outside the enterprise to ensure that control systems work effectively. For Internet offerings to be successful in a country like India, perhaps the greatest challenge is posed by the attitude of people towards technology[10]. The future is promising as the new generation is quicker in accepting and absorbing information technology.

## NOTES & REFERENCES

1. Financial products include financial instruments representing investments in debt, deposits, equity and other such forms.
2. The intended emphasis on Internet to be used for marketing of financial products in indicated by the fact that ICICI is targeting to generate 50% of total business on Net by the end of year 2000. For details see The Economic Times, Dec. 21, 1999.
3. A typical web site may cost about $100 to $400 per million characters space per year. Some of the vendors also bill according to the traffic load.
4. Setting up a web site enables a manager to run an information server that can be used for describing the product features. The E-mail drop boxes can be used for meeting the queries raised by potential investors. The investors can fill up on-screen order (not 'application') forms and get on line information regarding the pending call payments and other information that may ordinarily may take long time. The web sites also offer facility for regular feed back from investors regarding the financial products and services. These sites also enable the marketer to get quicker market response to proposed product innovations.
5. Kothari Pioneer Internet Opportunity Fund was offered for subscription online at the an Indian investment site named WalletWatch.com, see Economc Times February 14, 2000

6. Amazon.com had a market capitalization of more than 20 billion US dollars without having made any cent as profit.
7. Security and Exchange Board of India offers special facility for attending to complaints of overseas investors. Visit http://www.sebi.gov.in
8. The proposed Satyam Infoway will offer secure real time credit verification, authorization of credit card and transaction approval from the issuing bank. For details see Web Vision, Vol. 3, No. 34 Dec.6, 1999.
9. The Economist, Nov. 23 ,1996, p.102
10. Negriponte, Nicholas, "The e in e-commerce will go away" in Business Today, Dec. 7, 1999. pp. 105-111

# 7

# CORPORATE GOVERNANCE: BOARD STRUCTURING

*S.K. Tuteja*

Corporate governance' is the latest buzz word in India. It is a topic of concern and discussion amongst business chieftains, bureaucrats, financial institution heads and academicians alike. It is evident from the ongoing debate on the subject that people cherish divergent views with respect to its meaning, content and intent. But they all are unanimous that "the key to good corporate governance is a well-functioning Board of Directors.

The effectiveness of any company board is largely dependent on its structure. The present article, therefore, seeks to examine some of the theoretical considerations that must be kept in mind while constituting corporate boards. The aspects covered include the board size, the number of inside and outside board members, workers' representation on board, the age and retirement of directors, board members' qualifications, and the appointment, role and goal of professional as well as nominee directors. While there is no standard applicable to all companies and to all boards of directors, there are a number of basic considerations which every company should consider in tailoring its board. These have been discussed hereinunder.

**Board Size**

How big should the board of directors be? What should be the size of an idea) board? Should it be too small or unusually large? Is it possible to evolve any norms in this regard? According to Koontz, a celebrity on board structuring, although it is easy to state in principle the ideal size of a board of directors, it is less easy to put this principle into actual members. A board should neither be too small to permit proper representation of varied experience and points of view, nor too large and unwieldy to allow adequate free discussion of issues before the board". He suggests a minimum of 5 and not more than 13 as the board size for any organisation. According to Juran, another authority on the subject, a small number narrows the base of business knowledge available for decision-making. A large number broadens the base (and also simplifies getting a quorum present) but also reduces the personal opportunity for participation and discussion. This results in formal, dull meetings. Effective group action seems to be the main determinant of board size. There are factors like mergers, absence of age-limits, reluctance on the part of promoter- directors to retire, etc., which compel a company to deviate from a 'desirable' number of board members. Any move to reduce the board size to this norm is resisted by those who are likely to be dropped in the process and considerations like status and prestige attached to board membership justify the need to increase it. Koontz opines that, except for the compelling reasons of representation which may force a board to be larger than desirable, other reasons for excessive size should be relatively temporary. In these cases, those who lead large boards should look towards future reduction of board to a workable size, or else a large board be broken down into various committees. Normally, endowed with broad powers, subject to suitable restrictions, the executive committee may act for the entire board. It reports results of its deliberations to the full board and the latter endorses it.

Under this method, the actual size of the board ceases to be too significant. However, in view of personal liability of directors for board decisions, many board members do not favour it and feel that board's powers and action get dissipated through it.

It, thus, follows that "what really matters is not so much that the number for board size be thirteen or three; it is the long-run results that count". The decision on how many directors should be there on the board is arbitrary and should be tailor-made to fit each situation.

**The Board Composition**

Closely and intimately connected with the board size is the issue of board composition. It is not only the number of directors that determines the effectiveness of a board but also the facts like the quality, efficiency and ability to function harmoniously of these persons. Over-emphasis on one and under-statement of another is just not possible. The two have to go together. In other words, a proper balance between size and composition is to be created and maintained. According to Juran, there is need for several kinds of balance within the board membership if the board is to carry out its mission. These include balance as to skills, business experience, age, and the inside and outside directors.

**Inside Versus Outside Directors**

Perhaps the most contentious issue related to composition of boards of directors is the question of how many directors should be company insiders and how many should be outsiders. The problem is aggravated by the fact that even the definition of what is an 'insider' or an 'outsider' varies. The most usual definition which will be used here refers to 'inside' directors as those who are full-time employees of the company and 'outside' directors are those who do not have a full time commitment to the company. However, in adopting this definition one must recognise that many directors are classified as 'outsiders' but they do have an 'inside' interest. The crux is whether the director concerned is under the dominance of the inside executive group or enjoys independence.

The main advantage of an inside director emanates from his familiarity with the business, greater knowledge of the company operations as well as his involvement in- actions taken. Thus, he is expected to act more intelligently and be highly motivated while making company policy decisions. Further, he is more readily available for company board meetings and will give necessary study, thought and deliberation. Knowing fully that his own personal economic future is dependent on the company success, an inside board member would tend to serve the board with greater efficiency.

The insider directors have certain limitations too. Firstly, it is difficult for any insider to play the dual role, *i.e.*, to be a line manager for majority of time and be a director on the day of Board meeting forgetting such line interests and prejudices. Secondly, it is difficult for the chief-executive officer and his subordinate to reverse the roles at the time of board meeting with the result that insider sides with chief executive officer and becomes often a 'rubber stamp' for him. The decisions thus tend to be not 'independent'. The company is also deprived of drawing on the experience of outside directors.

The case for outside directors rests primarily on the argument that setting of policies and board directions will be done better when the base of judgment includes men drawn from a wide variety of fields of interest. The outside director does suffer from some disadvantages. He does not have the insider's intimate knowledge of a company's operations. It is, however, disputed by those who are of the opinion that too much knowledge of the company can be an obstacle in deciding major policy matters and can lead to 'inbred' types of decisions. They argue that intelligent men of board experience have an extraordinary ability to perceive problems, particularly, if their minds are not cluttered with operating details, personal loyalties, and the pressure of precedent which grows from past operating decision.

There have been pressures for increasing outside representation on boards of directors. The American Institute of Management, while appraising the quality of management of various companies, has rated down the corporations which do not include outside members on their boards. The pressure has also been mounted by shareholders, underwriters and other investors. Apparently, the belief is widespread that this is the best protection against insider myopia and abuse of power, and the best assurance of the necessary responsiveness of a company to the outside world in which it must live.

**Balancing Representation**

The conclusion, therefore, is that the ideal board should represent a balance between insiders and outsiders. There is a recognition that valuable contributions can be made by both types of directors. The focus, thus, has to be on 'balance' and the board should contain a judicious mixture of both kinds of directors. It may be noted that 'balance' does not mean the 'number game'. It actually refers to the fact that the board should not be dominated unduly either by insider or outsider views. The real problem in balancing inside and outside directors is to ensure their effectiveness. This depends in part upon the abilities and independence of individuals.

**Case for Workers Representation on Board**

*General considerations* - An off-shoot of the insider directors is the problem of worker directors which has gained considerable significance of late in the wake of demand for workers' participation in management. Workers' participation in management essentially implies the influence of workers in the decision-making process of an organisation. It is a mechanism for voicing their views in management of an organisation. It is advocated by social thinkers for 'achieving social justice' and social scientists etc. on the ground of 'humane approach'.

The scope, extent and the form of workers' participation depends to a great deal on the employees, the employer and the government. It has taken several forms based on the political and socio-economic conditions in different countries. The typical forms of participation may be indicated as self-management in Yugoslavia, co-determination in West Germany Joint Councils in Japan, Works Committees in France and Collective bargaining systems in USA.

*Worker Director:* Placing workers on the board of directors is an example of the participation at the apex level of an organisation. Involvement of worker directors is suggested with the aim of bringing in workers' perspective, help the workers transmit to their colleagues the larger environment, with its threats and opportunities and, thus, be an effective two-way communication link. Some other objectives of worker directors are : *(i)* a feeling of enhanced status for workers and their union, *(ii)* an active role for the workers in the formulation of company policies, particularly those areas where worker interests are involved and thereby minimise unjust treatment of the workers; *(iii)* actually involving the workers in the long-term strategies and decisions, which are decided by the board as would lead to industrial peace and consequent co-operation and viability of the enterprise.

On the other hand, there are certain apprehensions about worker directors: The most important amongst these is, the one relating to 'role-conflict' the difficulty of playing a dual role. Such a director is supposed to continue as a worker and yet at the same time, when he sits on a board meeting, he has to take a broader approach, rather than a segmented one. If he pursues either line of approach, he ignores or treads on the other. Further, the bargaining power of the unions may be reduced as the worker director may be able to get some of the worker demands accepted at the board level. There is also a fear that certain company secrets could be divulged to the union and the members. Some people feel that the concept of private enterprise would be eroded, if workers, who were a very distinct group, now become a part of the board resulting in a potential class conflict. A worker director may be ill-equipped to understand and deal with the intricacies of board level matters; and he may be a loner in the board because of the fact that he comes from a different social stratum coupled with inexperience and unfamiliarity with top management processes. It is alleged that he tends to take highly segmented approach rather than a broader view which is expected of a board member.

**The Age Composition of Board**

A Board must have a mix of experienced and young persons. It has been strongly advocated by Juran when he observed that 'we need experience and seasoning not only for today but for tomorrow. To have it for tomorrow, we need some young men on the board today'. Fortunately, young men are waiting for such an opportunity but the problem is how to make room for them. The advocates of a retirement rule are highly critical of over-aged directors arid try to emphasise their demand by pointing out that, generally, these directors have poor attendance record, fail to do their homework, virtually sleep through the meetings.

Some companies in the USA have started including age limit for directors either in the byelaws or through resolutions of the board. A few others have developed retirement plans applicable to directors. The most usual rule for the insider is that he must retire from the board at the same time that he retires from the executive job and make room for his successor. Chief executive officers are an exception to this rule and they are governed by the rule as is applicable to outside directors. These outsiders are retired on an age-limit basis, generally, at 70 or 72. However, the majority of companies still determine the tenure of directors either on a case-by-case basis or not at all.

The following new / innovative retirement age programmes merit our attention:

*(i)* A new programme of retirement shall not apply to those already on board. This -would dispel any feeling that the rule is aimed at any one currently on the board.

*(ii)* A retirement age plan shall become effective from a future date, say, 10 years from now, to those already on board, and with immediate effect for others;

*(iii)* Add younger men, if need there be, by enlarging the size of the board temporarily. Do not fill the vacancies when the retirements take place.

*(iv)* Persuade one of the oldest directors to introduce the resolution for retirement age and get him involved in the process;

*(v)* Create 'honorary directorships' or a new class of 'director emeritus' with all rights of a director (including sitting fee) except the right to vote.

The question of retirement age has been a moot point for a long time. Forcing a retirement age is fraught with several obvious problems, often difficult to tackle in practice. No doubt, an incapacitated or non-contributor director must make way for someone with more vigour and ability.

**Qualifications of Board Members**

It is commonly agreed that the question of the director's qualifications is far more important than a board's size, the age of members, or the balance of inside and outside directors, etc. An effective member of a board of directors will possess intelligence, judgment, ability to analyse problems and come to rational conclusions. He exhibits willingness to identify himself with the company and its shareholder interests, and displays ability to speak out independently during board deliberations. He is expected to be an individual of high personal integrity and character.

## Qualities Sought in Board Candidates

A wide variety of qualities and abilities may be listed as the desirable qualifications of a board candidate. The main specification for a director contains both a constant and a variable component. The constant part of the profile applies to directors for all companies. The variable portion is tailor-made, hi arriving at a general profile, a number of factors are weighed. These include practical experience, specialisation, independence, age and willingness to devote time, etc. A number of personal qualities are considered by chief executive officers as non-debatable attributes of a director. These include:

- *(a)* Honesty, integrity and a feeling of moral responsibility;
- *(b)* Analytical ability and incisiveness to ask discerning questions;
- *(c)* A constructive rather than a critical approach;
- *(d)* Taking the long-term view and being able to 'sense the winds of change;
- *(e)* Placing the company interests ahead of his own;
- *(f)* Emphasizing overall company performance, rather than performance of some speciality;
- *(g)* Being able to appraise men;
- *(h)* Being compatible in group activity; and
- *(i)* Possessing the spirit of enterprise.

Effectiveness of directors is said to be dependent upon the following related factors:

1. A background of experience and knowledge which enables them to understand board matters and to apply seasoned judgment to them;
2. A status and personal character which makes them outspokenly objective;
3. Availability of time to do justice to their duties as directors and willingness to devote the time to these duties.

When all of these conditions are met, we have the ideal director. Opinions differ widely as to how heavily the board should be packed with specialists in fields like law, finance, marketing, personnel, production, etc. Some people are of the opinion that it is desirable to have board members with considerable experience and judgment. The need is to balance specialised talents on the board. There are others who argue that specialised talent and advice can be hired, if the company can afford it. "The sound position for a company to take would be to select persons who can contribute most effectively to board deliberations and decisions, giving heavy emphasis to individuals with broad qualifications, particularly in the field of general management". The same principles should be applied in respect of persons with vested interests like the investment bankers, commercial bankers, lawyers, stock-brokers, vendors, etc. In certain cases, the companies have no choice and as per their contracts they have to place representatives of the vested group on their boards. Given the choice, the company should take into account the profile of the prospective director and match it with its requirements.

**The Share Qualification**

Whether a director should be a shareholder is a moot question. The members of a company would wish their company directors to hold at least a few shares. It is considered to be a means of displaying interest in the company. It is, however, argued that holding a small number of shares does not guarantee enhanced initiative and efficiency on the part of the directors. They may be more interested in short-term stock speculation rather than anything else. That is why most of the statutes governing companies throughout the world, including India, do not make it a requirement. Rarely companies make it obligatory on the part of directors to hold qualification shares through the Articles of Association.

**The Professional Director**

It is commonly suggested that to enhance board effectiveness companies should bring in outsiders of unusual competence and experience. They are expected to give the required time and attention to company matters more or less on a full time basis. Such people should treat this as their only profession. Thus, they are 'directors by profession' or 'professional directors'. According to Koontz, "the professional director is an individual who devotes all or most of his time to being a director, usually of several non-competing companies in which he holds no other executive position, and from each of which he receives a fairly handsome retainer.

The practice of having professional directors on board has long been followed in England though the experience has not always been too satisfactory. In some cases the salary and title have been used to pension members of the promoter family or bring to a board the prestige of one of the nobility. On the other hand, experts in general management and in various functional fields have also been associated and they served the companies with great distinction. Professional directors have not been widely utilised in the United States.

Executives of companies, generally, oppose the practice of using professional directors. They apprehend that such a director would intervene unduly in the administrative affairs of the business or would command a fee higher than he would earn. His position, thus, would be somewhere between an 'employee-director' and an 'outsider board member'.

From the foregoing it emerges that there is a considerable need for experienced, competent outsiders who would be prepared to accept the role and responsibilities of a professional director. Since there is no organised market for bringing the companies and the professional directors together, adequate care should be taken while selecting the tight individual for the position.

**Nominee Directors**

The term 'nominee director' refers to the director nominated by any of the lending financial institutions on the boards of assisted companies under contractual terms of loan and underwriting agreements. It does not include directors appointed not because of such agreements but through an informal understanding between the institutions and corporate managements, or on the strength of institutional voting power at an election of directors. The power of institutions to appoint nominee directors on the board of companies, thus, arises from the terms of the loan and underwriting agreements.

The system of the nominee director of a financial institution has assumed considerable importance of late as a powerful tool of project supervision. This is particularly so after the issue of guidelines by the Government of India in 1971 enjoining financial institutions to nominate directors on the boards of companies assisted substantially by them, and including in their loan agreement terms a clause for conversion of loan into equity. The relevant Acts constituting 'the financial institutions provide for appointment, retirement, qualifications, etc. of nominee directors in assisted companies. These provisions override the provisions of the Companies Act,

1956 and articles of associations of a company with respect to the said matters.

The need for a nominee director stems from the same consideration that underlie the appointment of directors in the ordinary course by shareholders, *i.e.*, to keep a watch over the stakes of the financial institutions in the assisted companies. In the case of companies of recent origin, where 80 to 85 per cent of the total cost is met by financial institutions, the rationale of appointing the so-called 'watch-dogs' hardly needs any advocacy.

Prior to the issue of guidelines, the financial institutions resorted to the appointment of nominee directors only in exceptional cases like unfavourable or continued unsatisfactory performance of an assisted company or when it is facing problems, etc. But after the issue of the said guidelines, such appointment is compulsory if the investment of the financial institution exceeds a specified amount or there is constant default in repayment of either the principal sum or the interest due thereon.

In the early phase of this institution, attention tended to be focussed on the legal obligations and the formal functions of the nominee director in terms of the company law and other regulations. There has been a sea-change in the matter over a period of time. The scope of the office of nominee director has broadened with the considerable increase in financial assistance by institutions, and the focus has shifted to the overall role and responsibilities of the office of nominee directors.

The ideal framework for the role of the nominee director is one in which he pays balanced regard to the claims and interests not only of the institutions which nominated him, but to the other corporate public, namely, the shareholder, the consumer of the company's products, the workers and the Government. These interests are not mutually exclusive but are often coincident, and the objective of the company director should be to work out optimum compromises among the various interests. In general, over the last few decades and over recent years the facts of ownership of and stake in industry have undergone a radical shift in favour of the community being the major partner in industry and business. The social obligations of business have, therefore, acquired a new relevance and edge, and the role of the nominee director needs to be reviewed in a broader and more comprehensive perspective.

## Conclusion

Good corporate governance, *inter alia,* is an offshoot of a well structured board, *i.e.*, a board with balance with regard to insiders and outsiders, competencies and qualifications, age, etc. It should include professionals and experts in various fields. Such a board would go a long way in improving the bottomlines of any organisation.

## NOTES & REFERENCES


1. Bhalla V.K., *Financial Management & Policy,* Anmol Publication, New Delhi, 1999.
2. Gopalsamy N., *Corporate Governance—The New Paradigm,* Wheeler Publishing, New Delhi, 1998.
3. Gupta, L.C., *Corporate Boards and Nominee Directors,* Oxford University Press, New Delhi, 1997.
4. Juran, J.M. and Louden, J.K., *The Corporate Director,* Taraporevala Publishing Industries (P) Ltd., Bombay, 1980.
5. Koontz, Harold, *The Board of Directors and Effective Management,* McGraw Hill, NY, 1967.
6. Thicker, Robert I., *International Corporate Governance,* Prentice Hall of India, New Delhi, 1998.
7. Tuteja, S.K., *Corporate Management Structure in India,* Deep & Deep Publications, New Delhi, 1992.

# 8

# IMPLICATION IN DEMERGER OF COMPANIES

*Girish Ahuja*

Demerger is relatively a new phenomenon in the Indian corporate sector. While there are no specific provisions under the Companies Act, 1956 governing demergers some transactions of this nature do take place through scheme of compromise or arrangement under sections 391 to 394 of the Companies Act.

With a view to recognise demergers, a number of amendments have been made by the Finance Act, 1999 on the basis of following broad principles:—

(a) Demergers, should be tax neutral and should not attract any additional liability to tax.

(b) In demergers tax benefits and concessions available to any undertaking should be available to the said undertaking on its transfer to the resulting company.

(c) Tax benefits to such business reorganisation should be limited to the transfer of business as a going concern and not to the transfer of specific assset which would amount to sale of assets and not a business reorganisation.

(d) The accumulated loss and unabsorbed depreciation, in a demerger, should be allowed to be carried forward by the resulting company if these are directly relatable to the undertaking proposed to be transferred. Where it is not possible to relate these to the undertaking, such loss and depreciation shall be apportioned between the demerged company and the resulting company in proportion of the assets coming to the share of each as a result of demerger.

(e) The Central Government, if it considers necessary, may prescribe certain guidelines or conditions to ensure that demergers are made for genuine business purposes.

(f) The benefit available for demergers are also proposed to be extended to Authorities or Boards set up by Central or State Governments. This will help unbuilding of State Electricity Boards and such other authorities and help them in corporatisation.

**Meaning of demerger [Section 2(19AA)]**

"Demerger", in relation to companies, means the transfer, pursuant to a scheme of arrangement under sections 391 to 394 of the Companies Act, 1956 by a demerged company of its one or more undertakings to any resulting company in such a manner that:—

(i) all the property of the undertaking, being transferred by the demerged company, immediately before the demerger, becomes the property of the resulting company by virtue of the demerger;

(ii) all the liabilities relatable to the undertaking, being transferred by the demerged company, immediately before the demerger, becomes the liabilities of the resulting company by virtue of the demerger;

(iii) the property and the liabilities of the undertaking

or undertakings being transferred by the demerged company are transferred at values appearing in its books of account immediately before the demerger;

(iv) the resulting company issues, in consideration of the demerger, its shares to the shareholders of the demerged company on a proportionate basis;

(v) the shareholders holding not less than three-fourths in value of the shares in the demerged company (other than shares already held therein immediately before the demerger, or by a nominee for, the resulting company or, its subsidiary) become shareholders of the resulting company or companies by virtue of the demerger, otherwise than as a result of the acquisition of the property or assets of the demerged company or any undertaking thereof by the resulting company;

(vi) the transfer of the undertaking is on a going concern basis;

(vii) the demerger is in accordance with the conditions, if any, notified under sub-section (5) of section 72A by the Central Government in this behalf.

**Points for consideration for demerger**

*(a) Meaning of undertaking being transfered [Explanation 1 to Section 2(19AA)]:* For the purposes of this clause, "undertaking" shall include any part of an undertaking, or a unit or division of an undertaking or a business activity taken as a whole, but does not include individual assets or liabilities or any combination thereof not constituting a business activity.

*(b) Meaning of liabilities referred to in sub-clause 2 section 2(19AA) above [Explanation 2 Section 2(19AA)]:* For the purposes of this clause, the liabilities referred to in sub-clause (ii), shall include—

(a) the liabilities which arise out of the activities or operations of the undertaking;

(b) the specific loans or borrowings (including debentures) raised, incurred and utilised solely for the activities or operations of the undertakings; and

(c) in cases, other than those referred to in clause (a) or clause (b), so much of the amounts of general or multipurpose borrowings, if any, of the demerged company as stand in the same proportion which the value of the assets transferred in a demerger bears to the total value of the assets of such demerged company immediately before the demerger.

*(c) Value of the property of the undertaking being transferred [Explanation 3 to Section 2(19AA)]:* Section 2(19AA)(iii) specifies that the value of the property and the liabilities of the undertaking(s) being transferred by the demerged company should be at book value appearing in books immediately before demerger. This is also required to be read with Explanation 3 to section 2(19AA) which specifies that any change in the value of assets consequent to revaluation shall be ignored.

*(d) Benefit of demerger also available to certain authorities or Boards [Explanation 4 to Section 2(19AA)]:* For the purposes of this clause, the splitting up or the reconstruction of any authority or a body constituted or established under a Central, State or Provincial Act, or a local authority or a public sector company, into separate authorities or bodies or local authorities or companies, as the case may be, shall be deemed to be a demerger if such split up or reconstruction fulfils the conditions specified.

*(e) Shares to be issued on a proportionate basis:* Under the

provision of section 2(19AA) the resulting company should issue shares on a proportionate basis to the shareholders of demerged company.

**33.8c Meaning of demerged company [Section 2(19AAA)]:** "Demerged company" means the company whose undertaking is transferred, pursuant to a demerger, to a resulting company.

**33.8d Meaning of resulting company [Section 2(41A)]:** "Resulting company" means one or more companies (including a wholly owned subsidiary thereof) to which the undertaking of the demerged company is transferred in a demerger and, the resulting company in consideration of such transfer of undertaking, issues shares to the shareholders of the demerged company and includes any authority or body or local authority or public sector company or a company established, constituted or formed as a result of demerger.

**Case study**

From the following details submitted by R Ltd before demerger, determine the value of shares to be issued by the resulting company (say G Ltd.) to the shareholders of R Ltd. assuming division II is proposed to be hived off.

| *Description* | *Divisions I* | *Division II* | *Head office. i.e. Common to to both divisions* | *Total* |
|---|---|---|---|---|
| Fixed Assets after depreciation | 15,00,000 | 10,00,000 | 4,00,000 | 29,00,000 |
| Current Assets | 10,00,000 | 5,00,000 | 1,00,000 | 16,00,000 |
| Total | 25,00,000 | 15,00,000 | 5,00,000 | 45,00,000 |
| Share capital | | | 20,00,000 | 20,00,000 |
| Reserves & surplus | | | 7,00,000 | 7,00,000 |

*cont...*

| *Description* | *Divisions I* | *Division II* | *Head office. i.e. Common to to both divisions* | *Total* |
|---|---|---|---|---|
| Loans | 3,00,000 | 2,00,000 | 4,00,000 | 9,00,000 |
| Current Liabilities | 4,00,000 | 3,00,000 | 2,00,000 | 9,00,000 |
| Total | 7,00,000 | 5,00,000 | 33,00,000 | 45,00,000 |

Also determine the ratio of shares of the resulting company to be issued to the shareholders of demerged company assuming the shareholders of R Ltd. held the shares as under:

(a) Promoters 40%
(b) Financial Institutions 25%
(c) Public 35%

**Solution**

| | Rs. | Rs. |
|---|---|---|
| Value of Asset of Division II | | 15,00,000 |
| Less: Liabilities of division II | 5,00,000 | |
| Proportionate liabilities of Division II out of common liability of R Ltd. | | |
| $\text{Common Liability} \times \dfrac{\text{Book value of assets transferred}}{\text{Total value of assets of R Ltd}}$ | | |
| $6{,}00{,}000 \times \dfrac{1500000}{4500000}$ | 2,00,000 | 7,00,000 |
| Balance | | 8,00,000 |

The resulting company i.e. G Ltd shall issue shares of Rs. 8,00,000. These will be issued on the same basis which the existing shareholders of the demerged company have in the share capital of the company.

| | Rs. |
|---|---|
| Promoters $8,00,000 \times \frac{40}{100}$ | 3,20,000 |
| Financial Institutions $8,00,000 \times \frac{25}{10}$ | 2,00,000 |
| Public $8,00,000 \times \frac{35}{100}$ | 2,80,000 |
| Total | 8,00,000 |

**Tax concession/incentives in case of demerger**

If any demerger takes places within the meaning of section 2(19AA) of the Income-tax Act, the following tax concession shall be available.

(1) Tax concessions to demerged company.

(2) Tax concessions to shareholders of demerged company.

(3) Tax concessions to resulting company

These concessions are on similar lines as are available in case of amalgamation discussed earlier. However some concessions available in case of amalgamation are not available in case of demerger.

***(1) Tax concession to demerged company***

(i) Capital gains tax not attracted [Section 47(vib)]: According to section 47(vib) where there is a transfer of any capital asset in a demerger by the demerged company to the resulting company, such transfer will not be regarded as a transfer for the purpose of capital gain provided the resulting company is an Indian company.

(ii) Tax concession to a foreign demerged company [Section 47(vic)]: Where a foreign company holds any shares in an Indian company and transfers the same, in a demerger, to another resulting foreign company, such transaction will not be regarded as transfer for the purpose of capital gain under section 45 if the following conditions are satisfied:

(a) at least seventy-five per cent of the shareholders of the demerged foreign company continue to remain shareholders of the resulting foreign company; and

(b) such transfer does not attract tax on capital gains in the country, in which the demerged foreign company is incorporated.

(iii) Reserves for shipping business: Where a ship acquired out of the reserve is transferred in a scheme of demerger, even within the period of eight years of acquisition there will be no deemed profits to the demerged company.

***(2) Tax concessions to the shareholders of the demerged company [Section 47(vid)]:*** Any transfer or issue of shares by the resulting company, in a scheme of demerger to the shareholders of the demerged company shall not be regarded as a transfer if the transfer or issue is made in consideration of demerger of the undertaking.

In the case of demerger the existing shareholder of the demerged company will now hold:

(a) shares in resulting company; and

(b) shares in demerged company.

and in case the shareholder transfers any of the above shares subsequent to the demerger, the cost of such shares shall be calculated as under:—

Cost of acquisition of shares in the resulting company

[Section 49(2C)]: It shall be the amount which bears to the cost of acquisition of shares held by the assessee in the demerged company the same proportion as the net book value of the assets transferred in a demerger bears to the net worth of the demerged company immediately before such demerger.

Cost of acquisition of shares in the demerged company [Section 49(2D)]: The cost of acquisition of the original shares held by the shareholder in the demerged company shall be deemed to have been reduced by the amount as so arrived at under section 49(2C) above.

> For the above purpose net worth shall mean the aggregate of the paid up share capital and general reserves as appearing in the books of account of the demerged company immediately before the demerger.

Period of holding of shares of the resulting company [Section 2(42A)(g)]: In the case of a capital asset, being a share or shares in an Indian company, which becomes the property of the assessee in consideration of a demerger, there shall be included the period for which the share or shares held in the demerged company were held by the assessee.

***(3) Tax concession to the resulting company:*** The resulting company shall be eligible for tax concessions only if the following two conditions are satisfied:

(i) The demerger satisfies all the conditions laid down in section 2(19AA); and

(ii) The resulting company is an Indian company.

The following concessions are available to the resulting company pursuant to a scheme of demerger:

*(a) Expenditure on acquisition of patent rights or copy rights [Section 35A(7)]:* Where the patent or copyrights acquired by

the demerged company is transferred to any resulting Indian company, the provisions of section 35A which were applicable to the demerged company shall become applicable in the same manner to the resulting company consequently:

(i) The expenditure on patents copyrights not yet written off shall be allowed to the resulting company in the same number of balance instalments.

(ii) Where such rights are later on sold by the resulting company, the treatment of the deficiency/surplus will be same as would have been in the case of demerger company.

However, if such expenditure is incurred by the demerged company after 31-3-1998, deduction under section 35A is not allowed, as such expenditure will be eligible for depreciation as intangible asset. In this case, provisions of depreciation shall apply.

*(b) Expenditure on know-how [Section 35AB(3)]:* W.e.f. 000assessment year 2000-2001, where there is a transfer of an undertaking under a scheme of demerger, the resulting company shall be entitled to claim deduction under section 35AB in respect of such undertaking to the same extent and in respect of the residual period as it would have been allowable to the demerger company, had such demerger not taken place.

However, if such expenditure is incurred by the demerger company after 31-3-1998, deduction under section 35AB is not allowed, as such expenditure will be eligible for depreciation as intangible asset. In this case provisions of depreciation shall apply.

(c) Expenditure for obtaining licence to operate telecommunication services [Section 35ABB(7)]: Where in a scheme of demerger, the demerged company sells or otherwise transfer its licence to the resulting company (being an Indian company), the provisions of section 35ABB which were applicable to the demerged company shall become applicable in the same manner to the resulting company, consequently:

(i) The expenditure on acquisition of licence, not yet written off, shall be allowed to the resulting company in the same number of balance instalments.

(ii) Where such licence is sold by the resulting company, the treatment of the deficiency/surplus will be same as would have been in the case of demerged company.

(d) Treatment of preliminary expenses [Section 35D(5A)]: Where the undertaking of an Indian company which is entitled to deduction of preliminary expenses in transferred before the expiry of ten years/5 years, as the case may be, to another company in a scheme of demerger, the preliminary expenses of such undertaking which are not yet written off shall be allowed as deduction to the resulting company in the same manner as would have been allowed to the demerged company. The demerged company will not be entitled to the deduction thereafter.

(e) Treatment of expenditure on prospecting, etc. of certain minerals [Section 35E(7A)]: Where the undertaking of an Indian company which is entitled to deduction on account of prospecting of minerals, is transferred before the expiry of period of 10 years to another company in a scheme of demerger, such expenditure of prospecting, etc. which is not yet written off shall be allowed as deduction to the resulting company in the same manner as would have been allowed to the demerged company. The demerged company will not be entitled to the deduction thereafter.

(f) Treatment of bad debts [Section 36(1)(vii)]: Where due to demerger the debts of the demerged company have been taken over by the resulting company and subsequently by such debt or part of debt becomes bad such bad debt will be allowed as a deduction to the resulting company. This is based upon the decision of the Supreme Court in the case of CIT v Veerabhadra Rao (T.), K. Koteswara Rao & Co. (1985) 155 ITR 152 (SC) which was decided in the case of amalgamation of companies.

(g) Amortisation of expenditure in case of demerger [Section 35DD]: (1) Where an assessee, being an Indian company, incurs any expenditure, on or after the 1st day of April, 1999, wholly and exclusively for the purposes of demerger of an undertaking, the assessee shall be allowed a deduction of an amount equal to one-fifth of such expenditure for each of the five successive previous years beginning with the previous year in which the demerger takes place.

No deduction shall be allowed in respect of the expenditure mentioned in sub-section (1) under any other provision of this Act.

(h) Carry forward and set off of business losses and unabsorbed depreciation of the demerged company [Section 72A(4) & (5)]: The accumulated loss and unabsorbed depreciation, in a demerger, should be allowed to be carried forward by the resulting company if these are directly relatable to the undertaking proposed to be transferred. Where it is not possible to relate these to the undertaking, such loss and depreciation shall be apportioned between the demerged company and the resulting company in proportion of the assets coming to the share of each as a result of demerger.

**Other points for consideration**

(A)(1) "Actual cost" of assets in a demerger to the resulting company: Where, in a demerger, any capital asset is transferred by the demerged company to the resulting company and the resulting company is an Indian company, the actual cost of the transferred capital asset to the resulting company shall be taken to be the same as it would have been if the demerged company had continued to hold the capital asset for the purpose of its own business.

However such actual cost shall not exceed the written down value of such capital asset in the hands of the demerged company.

(2) "Written down value" of assets in a demerger to the resulting company: Where in a previous year, any asset forming part of a block of assets is transferred by a demerged company to the resulting company, then, notwithstanding the actual cost discussed above, the written down value of the block of assets in the case of the resuting company shall be the value of the assets as appearing in the books of account of the demerged company immediately before the demerger.

However the value of the assets as appearing in the books of account of the demerged company immediately before the demerger exceeds the written down value of such assets in the hands of the demerged company, the amount representing such exceeds shall be reduced from the written down value of the assets.

(3) "Written down value" of assets in a demerger to the demerged company: Where in any previous year, any asset forming part of a block of assets is transferred by a demerged company to the resulting company, then, notwithstanding the actual cost discussed above the written down value of the block of assets of the demerged company for the immediately preceding previous year shall be reduced by the book value of the assets transferred to the resulting company pursuant to the demerger.

*(B) Recovery of any allowance/deduction earlier allowed to the demerged company [Section 41(1)]:* Where a demerged company was earlier allowed any allowance/ deduction in respect of loss, expenditure, or trading liability and subsequently the resulting company has obtained/recovered whether in cash or in any other manner any amount in respect of which any allowance/deduction was allowed to the demerged company, such amount shall be deemed to be the profits and gains of business or profession of the resulting company of the previous year in which it is obtained or recovered.

## NOTES & REFERENCES

1. Ahuja, Girish and Ravi Gupta: *Systematic Approach to Income Tax,* Bharat Law House, New Delhi, 1999.
2. Bhalla, V.K.: *Financial Management and Policy,* Anmol Publication Pvt. Ltd., 1999.
3. Ghosh, T.P.: Accounting Standard and Corporate Accounting Practices, Taxmann Allied Services (P) Ltd., New Delhi, 1997.
4. Kretlow: *Contemporary Financial Management,* West Publicity Company, 1990.

# 9

# STRATEGIC PLANNING AND MANAGEMENT

*Subhash Mahajan*

Global aspirations of companies everywhere constitute a major force that is reshaping the world economy. Domestic markets can no longer be understood—or operated within—unless they are seen in connection with all other economies. No firm can ignore the international dimensions. Even the most domestically oriented business is likely to find that it is operating in somebody else 's international market. This interlinked economic transformation of the world economy has been so rapid that they have to reassess their products, their customers, their markets, and their rivals. It has driven them to prove their skills against the most demanding customers worldwide.

International managers, forced by the increasing intensity of the global competition, face a number of critical challenges, including competitors, customers, financial institutions, and governments across cultures, in managing a wide number of separate operations. Yet, despite this multitude of challenges and activities, successful international managers are expected to evolve their strategies in multiple environments. Although their strategies may differ from country to country, the basic concepts of international management remains same. To develop a sustainable strategy and to lead by strength, they try to focus on the implications of competitive strategies. It is well recognised that strategic planning is the process of determining an organisation's basic mission and long-term objectives, followed by implementation of action plan for accomplishing the mission and attaining the objectives. As a company goes international this process takes on new dimensions. One of the most interesting is that of going where action is, by setting up operations near world class competitors. The strategic planning process and resource allocation based on it can be used as a catalyst to achieve convergence among managers on key decisions and consensus—building among executives whose priorities and perceptions vary widely. It can create pressures for interaction among managers, for convergence of views, and for conflict resolution. A reward system for effective participation in the planning process and for achievements of goals and sub-goals fosters such a business climate.

Integrated planning involves global unification of functional, product or other strategies, and centralisation of decisions, particularly in production, finance, R&D, and investments. Adaptive planning comprising differentiation and responsiveness to diversity of country environments, multinational companies characterised by high technology or rapid technological change, complex sourcing, and high economies of scale often require integrated planning. On the other hand, firms with somewhat limited economies of scale, mature products in the product cycle, and major emphasis on marketing, and those facing diversity in consusmer tastes and government regulations need considerable adaptive planning. Most multinational companies have to achieve some balance between integration and adaptation in their strategic planning and operational decisions.

Through portfolio planning and hard-headed management, multinational companies have strives to increase their returns on investments by concentrating on their profitable and promising product lines and diversify country and product operations that have not been achieving their earning goals or that do not fit within their long-term company mission or definition of their business. These companies have been given more attention to international risk management and exploitation of their unique advantages. Portfolio planning can be illustrated by a Product Grid matrix of the Boston Consultancy Group, used since 1977 by a number of multinational companies. The companies utilising portfolio planning typically evaluate the position of each strategic business unit by using a 4-box matrix based upon relative market share and market growth. The box establishes the business units as (1) stars and candidates for investment and building markets; (2) cash cows to maintain the franchise for selective investments and positive cash flows; (3) problem children to watch carefully; and (4) dogs, to optimise cash, minimise investment, maximise profit rather than share of market and consider for possible divestment.

The company evaluates the performance of strategic business units (products/brands in country markets) in the past, present and future. The management attempts to ascertain whether the strategic business units are going to experience a success sequence-moving from problem children to stars—or a disaster sequence-moving from stars to problem children and dogs. The top international management works with the country and the regional managers in the evaluation process that considers the importance of each product/brand, the outlook for innovation, the relationship between various brands, current and future competition, and risk in various country markets in resource allocation. The process requires the management to make judgements on how the multinational company plans to manage its portfolio of strategic business units, with evaluation of appropriate trade-offs. This portfolio planning process provides a role for each product/brand in country markets and results in a means of allocating resources clarifying priorities and fostering communications.

Some companies experience difficulties in coordinating portfolio planning for their domestic and overseas units as a result of major differences in country characteristics and variation in risk. Managers can also encounter difficulties in resource allocation to strategic business units where facilities and resources are shared among these units. Further, portfolio planning may not be suitable for many new international activities or for those that require a period of nurturing before explosive growth takes place. Portfolio planning has to be integrated with the management process; it has to have a specific time frame for actions and implementation. Functional support is essential, alongwith patience and flexibility. Further, the top management has to have an effective system of strategic review and control of performance.

Faced with increased change and uncertainty and a more competitive international environment, multinational companies have been fine-tuning their strategic planning systems. A number of them have been moving into more integrative planning in order to rationalise utilisation of resources on a global basis. Another trend has been to develop more formalised strategic planning with line and staff managerial involvement at headquarters, regional and country levels.

Certain multinational companies try to ascertain the key strategies of major competitors in product/country markets in order to respond to them better. The strategic plan can take on an economic focus, a political focus, a quality focus, an administrative coordination focus, or some variation of the four. In addition, the global companies are typically predisposed toward an ethnocentric, polycentric, regiocentric, or geocentric orientation. The companies may use a combination of these orientations to evolve strategies for effective risk containment and opportunity exploitation. The process in itself, however, does not enable the management of a company to foresee and develop strategies to deal with the consequences of certain major political and economic changes. Nevertheless, a number of multinational companies have been utilising early warning systems focussing on key indicators — which they relate to contingency plans and action programmes.

All in all, the threat/opportunity analysis provides a major systematic way for multinational companies and its international product and strategic business units' managements to undertake more effective international risk management in the strategic planning process. However, the system requires sophisticated forecasting, comprehensive evaluation of key environmental factors and sound management judgement. It also requires periodic re-evaluation, alongwith comprehensive assessment of future political risk, socio-economic changes, competitive developments, contingency planning, and effective strategic and operational control.

The competitive audit assesses actual and potential competition faced by the corporation in countries, region and worldwide, particularly in major country markets. The audit involves analysis of industry, technology, product cycle and product development, and of substitute product trends in major markets. The auditing company then identifies major competitors in country markets, their types of operation, their business policies and practices, and their key strengths and weaknesses. The performance of units of the company is compared with that of competitors in matters such as sales growth, share of market, market/expense costs, quality of products, product change and innovation, better productivity, costs of manufacturing, physical facilities and scale of operations, profit margins, various measures of profitability, and competence of management and personnel. The analysis should also deal with companies that are producing and marketing substitute products and with potential competitors in national markets.

From the analysis of key environmental factors in major countries, combined with managerial and competitive audits and a focus on strategic issues, multinational corporations can generally pinpoint the countries with the most promising opportunities in relation to risk. Many companies have adopted strategic portfolio planning, however, which is a more sophisticated approach to determining priorities for allocation of corporate resources in complex enterprises with a portfolio of businesses. This approach establishes criteria for evaluating, allocating resources to, and planning the future direction of a portfolio of businesses involving a combination of several product lines in a number of countries.

## NOTES & REFERENCES


1. Asian Development Bank (ADB): *Asian Development Outlook*, Oxford University Press, New York, 1999.
2. Bennet, R.: *Managing People*, Kogan Page Ltd., 1989.
3. Bhalla, V.K.: *International Business Environment of Management*, Anmol Publication Pvt. Ltd., Delhi, 2000.
4. Cummings, Tomas G. and Edgar F. Huse: *Obligation Development and Change*, West Publishing Company, 1989.
5. Drucker, Peter F.: "The Practice of Management, Allied Publihsers Pvt. Ltd., Delhi, 1970.
6. Dunning, John H.: *The New Globalism and Developing Countries*, Bookwell, Delhi, 1998.
7. ———,: *Multinational Enterprises and the Global Economy*, Addison-Wesley, 1993.
8. ILO: *Employability in the Global Economy How Training Matters*, 1999.
9. Katy, Robert L.: "Management of Total Enterprise, Prentice-Hall, Inc., Englewood Cliffs, New Jersey, 1970.
10. Rojec, Matija: *Restructuring with Foreign Direct Investment*, Institute of Macroeconomic Analysis and Development, 1998.
11. UNCTAD: *Transnational Corporation Market Structure and Competition Policy*, 1998.
12. Weibrich, H. and H. Koontz: *Management: A Global Perspective*, McGraw-Hill, Inc., 1994.

# 10

# HUMAN RESOURCE DEVELOPMENT: A CASE STUDY OF DELHI UNIVERSITY

*J.P. Sharma*

The University of Delhi is made of four Campuses, *and* almost all the Faculties, University Departments as well as the University Hall of Residence, are located on the Main Campus.

Since the demand for establishment of an additional University for South Delhi did not find the favour of Government of India and the U.G.C., it was later modified into a modest proposal to set up South Campus for post-graduate teaching. The South Campus made a beginning in 1970, with a view to limit the growing size of the post-graduate classes in the Main Campus and easing transport problems for students residing in South Delhi colonies, and as a part of University's phased programmes to develop Multi-Campus System. A beginning has also been made to establish East and West Campuses. The East campus is being developed with the University College of Medical Sciences, as its Nucleus, while the West Campus will have its focus on sciences related to Engineering and Technology.

Of the 81 Colleges and other Institutions including eleven Evening Colleges, only a few are located on the Main Campus while the remaining, are spread all over the city of Delhi, with some of them situated at a distance of 25 to 30 kms, from the Main Campus. Of these 81 Colleges! Institutions, 19 are University maintained, 41 of Government of NCT and remaining 21 are Trust Colleges.

While the University was founded in 1922, the number of students studying in the University was 750. The student population remained below 2000 all through the twenties but exceeded this figure in the 1930s. At the beginning of Second World War, student enrolment in this University was below 3000. In 1996-97, the University had about 2,36,000 students enrolled, with approx. 20000 (including nearly 4000 research students of Ph.D. and M.Phil) as post-graduate students. There were 1,17,736 students enrolled in non-formal education programmes. 1150 foreign students enrolled with the University representing over 50 countries, provide a contemporary global perspective.

**TABLE 1**

**Students Enrolment 1996-97**

*(Regular and Non-Formal)*

| | *Under-Graduate* | *Post-Graduate* | *Total* |
|---|---|---|---|
| Regular | 1,02,945 | 15,592 | 1,18,537 |
| Non-Formal External | 10,839 | 912 | 11,751 |
| Correspondence | 91,426 | 2,908 | 94,334 |
| Non-Collegiate | 11,071 | 616 | 11,687 |
| Total | 2,16,281 | 20,028 | 2,36,309 |

*Source:* Planning Development and International Cell, Delhi University 1996-97.

## ACADEMIC STAFF

Academics in Delhi University by and large function as employee either of the University or of Constituent and Affiliated Colleges. There are thus two categories of University academics — those, who are employees of the University Departments and those of Colleges and teach at the Constituent or Affiliated Colleges. College teachers working in Undergraduate Colleges constitute nearly 85% of the total teaching community. University teachers have better remuneration, better working conditions, better office facilities and enjoys a higher professional status as compared to College teachers.

The teachers in University Departments belong to three grades i.e. Lecturer at the bottom of the hierarchy, Reader, and at the top of the hierarchy, is Professor. Rastogi Pay Review Committee has recommended two more grades for University teachers i.e. the grade of Senior Reader and Senior Professor. At present, the teachers in Colleges have three grades i.e. grade of Lecturer, Senior Lecturer and Reader. In the case of College teachers also, Rastogi Committee recommended one more grade of Senior Reader but the Ministry of HRD ultimately rejected the recommendation. Ministry of HRD in Oct. 1999, after accepting. The UGC proposal, has introduced Professorship by promotion, both in University Departments and Colleges.

**Strength of Academic Staff**

The strength of academic staff in the University Departments, in 1922, was only two teachers, and it increased to 208 in 1955-56, 626 in 1980 and in 1996 the sanctioned strength was 967 out of which 225 posts were lying vacant. The strength of teachers in Colleges, in 1922, numbered only 76, rose to 613 in 1955-56 and almost doubled itself in 1962-63, reached 4505 by 1980 and now it is around 8000. A detailed picture of the strength of University appointed teachers in 86 Departments of the University and College appointed teachers in 81 Colleges affiliated to Delhi University, is presented in the following three tables.

**TABLE 2**

**Strength of University Appointed Teachers**

| | *As on 30.09.1998* | | *As on 31.12.1998* |
|---|---|---|---|
| | *Sanctioned* | *Vacant* | |
| Professors | 172 | 52 | 341 |
| Readers | 373 | 87 | 202 |
| Lecturers | 376 | 73 | 187 |
| Research Asstt. | 46 | 13 | |
| Total | 987 | 225 | 730 |

* indicates actual strength of University appointed teachers as per 1998 AC/EC electoral rolls

*Source:* Planning, Development and International Unit, University of Delhi.

As most of the Readers in the University departments have been promoted as Professors under MPS, the actual strength of Professors in 1998 was 341 as compared to the sanctioned strength of 172, which is almost double of the sanctioned posts. The table reveals that a large number of posts of Professors, Readers and Lecturers in the Departments are lying vacant. The reason for this is that due to inordinate delay in the finalization of Visitor's nominees for the selection committees, the University could not hold selections for these posts.

In 1996 University of Delhi had a workforce of about 3200 university appointed and nearly 5000 college appointed non-teaching staff spread over 86 university departments and 81 colleges/institutions. The staff of university and its departments comprises the Vice-Chancellor and his team members, Registrar, Deputy/Assistant Registrars, Controller/Dy. Controller/Asstt. Controller of Examinations, Section Officers, PAs, Sr. Assistants, Assistants, Security Officers, Stenographers, and other lower staff. The staff in colleges comprises

Administrative Officers, Office Superintendent, Section Officers, Sr. Assistants, Assistants, PAs, Clerks, Library and Laboratory Staff and other lower staff.

**TABLE 3**

**Department-wise Strength of University Appointed Teachers As on 31st December 1998**

| | *Department* | *Professor* | *Reader* | *Lecturer/RA* | *Total* |
|---|---|---|---|---|---|
| 1 | Physics | 30 | 9 | 8 | 47 |
| 2 | Chemistry | 15 | 8 | 7 | 30 |
| 3 | Botany | 14 | 4 | 2 | 20 |
| 4 | Zoology | 9 | 3 | 5 | 17 |
| 5 | Anthropology | 14 | 5 | 3 | 22 |
| 6 | Geology | 10 | 4 | 1 | 15 |
| 7 | Philosophy | 7 | 8 | 2 | 17 |
| 8 | Education | 10 | 11 | 14 | 35 |
| 9 | Psychology | 9 | 4 | 5 | 18 |
| 10 | English | 10 | 3 | — | 13 |
| 11 | Persian | 2 | 5 | 3 | 10 |
| 12 | Arabic | 2 | 2 | 1 | 5 |
| 13 | Urdu | 5 | 5 | — | 10 |
| 14 | Hindi | 3 | 4 | 2 | 9 |
| 15 | Budhist | 1 | — | 4 | 5 |
| 16 | Sanskrit | 12 | 1 | — | 13 |
| 17 | German & Roman | 3 | 5 | 3 | 11 |
| 18 | M I L | 6 | 5 | 6 | 17 |
| 19 | Linguistics | 4 | 2 | 1 | 7 |
| 20 | Chinese & Japanese | 2 | 4 | 14 | 20 |
| 21 | Slavonic Studies* | 3 | — | 5 | 8 |
| 22 | Punjabi | 5 | — | — | 5 |

*cont...*

| | Department | Professor | Reader | Lecturer/RA | Total |
|---|---|---|---|---|---|
| 23 | Computer Science | 1 | 2 | 2 | 5 |
| 24 | Sociology | 6 | 3 | 9 | 18 |
| 25 | Lib. Inf. Science | 4 | 2 | 2 | 8 |
| 26 | Mathematics | 10 | 5 | 1 | 16 |
| 27 | Operational Research | 6 | 1 | 2 | 9 |
| 28 | Management Studies | 15 | 11 | 6 | 32 |
| 29 | Music Fine Arts | 3 | 10 | 7 | 20 |
| 30 | History | 11 | 8 | 2 | 21 |
| 31 | African Studies | 3 | 3 | 2 | 8 |
| 32 | Pol. Science | 9 | 3 | — | 12 |
| 33 | Commerce | 11 | 6 | — | 17 |
| 34 | Social Work | 6 | 5 | 2 | 13 |
| 35 | Economics | 9 | 9 | - 8 | 26 |
| 36 | Business Economics* | 3 | 2 | — | 5 |
| 37 | Campus Law Centre | 8 | 7 | 16 | 31 |
| 38 | Genetics* | 2 | 1 | 2 | 5 |
| 39 | Micro-Biology | — | 1 | 3 | 4 |
| 40 | Electronic Science | 6 | 6 | — | 12 |
| 41 | Bio- Chemistry | 2 | 2 | — | 4 |
| 42 | Plant Molicul Biology | 2 | 3 | 1 | 6 |
| 43 | Bio- Physics* | — | — | 1 | 1 |
| 44 | Adult Education | — | 1 | — | 1 |
| 45 | Mathematical Statistics | 6 | — | 2 | 8 |
| 46 | Geography | 4 | — | 4 | 8 |
| 47 | Lib. System | 22 | — | — | 22 |
| 48 | Sports Council | — | 3 | — | 3 |
| 49 | B.R. Ambedkar Centre | — | 1 | 2 | 3 |
| | | 341 | 202 | 187 | 730 |

*Source:* Electoral Rolls AC/EC, 1998 indicates Courses run in South Campus

**TABLE 4**

**Strength of Teachers in Colleges/Institutions Affiliated to University of Delhi**

| | *Colleges* | *Reader* 1994 | *Reader* 1998 | *Lecturer/Sr Lecturer/* 1994 | *Lecturer/Sr Lecturer/* 1998 | *Total* 1998 |
|---|---|---|---|---|---|---|
| | 1 | 2 | 3 | 4 | 5 | 6 |
| 1. | Acharya Narenderdev | - | - | 29 | 56 | 56 |
| 2. | A.R.S.D. | 75 | 66 | 44 | 25 | 91 |
| 3. | Unanani Tibbia** | 1 | - | 27 | 28 | 28 |
| 4. | Bharati Mahilla | 39 | 36 | 2 | 29 | 56 |
| 5. | Bhim Rao Ambedkar | 1 | - | 32 | 46 | 46 |
| 6. | College of Applied Sciences for Women* | - | - | 10 | 11 | 11 |
| 7. | College of Arts** | 8 | 8 | 9 | 1 | 9 |
| 8. | College of Business Studies* | - | - | 13 | 12 | 12 |
| 9. | Vocational College | 18 | 46 | 48 | 21 | 67 |
| 10. | College of Pharmacy** | 2 | 6 | 17 | 13 | 19 |
| 11. | Daulat Ram | 126 | 100 | 27 | 33 | 133 |
| 12. | Deen Dayal* | 1 | 1 | 46 | 60 | 61 |
| 13. | Deshbandhu | 54 | 70 | 81 | 58 | 137 |
| 14. | Deshbandhu (E) | 37 | 38 | 24 | 12 | 50 |
| 15. | Dayal Singh | 76 | 75 | 52 | 64 | 139 |
| 16. | Dayal Singh (E) | 29 | 21 | 14 | 25 | 46 |
| 17. | Delhi College of Arts & Commerce | 33 | 41 | 40 | 36 | 77 |
| 18. | Delhi College of Engineering** | 40 | 4 | 34 | 73 | 79 |
| 19. | Delhi Institute of Technology** | 15 | 3 | 15 | 35 | 38 |
| 20. | Gargi | 82 | 84 | 25 | 71 | 155 |

*cont...*

| 1 | 2 | 3 | 4 | 5 | 6 |
|---|---|---|---|---|---|
| 21. Hindu | 41 | 55 | 47 | 46 | 101 |
| 22. Hans Raj | 95 | 104 | 40 | 33 | 137 |
| 23. I.P. College | 75 | 63 | 24 | 35 | 108 |
| 24. Home Economics | 20 | 23 | 22 | 32 | 55 |
| 25. Indira Gandhi Inst. of Physical and Sports Sciences* | - | 3 | 18 | 20 | 23 |
| 26. Janki Devi | 80 | 62 | 32 | 44 | 106 |
| 27. Jesus & Marry | 35 | 20 | 74 | 85 | 105 |
| 28. Keshav Mahavidyala* | - | - | 20 | 21 | 21 |
| 29. K.M. College | 72 | 62 | 60 | 76 | 138 |
| 30. Kalindi | 10 | 78 | 76 | 30 | 108 |
| 31. Kamala Nehru | 73 | 80 | 22 | 23 | 103 |
| 32. Lady Irwin | - | 40 | 56 | 31 | 71 |
| 33. Lady Shri Ram | 69 | 72 | 40 | 36 | 108 |
| 34. Laxmi Bai | 88 | 84 | 22 | 33 | 117 |
| 35. Lady Harding Medical** | 63 | 11 | 22 | 93 | 103 |
| 36. Mata Sundari | 81 | 97 | 37 | 27 | 124 |
| 37. Maitreyi | 71 | 85 | 52 | 43 | 128 |
| 38. Miranda House | 79 | 76 | 40 | 59 | 135 |
| 39. Moti Lal Nehru | 66 | 65 | 26 | 29 | 94 |
| 40. Moti Lal Nehru (E) | 30 | 40 | 20 | 17 | 57 |
| 41. Maulana And Medical | 12 | 10 | 140 | 152 | 162 |
| 42. Nehru Homeopathy | 13 | - | 12 | 25 | 25 |
| 43. P.G.D.A.V | 54 | 48 | 35 | 55 | 103 |
| 44. P.G.D.A.V.(E) | 31 | 29 | 21 | 28 | 57 |
| 45. Ramjas | 81 | 73 | 36 | 53 | 126 |
| 46. Rajdhani | 72 | 74 | 28 | 36 | 110 |
| 47. Ram Lal Anand | 34 | 32 | 15 | 27 | 59 |
| 48. Ram Lal Anand (E) | 18 | 19 | 17 | 24 | 43 |
| 49. Amrit Kaur Nursing ** | 23 | - | 4 | - | 34 |
| 50. Satyawati | 45 | 50 | 38 | 54 | 104 |
| 51. Satyawati (E) | 23 | 28 | 36 | 41 | 69 |

| 1 | 2 | 3 | 4 | 5 | 6 |
|---|---|---|---|---|---|
| 52. Correspondence | 58 | 70 | 36 | 20 | 90 |
| 53. Shivaji | 77 | 76 | 47 | 37 | 113 |
| 54. Stephans | 22 | 28 | 46 | 45 | 73 |
| 55. Shri Ram College | 51 | 41 | 25 | 43 | 84 |
| 56. S.P.M. | 60 | 61 | 32 | 61 | 122 |
| 57. Khalsa | 69 | 69 | 50 | 60 | 129 |
| 58. Khalsa (E) | 26 | 48 | 45 | 28 | 76 |
| 59. Venkateshwara | 59 | 70 | 70 | 71 | 147 |
| 60. Shradhanand | 73 | 80 | 28 | 37 | 117 |
| 61. Shyam Lal | 63 | 55 | 8 | 20 | 75 |
| 62. Shyam Lal (E) | 27 | 27 | 2 | 11 | 38 |
| 63. Aurobindo | 34 | 36 | 26 | 58 | 94 |
| 64. Aurobindo (E) | 5 | 12 | 22 | 35 | 47 |
| 65. Bhagat Singh | 64 | 59 | 24 | 29 | 88 |
| 66. Bhagat Singh (E) | 15 | 21 | 25 | 36 | 57 |
| 67. Guru Govind Singh | - | 2 | 31 | 45 | 47 |
| 68. U.C.M.S.** | 58 | 51 | 43 | 55 | 106 |
| 69. Vivekananda | 45 | 53 | 25 | 30 | 83 |
| 70. Patel Chest* | 4 | 7 | 4 | 4 | 11 |
| 71. Aditi College Bawana* | - | - | 7 | 36 | 36 |
| 72. Zakir Hussain | 62 | 72 | 88 | 61 | 133 |
| 73. Zakir Hussain (E) | 49 | 47 | 11 | 26 | 73 |
| 74. GB Pant | | | - | - | 58 |
| 75. Agriculture Economics Research Centre** | - | - | - | - | 5 |
| 76. Bhagni Nivedita * | - | - | - | 26 | 26 |
| 77. Bhaskarachraya College | - | - | - | 21 | 21 |
| 78. Maharaja Agrasen* | - | - | - | 47 | 47 |
| 79. Maharishi Valmiki College* | - | - | - | 11 | 11 |

*Indicates newly established Colleges
**indicates professional Colleges
*Source:* Electoral Rolls 1994 and 1998 for the election of AC/EC

**Administrative Staff**

The university, on the basis of pay scales, has placed all these staff members in five different cadres. These cadres of employees of group A, B, C, D and E are as follows:

**Group A:** In this group, the employees working in the pay scale of 8,000- 13,500 and onwards are covered. They are Registrar, Controller of Examinations, Finance Officer, Deputy Registrar, Deputy Controller of Examinations, Deputy Finance Officer, Development Officer, Deputy Director, Assistant Registrar, Administrative. Officer, Assistant Controller of Examinations, Assistant Finance Officer, Accounts Officer, Internal Audit Officer, etc.

**Group B:** In this group, the employees working in the pay scale of 6,500- 10,500 are covered. They are Section Officer, Private Secretary, Senior Personal Assistant, etc.

**Group C:** In this group, the employees working in the pay scale of 5,000- 8,000 are covered. They are Senior Assistant, Assistant, Upper Division Clerk, Junior Assistant-cum-Typist/Clerk, Personal Assistant, Stenographer, etc.

**Group D:** In this group; the employees working in the pay scale of 3,050- 4,900 are covered. They are Lab Attendants and Library Attendants.

**Group B:** In this group, the employees working in the pay scale of 2,500- 4,400 are covered. They are class fourth employees e.g. Peons, Chaukidars, Mali, etc.

***Strength of University Appointed Staff***

The strength of university appointed administrative staff is depicted in Table 5.

The Table 5 reveals that the strength of male employees as compared to their female counter pans, is substantially high. Similarly, at the senior positions of the administration, only a small number of female employees work as compared to their male counter pans. It further indicates that most of the employees of the university fall in the category of group C and infact they form the backbone of the university administration.

**TABLE 5**

**University Appointed Administrative Staff (as on 30.06.1996)**

| *Group* | *Male* | *Female* | *Total* |
|---|---|---|---|
| Group A | 556 | 018 | 574 |
| Group B | 226 | 071 | 297 |
| Group C | 1242 | 274 | 5516 |
| Group D | 5004 | 025 | 1025 |
| Group E | 145 | 055 | 156 |
| Total | 2769 | 399 | 3168 |

*Source:* Planning. Development and International Relations au. Delhi University.

## IV. IMPLEMENTATION OF PROFESSIONAL DEVELOPMENT SCHEME IN UNIVERSITY OF DELHI

To meet the challenges of change and to operate successfully in the ever changing and dynamic environment, both teaching and administrative personnel of the university need to be equipped with the requisite knowledge, skills and attitude. It is to meet the above needs that the University of Delhi set up two Centres-I, the Centre for Professional Development in Higher Education (CPDHE) and II, the Centre for Human Resource Development (CHRD).

### I. Centre for Professional Development in Higher Education (CPDHE)

The National Policy of Education (1986) proposed to organize especially designed orientation programmes in teaching methodologies, pedagogy, educational psychology etc. for all new entrants at the level of lecturers and to organize refresher courses for serving teachers to cover every teacher in five years. As a consequence of the above; in 1987, UGC asked the University of Delhi to set up an Academic Staff College.

The University of Delhi after examining the proposal of the UGC sent a counter proposal for setting up a Centre for Professional Development in Higher Education (CPDHE) with a different pattern of staffing and functioning to achieve not only the objectives of faculty rejuvenation as outlined in the UGC proposal but also to understand and accomplish the broad aims of Higher Education system in India. The proposal for setting up of such a Centre was framed within the framework of the ethos of Delhi University, which has the distinction of having a large faculty with a high degree of academic capabilities. The university has nuclei of scholars in many departments with academic achievements of significance. It has a number of advance centres, centres of special assistance and of research projects along the frontiers of knowledge. Its intellectual resources are rich and have a potential for augmentation from other centres of higher learning in the city and elsewhere. The university was therefore, having a right climate for launching a scheme of professional development in Higher Education in a unique manner. The UGC accepted the proposal of Delhi University to start a Centre for Professional Development in Higher Education (CPDHE). The CPDHE started functioning in 1988.

The CPDHE has now been functioning for more that 10 years and it is the first major step in the University to tackle the problems relating to academic obsolescence and apathy. As stipulated and envisaged by the Expert Committee and the Executive Council, the CPDHE undertook the responsibility of conducting orientation and refresher courses for the university and college teachers. These courses are based on the framework of modern techniques and methodologies including Computer Assisted Learning (CAL) with respect to various disciplines.

### *Administrative Structure of CPDHE*

To ensure smooth functioning of Academic Staff Colleges (CPDHE in the case of Delhi University), the UGC has decided the following structure:

(i) An advisory committee for each ASC to advise on the courses and appoint the resource persons

(ii) A full time director to look after its functioning and implement the decisions taken

(iii) A course coordinator for each course

(iv) A standing committee to guide and monitor the functioning and working of Academic Staff College

At the time of the establishment of CPDHE, the UGC proposed altogether different structure than the one that exists at present. The UGC proposed four administrative posts namely Director, Deputy Director, Assistant Director and Section Officer. But Delhi University in 1988 remodeled the proposed structure and created the post of Academic Secretary in place of Assistant Director. Initially, Executive Council of Delhi University decided to have part-time Director and appointed Professor N.K. Roy as its first part-time Director. Subsequently, the university convened the post into fulltime one and Dr. N.K. Oberoi, Principal of Hans Raj College joined as its fulltime Director. After the retirement of Dr. N.K. Oberoi in June 1996, Professor S. Neelamegham took over the additional charge of CPDHE. Since than, Prof. Neelamegham who is professor in the Faculty of Management Studies and Dean of Planning and also Director of CHRD, is holding additional charge of CPDHE.

The programmes of the Centre are being managed by a Course Incharge who is normally a senior professor of a university department. The Course Incharge contacts the resource persons, draws programme schedules and decides course contents. The course coordinator who is a senior faculty member from a college, supports the Course Incharge in the conduct of the programme.

As regards advisory committee of CPDHE, very important persons including senior officials of the university, are the members of the advisory committee.

The following Figure gives an idea of the organisational structure of CPDHE.

***Courses Conducted***

The CPDHE has been conducting three kinds of courses: orientation courses having general and subject components, refresher courses in subjects like Physics, Chemistry, Commerce, Economics, English, Hindi, Botany, Microbiology, Mathematics, Political Science, History etc. and the special courses. The orientation and refresher courses are conducted in pursuance of the UGC requirements and are meant besides the teachers of the Delhi University, for the faculty from universities of North, Central and Western zones of the country. The special courses are meant only for the teachers of Delhi University and mostly cover inter-disciplinary areas. Orientation courses are meant for younger teachers and cover pedagogy, teaching methodology, educational psychology and management issues. The refresher and special courses are updating programmes for the serving faculty.

CPDHE

| Organisational Structure | Programme Mnagement |
|---|---|
| Director | Director |
| ↓ | ↓ |
| Dy. Director | Dy. Director |
| ↓ | ↓ |
| Academic Secretary | Academic Secretary |
| ↓ | ↓ |
| Sr. Technical Asstt. | Course Incharge |
| ↓ | ↓ |
| Computer Asstt. | Course Coordinator |
| ↓ | |
| Programmer | |
| ↓ | |
| Atendants | |

**Figure :** Organisational Structure of CPDHE

Each course has a curriculum with a definite focus. The orientation courses has a curriculum which is split up into various units—Societal Context of Higher Education, Management of Higher Education, Psycho-sociological Dimension of University Education, Functions of Teachers in Higher Education and Service Conditions of Teachers. The subject specific components of the orientation course deals with the methodology of break up of syllabus into teaching units, preparation of synopsis of lectures and reading lists, identification of topics for tutorials, seminars and framing question papers and objective tests.

In refresher courses, for example, in the course of Commerce teachers, the focus is on updating knowledge in accounting and finance and computer applications in these areas. The teacher participants undergo training in the form of workshops on various software packages like MS-DOS, Wordstar, Lotus 1-2-3,

Dbase-III etc. Likewise, the course on current trends in Chemistry has two important components namely fabrication of low cost instruments and computer applications in chemistry. Teachers are trained in the use of software packages like MS-DOS, Wordstar, Lotus 1-2-3 and other packages of use in Chemistry.

Since the courses, as explained above, are participative in nature, approximately half of the time is devoted for discussion between the participants and the resource person and amongst the participants. The faculty for various courses is drawn from amongst eminent scholars of the country. Senior teachers of the departments of Delhi University are associated with the Centre as 'Course Incharge' and senior teachers of colleges of Delhi University act as course coordinators.

Another important function of the CPDHE is the production of teaching materials for higher education. The Centre has prepared the monographs on subjects related to different components of orientation courses and refresher courses conducted by it.

***Number of Programmes Conducted***

Since its inception in 1987 till April 1996, the CPDHE has conducted 170 programmes including 30 orientation, 118 refresher and 22 other training programmes respectively. 4625 teachers of University of Delhi and other universities have participated in these programmes (see Table 6)

**TABLE 6**

**Total Programmes Conducted during 1987 and April 1996**

| | *Programme* | *No.* | *Participants* |
|---|---|---|---|
| 1. | General Orientation | 30 | 812 |
| 2. | Refresher Course | 118 | 2802 |
| 3. | Training Programmes | 22 | 1011 |
| | Total | 170 | 4625 |

*Source:* CPDHE Annual Report

### *Subjectwise Details of Participants*

It is necessary to obtain an understanding of subjects wise participation of

It is evident from Table 7 that very few teachers participated in the orientation programmes on subject like law, punjabi, computer science, library science, statistics, music, sociology, buddhist, stenography and just one teacher participated in the programmes conducted for tamil language, behavioural sciences, anthropology, bio-chemistry, ecology, philosophy-energy environment and military science. One reason for such a low participation may be either the small size of the college sponsoring the participants; or very small size of department in the college. Some departments of colleges have only one or two teachers and that department, with no possibility of finding substitute teachers, can not afford sending teacher for such programmes. Another reason may be the inadequate support from CPDHE officials for running programmes in such courses. The UGC may consider either shifting such courses in the Academic Staff College of some other universities or instead of all the ASCs conducting such programmes only four or five ASCs in the country may be asked to conduct programmes for such courses on the basis of regional demands.

**TABLE 7**

**Subject-wise Details of Participants**
**(1st April 1992 to March 1997)**

| *Name of subject* | *No. or participant* |
|---|---|
| 1 | 2 |
| **I. Orientation Programme** | |
| English | 38 |
| Economics | 59 |
| Law | 05 |
| Home Science | 08 |

| 1 | 2 |
|---|---|
| Zoology | 23 |
| Commerce | 55 |
| Maths | 20 |
| Botany | 49 |
| Hindi | 47 |
| Chemistry | 28 |
| Political Science | 30 |
| Punjabi | 06 |
| History | 22 |
| Microbiology | 15 |
| Psychology | 15 |
| Computer Science | 02 |
| Education | 08 |
| Tamil | 01 |
| Sanskrit | 11 |
| Physical Education | 94 |
| Behavioural Science | 01 |
| Library Science | 02 |
| Physics | 38 |
| Geography | 12 |
| Statistics | 06 |
| Anthropology | 01 |
| Music | 05 |
| Sociology | 02 |
| Buddhist | 02 |
| Bio-Chemistry | 01 |
| Ecology | 01 |
| Stenography | 03 |
| Philosophy | 01 |
| Energy Environment | 01 |
| Military Science | 01 |
| **II. Refresher Programme** | |
| Chemistry | 750 |

| 1 | 2 |
|---|---|
| Maths | 213 |
| Computer awareness | 169 |
| Commerce | 146 |
| Economics | 117 |
| Political Science | 89 |
| Physics | 70 |
| Bio-chemistry | 67 |
| English | 42 |
| History | 35 |
| Linguistics | 31 |
| Botany | 24 |
| International courses in chemistry | 19 |

*Source:* CPDHE, Annual Reports—1997-98.

## II. CENTRE FOR HUMAN RESOURCE DEVELOPMENT (CHRD)

### Organisational Structure of CHRD

The Centre for Human Resource Development (CHRD) is presently located at the administrative block of the main campus of the University of Delhi. Like Centre for Professional Development in Higher Education (CPDHE), Centre for Human Resource Development (CHRD) does not have a separate building of its own equipped with facilities like, its own conference hall and public address system, visual aids, computer room, library and separate administrative office.

The University of Delhi has constituted an advisory board of eminent people under the chairmanship of the Vice-Chancellor to advise him on the functioning of CHRD. Besides the advisory board, the staff of CHRD comprises Hony. Director, Deputy Director, Station Officer, Senior Assistant, Assistant, P.A., Typist and a peon. The following figure depicts the administrative structure of CHRD

**Administrative, Structure of CHRD**

Hony. Director

Dy. Director

Section Officer

Sr. Asstt. | Asstt. | P.A. | Typist | Peon

The working of Centre for Human Resource Development (CHRD) is explained in the following paragraphs.

### *Identification of Needs*

As a first step, a group of administrators from different faculties, departments and colleges are contacted in order to bring awareness amongst them that a need for training and development does exist and this interaction helps in identifying the training needs. These discussions with the various officers of the university have been extremely fruitful as they create a desire to attend these training programmes. There exists a process of consultations by short meetings prior to designing of a course and desired alterations and modifications in the course contents are made during the discussion process.

The need for the training programmes is also there because of the university's requirement of completing two such programmes for promotion of Assistant Registrar and onwards. Due to such requirements in the career advancement scheme of the University of Delhi and other institutions of higher learning in the country, there is a considerable demand for these training programmes and at times, CHRD is not able to accommodate all the applicants.

### *Training Programmes Offered by CHRD*

The Centre conducts £fresher courses for educational administrators, including Deputy Registrars, Assistant

Registrars, Deputy Controller and Assistant Controller of examinations, Section Officers, Administrative Officers, Security Personnel of the university, P.A.'s and Senior Assistants. A group of 20 to 25 administrators participate in a programme and the Centre conducts on an average 4 to 5 programmes every year depending upon the availability of venue for the programmes.

Though the programmes organised by CHRD are intended mainly for administrators of the University of Delhi, a few seats are reserved in each programme for participants from other higher educational institutions located in Delhi and outside; The participants of the training programmes, in September 1995 included the administrators of reputed institutes like National Dairy Research Institute, Karnal, Ranchi University, Lucknow University, Mother Teresa Women University, Madras, UT Bombay, Rajasthan Agricultural University Bikaner, Amrawati University, Gujrat Vidyapeeth Ahmedabad, IARI New Delhi and Central University Hyderabad.

275 administrators specially from Delhi University, participated in various programmes of C during its initial period of establishment i.e. from 1989 to 1991 (See Table 8). Another over 200 administrative personnel have participated during 1992 and 1994. The details for years after 1994 are not available in the records of CHRD, as it has not maintained any database for the programmes conducted and the number of participants for each year.

Since the inception of CHRD, over 700 administrators from Delhi University and other institutes of higher learning, have attended the courses. The CHRD had drawn up an ambitious plan of conducting as many as seven training programmes, for the year 1997-98 but due to non-availability of suitable venue, the Centre could conduct only two programmes. Similarly, for 1999-2000, there is a proposal to hold eleven training programmes for DR/AR/Junior Officers/ SOs/ Assistants and Administrative Officers of colleges, but again owing to space problem and other infrastructural problems there is a possibility that the Centre may not be able to hold any of these programmes.

**TABLE 8**

**Participants Details of Programmes of CHRD During 1989-1991**

| *Year* | *Participants* | *Designation* |
|---|---|---|
| June 1989 | 20 | AR/AO/Asstt. Controller Exams. |
| Sept. 1989 | 22 | Section Officers |
| Nov. 1989 | 21 | AR/AO/SO/Asstt/Security Officers |
| Dec. 1989 | 12 | SR. PA/PA/Steno |
| June 1990 | 20 | AR/SO |
| Nov. 1990 | 29 | PS/Sr. PA/PA |
| Jan. 1991 | 23 | PS/Sr PA/PA/Steno |
| Sept. 1991 | 39 | DR/AR/Statistician/SO/ and AR of H.P/Kakatia/IIT Kharagpur |
| Nov. 5991 | 43 | S.O./Sr. P.A/P.A. |

*Source:* CHRD Annual Reports.

## CONCLUSION AND RECOMMENDATIONS

The various issues and recommendations connected with the working of these two Centres have been dealt within the following paragraphs separately.

### I. CPDHE

While it is essential that structural provisions and external interventions are made available with adequate resources, it cannot be taken for granted that the programmes conducted by the CPDHE would have the desired outcomes. Infact the whole emphasis should be on making the HRD efforts more effective and qualitative. The need for making the training effective requires that the training should not only be systematic but the capacity and resources available must also he optimally utilised. This brings out the following issues and recommendations:

***1. Creating required Climate within the Organisation***

First of all, college principals and head of departments need to be actively involved in the ongoing HRD movement in the University so that these principals and head of departments have a better appreciation of HRD movement and CPDHE in particular. This would ensure greater success of the movement itself besides making them more participative than before. To make this idea operational, it would be worthwhile to consider the formation of Steering Committee at apex level of the University.

There are at present 86 university departments and over 80 colleges and obviously it may be difficult to have a Steering Committee with such a large number of constituents. To obviate this problem, the Committee's size be suitably restricted to say 50. Half of the members should retire every year. This Steering Committee should also have a few HRD experts. Their guidance and expert advise will enrich the deliberations and could help in better designing and improvement of HRD programmes.

It is also desirable to have a newsletter to serve as a communication tool of the goings on in the CPDHE and CHRD to be widely circulated among the colleges, departments and various other institutions in the University.

***2. Strengthening the Organisation Structure***

The CPDHE should be granted more autonomy on the line of other autonomous departments of the University. The job of the Director necessitates that he is on a wholetime basis and does not hold it as an additional responsibility. The Centre should thus be headed by a full-time Director who should be granted statutory recognition as a member of Vice-Chancellor team so that he can participate in all the statutory bodies of the University, as well as function independently. The post of Deputy Director and Section Officer, presently lying-vacant, be filled up without delay. This will go a long way in boosting up the motivation and morale of the present staff.

### 3. Identification of Training Needs

So far there is no systematic method of identifying the teachers who have to be imparted training either on the basis of felt need or as a measure which is mandatory. Thus whatever number of teachers have been covered so far, seems to have been done in a haphazard manner. Since these programmes have been prescribed under a UGC scheme, it is imperative that the selection of teachers for these programmes atleast meets the above criteria. The College/Department should draw up a training plan based on its own need assessment. This should be communicated to the CPDHE to incorporate these requirements in its own training programme and prepare the calendar of training programmes accordingly.

### 4. Course, Duration, Design and Contents

Course, duration, design and contents constitute very significant components of the entire training process, since it is the quality and coverage of these inputs which is going to make the desired impact on the participants. The suggestions are:

*Review of Programme Duration*

Most of the refresher courses were conducted for 21 days. Adding the days of travel, the outstation teachers were away from their colleges for as much as four weeks depending on the distance and possible mode of travel between their colleges and CPDHE. On the other hand, coordinators and resource persons who were invited for several sessions, were partially away from their workplace for say S to 20 days. Can the refresher course be for 15 days? There are small colleges having I to 10 or even less teachers in a department, with no possibility of finding substitute teachers. The refresher courses cannot always be conducted in vacation. The pattern of refresher courses can be changed and duration of 21 days can be shortened.

*Focus on Thrust Areas*

If it is possible, the thrust areas of Refresher Courses can be announced beforehand and only those teachers in need of updating the knowledge in announced thrust areas can be encouraged to participate.

*Review of Curriculum*

The curriculum is an important ingredient of any academic institution. Large number of participants suggested that CPDHE should keep on revising the curriculum constantly and should add new topics in the curriculum. The planning of course curriculum should be in such a way as to relate it to changing needs.

### 5. *Evaluation of Training Programmes*

Evaluation of training programmes is a weak area in CPDHE. The deficiencies are:

1. inadequate coverage of all the aspects of training programme.
2. inadequate schedule for assessing the effectiveness of course; and
3. No evidence of evaluation being conducted at all the levels namely immediate, inter-mediate and ultimate level.

The criticality of evaluation cannot be understated because it provides a very significant tool of feedback mechanism which goes directly into the overall training process. Notwithstanding the fact that an effective feedback mechanism is found wanting more as a general practice rather than an exception, it is highly desirable that CPDHE handles this critical component of training with greater sense of responsibility. Our resources are extremely limited and we have more miles to go.

***6. Other Issues***

*(i) Need for Stepping up the Number of pProgrammes*

In view of the knowledge explosion whereby new knowledge is replacing the earlier one much faster today than ever before, the training cycle itself may have to be repeated more than once or twice.

So far, CPDHE has not envisaged training programmes for Principals and Heads of Departments which have a dual role to play namely academics as well as administrative. The future plan should he to have an orientation programme for Principals, Head of Departments and other cadres of teachers so as to make them aware of its importance and utility. Teachers with more than eight years experience may also be considered for admission to orientation programmes.

Under the present rules, a newly appointed Ph.D. teacher is placed in the senior scale after 4 years when he completes two courses. As per CPDHE requirements such a teacher is entitled for one orientation programme and is not entitled for refresher courses till he or she completes 4 years. This is an anomaly which should be removed. The UGC should think of reducing the service limit for attending refresher courses at least in the case of Ph.D. holders to 213 years. Further anyone who teaches should be asked to undergo an orientation programme irrespective of the fact that the teacher is part-time or ad-hoc.

Out of 8000 teachers, the strength of commerce teachers in Delhi University is more than 900 which constitutes the largest single block of teachers. There seems to be quite huge backlog of teachers specially commerce teachers yet to he exposed to systematic training both orientation as well as refresher. Therefore, there is a special need for stepping up the number of programmes in order to cover more and more commerce teachers.

*(ii) Problem of Oversized Groups*

The practice of training oversized groups i.e. by including as many as 45 participants against the norm of 20 is not going to give effective results. This problem is really attributed to (i) shortage of space and (ii) demand rush of teachers (so as to complete training to be eligible for higher promotion). In the process, both the quality and effectiveness of training suffers. Till such time the infrastructure facilities remain inadequate, the desirability of organising courses of shorter duration should he considered. Even otherwise a quality training for 15 days can prove to be more rewarding than a generalised training of 21 days catering to oversized groups housed in cramped accommodation.

*(iii) Need to Create Library Facilities*

The CPDHE library at present is housed in a small room without any sitting facility so it cannot be called a library—just a collection of hooks locked in almirahs. This needs urgent attention. The minimum that can be done is to create a reference facility with sitting arrangement. Further, subjectwise training programme's latest available publications may be borrowed from the sister libraries within and outside the university system so that such books and material can be made available for reference and reading by the participants.

Another important aspect of training is the reading material made available to the participants of training programmes.

Based on the feedback given by the participants, the quality of reading material needs to be improved a lot. There is no evidence of any new material being added from time to time and also there is no proper record of the reading material which has been produced in the past. To systematise the whole process of producing reading material, there is need to organise proper documentation of the material already produced and new material to be generated so that every time a particular training programme is held, only such material is selected which is most appropriate.

*(iv) Putting Computer to Effective Use*

The CPDHE should maintain a suitable database of teachers already trained as well as to be trained. This would enable the Centre to set proper targets and plan its programme more systematically and methodically. Infact this issues is closely related to the process of Human Resource Planning and its relevance to HRD which process is practically non-existent at present.

*(v) Need for Continuous Development*

It is almost common place these days to hear the view that training should be a continuous process. This is prompted by the suggestion that employees cannot in a rapidly changing world rely on the knowledge and skill acquired initially but keep such knowledge and skills updated by training and retraining on continuous basis. This brings into focus the need for developing the CPDHE into a permanent, full-fledged and self contained staff college with a permanent building of its own, hostel facility for the participants and staff quarters.

*(vi) Review of CPDHE Working*

Academic Staff Colleges (CPDHE in the case of Delhi University) all over the country are working subject to review by an independent body namely National Institute of Educational Planning and Administration (NIEPA). NIEPA under the directions of UGC produced the review report in 1992 with certain recommendations. The Review Committee observed that since the performance of some of the Academic Staff Colleges had not been so satisfactory in relation to organisation of programmes, they should be reviewed after one year and in case their performance continued to be unsatisfactory, they should he closed. The committee also decided to discontinue three staff colleges where no programmes were conducted. Another committee constituted by UGC to review the functioning of these staff colleges submitted its report in December 1997, but it is not known what follow-up action is taken on such reports in order to improve the work and performance of ASCs and CPDHE. It is suggested that Delhi University may also take up a detailed review of the working of CPDHE and it could be one of the role which could be assigned to the proposed Steering Committee (HRD).

**II. CHRD**

Much of the issues concerning the working of CHRD are the same as mentioned against CPDHE namely, inadequate infrastructural facilities, lack of support from the top management, outdated course contents, absence of proper evaluation mechanism and financial problems. However, since CHRD is again a distinct Centre under the scheme, it has also got certain specific issues pertaining to its working. They are briefly summarized below:

***1. Widening the Scope of Programmes***

CHRD conducts programmes only for DRs/ARs/SO's/PAs/Stenos/Asstts. and Security personnel. It has no scheme of training programmes for senior officials of the University e.g. Registrar, Dean of Faculties, Head of Departments, Director of Institutes and Principal of Colleges. Since most of the above mentioned posts are term posts, every new incumbent who joins the post requires at least some training to improve the performance on the job.

The principals of colleges are held responsible to face and solve problems related to students admissions, elections to students union, conduct of examinations, maintenance of discipline, issues raised by the associations of teachers and karamcharis, holding functions in the college. They have to exercise leadership functions in many areas. All this requires a proper and systematic training, for which presently there is no mechanism in the training system of CHRD or CPDHE.

Similarly the Registrar, Controller of Examinations, Dean of Faculties and Head of Departments, the vice-chancellor and his team members in the University are always encircled by piles of files and documents on their table. Their jobs are tiring and time-consuming which involves careful scrutiny and continuous supervision. Since they are usually from academic having no administrative experience, training for them becomes imperative.

### 2. *A Case for Making the CHRD Self Supporting*

The main source of finance of the CHRD is funds made available by the University. The Centre also collects fees from outside participants. Unlike CPDHE, CHRD is not directly funded by UGC. This is the reason, the CHRD lacks even the minimum infrastructural facilities. There are complaints of the delay in the release of grants from the finance branch. Some of the programmes are either postponed or cancelled by the CHRD due to this problem. It is therefore suggested that the CHRD should be directly financed by UGC on the line of CPDHE.

It is also suggested that there should be a financial review of the working of CHRD in order to examine whether the Centre should be run on self supporting basis or should be run on straight lump sum grants worked out on the basis of its legitimate operative requirements.

### 3. *Need for Cost Benefit Analysis*

From the details mentioned earlier it would be seen that out of the total expenditure of CHRD a large chunk goes towards salaries of staff whereas only a small component is incurred on conducting the training programme numbering on an average of 4 per year. It is felt that the output of this Centre in terms of training programmes and persons trained is not at all commensurate with the resources spent on running the Centre. There is thus a need to examine various options towards making this Centre cost effective by either increasing its productivity or allocating more resources to develop it a full-fledged staff training centre.

### 4. *Top Management Involvement*

There should be an effective communication between the university senior officials and the training system in CHRD. As already mentioned, a high powered Steering Committee (HRD) should meet periodically to decide on training priorities, plans and to their review. This will demonstrate the necessary top management involvement and support.

### 5. *Training Need Identification*

In the CHRD, training need identification is not systematically done; as a result training system and operational sides tend to move in different directions. Therefore, the Centre should have continuous interaction with college principals, heads of the university departments, and senior officials of the university so that it is able to design training programme to meet the training needs of the non- teaching staff

### 6. *Use of Current Technology to Aid Training*

Developments in the field of electronic are now bringing about a revolution in the field of training. Modern equipments like TV, Radio, Video and computers are now making their way into classrooms. Accordingly, the CHRD also needs to go in for these new training tools.

### 7. *Review of the Working of CHRD*

During the course of study and from the discussion held, an impression is gathered that the CHRD has not been preparing its annual reports on a regular basis. The only report on record are the reports prepared for the year 1994-95 and 1995-96, even though the Centre was established in the year 1987. It could not be ascertained if there might exist any other mechanism of reporting its activities to the highest body in the university namely the University Court. It is also not know whether there exists any reporting relationship between the CHRD and the Executive Council of Delhi University. This implies that neither the performance of this Centre nor the problems and difficulties that it experiences get into the notice of the higher authorities. It is suggested that the management may take up a detailed review of the working of CHRD on priority basis, so that any impediments in further growth and development of an otherwise good Centre can be effectively removed.

## LOOKING AHEAD

It is said that:

(i) The aim of education is essentially three-fold

(a) to improve intellectual excellence and individual happiness and to sensibilize to ethical, cultural and social values to make one enlightened;

(b) to acquire knowledge, skill, enterprise and scientific attitudes to be self-competent and self-reliant thereby contributing to development;

(c) to be responsible for and responsive to the

needs and demands of the society and the world.

(ii) Education should be perceived as a seamless continuum of lifelong learning for Human Development.

CPDHE and CHRD have amply justified their existence all these years, even though there is considerable scope for improvement. In the light of this study, and the issues and recommendations brought out above, if necessary follow up action is also taken by the concerned authorities, than there is every hope that these two Centres of learning are going to emerge as Centres of excellence to attain the above mentioned aims and objectives.

## REFERENCES

Bali, Arun P. (1986), "College Teachers—Challenges and Responses—A Study in Context of Delhi University, p. 27-45.

Benakanal, V.A. and Sahoo, P.K. (1994), "Faculty Development and Academic Staff colleges," *University News,* December 19.

Centre for Human Resource Development "Annual report 1995-96."

CPDHE, "Annual Report—1997-98," p. 2.

Delhi University (1988), "Calendar Vol. I—The Act, Statutes and Ordinances.

Delhi University "72nd Annual Report, 1994-95."

Indiresan, J. (1991), "Faculty Development," *University News,* January 14.

Internatinal Labour Office (1987), "Teaching and Trainign Methods of Management Development" Geneva.

Joshi, K.G. (1998), "Refresher Course—An Opportunity for Improvement in Academics of Teachers," *University News,* March 16.

Kapur, J.N. (1991), "Teacher Training in Higher Education," *University News,* June 24.

Kashinath, H.M. (1995), "Pre-induction Course to Improve Teaching," *University News,* Jan., 9.

NIEPA (1992), "Planning and Implementation of Academic Staff Development Programme," *NIEPA Report.*0

NIEPA (1992), "Review Meeting of Directors of Academic Staff Colleges."

Pal, Rajindra (1988), "Evaluation of Academic Staff College," M.Ed. Dissertation.

Passi B.K. and Pal, Rajindera (1991), "Relevance of Existing Curriculum of Academic Staff Colleges," *University Lecturers," University News*, June 10.

Pattansheti, M.M. and Gowda, J.M. (1998), "Induction Training Programme for Newly appointed College and University Lecturers," *University News*, Feb.

Rastogi, S. an᠎d kantharia, K.G. (1998), "Human Relationin India Universities." *University News*, Nov.. 30.

Singh, P.N. (1984), "Trainign for Management Development," p. 125.

Singh, A.K. (1990), "Emerging Areas of Research on Audio Visual Education," *University News*, Dec., 24.

Sunil Kumar (1991), "Teacher Development," *University News*, May 13.

Uberoi, U.N. (1990) "Centre for Professional Development—

A New Experiment at Delhi University," *University News*, June 4.

UGC (1997), "On Pay Scales," *UGC Review Report*, Dec.

University of Delhi Information Bulletin Published by Planning Development and International Relaitons Cell, 1996-97.

University of Delhi (1989), "Centre for Human Resources Development—Brochure."

University of Delhi (1989), "Centre for Professioanl Development in Higher Education—Reort One."

Valicha, Kishore (1990), "You canot tech without training," *University News*, July 2.

Verma, Yogendra (1990), "Orientation for Quality in Higher Education," *University News*, March 26.

# 11

## WTO AND NON-TARIFF BARRIERS

*Devendra Kumar, J.P. Sharma and V.P. Bansal*

The recognition of the economic superiority of tariffs over quotas as instruments of trade protection is incorporated in the form of Article XI of GATT 1994. This is one the basic principles of WTO. Two exceptions to this general rule take the shape of Article XII (balance of payments difficulties) and Article XVIII (greater flexibility for developing countries). The aim of trade liberalization is sought to be achieved through further non-increase of tariff levels through the technique of tariff bindings with the declared objective of ultimately reducing their levels in the long run.

The first five years of WTO have witnessed that while many countries have reduced tariff levels to very low levels on industrial goods, non-tariff measures are increasingly being relied upon as neo-protectionist measures. These measures fall within the agreements on Sanitary and Phytosanitary Measures (SPS), Technical Barriers to Trade (TBT), Anti-dumping measures, and Rules of Origin. Additionally, there are attempts to enlarge the canvas in terms of 'new issues' like core labour and environmental standards.

Based on Article XX (b) of GATT 1994, the SPS agreement recognizes the right of members to take measures necessary for the protection of human, animal or plant life or health provided such measures are based on "sufficient scientific evidence" [Article 2(2)] and are "not applied in a manner which would constitute a disguised restriction on international trade" [Article 2(3)], in order to prevent the use of SPS measures as arbitrary protectionist actions. In addition, SPS must equally apply to domestically produced goods and goods from all other countries, in accordance with the two other basic principles of GATT 1994, the most favoured nation rule (MFN) [Article I] and the national treatment rule [Article III].

The area covered by the SPS agreement relates to agriculture alone and is specifically confined to risks to animal or plant life or health from diseases and pests as well as "risks arising from additives, contaminants, toxins or disease carrying organisms in foods, beverages or feedstuffs."

The last five years of WTO experience are replete with allegations of misuse of the provisions of the SPS agreement with many SPS actions being characterized as non-tariff barriers.

A landmark objection was the European Union's ban on import of hormone treated beef from USA and Canada. The European Scientists believed that hormone treated beef could endanger human health, while Canadian and US scientists questioned this view on the basis of inadequate evidence. WTO's Dispute Settlement Body has decreed in favour of USA and Canada in a highly controversial ruling. The EU has preferred to pay compensation rather than allow entry of the product into its borders.

For some time, the Philippines has been making strong criticism of Australian SPS measures directed against its fruit exports. Australia relied on its quarantine rules to erect non-tariff barriers. For instance, it took a long nine -year period tc evaluate and finally rule out the possibility of risk from Philippines mangoes. The a large number of preconditions were imposed along with the condition that only mangoes from a particular area—Guimaras Island—could be exported to Australia. Later, Australia determined that a minimum period of 26 months was to be required for assessing the risk from Philippine bananas. Philippine pineapples also faced SPS barriers in Australia. As a retaliatory measure, in June 2000, Philippines announced a 20% cut in imports of cattle from Australia. This was a significant action hurting Australia because Philippines is the main destination for Australian cattle exports. This led to immediate negotiations between the two countries and Australia agreed cut the time required by conducting the quarantine tests simultaneously for different fruits when earlier they insisted on these tests being carried out only one by one. However, Philippines is not revising its decision to go to WTO's Dispute Settlement Body against Australian testing of imported fruit.

The agreement on Technical Barriers to Trade (TBT) recognizes the sovereign rights of members to take measures necessary "to ensure the quality of its exports, or for the protection of human, animal, or plant life or health, of the environment, or for the prevention of deceptive practices." Towards this end, a member may stipulate "technical regulations and standards, including packaging, marking and labeling requirements, and procedures for assessment of conformity with technical regulations and standards." These rights are subject to the provisio that they "do not create unnecessary obstacles to international, trade."

The experience of the first five years of WTO points to an increasing feeling among members that frequently technical regulations are a disguised attempt to build non-tariff barriers.

In June 2000, the Mercosur representatives (comprising Argentina, Brazil, Paraguay and Uruguay), have been negotiating with the EU to liberalize health and environment rules and customs procedures in an attempt to build up a free trade zone covering the EU and the Mercusor countries with a joint population of 680 million. The target date for this is 2005. Technical norms especially those relating to animal and plant health in this context are viewed, not as pre-requisites for the protection of standards but as negotiable trade barriers, which can be adjusted on the basis of a quid pro quo. However, the agreement on TBT does provide for differential treatment on the basis of conditions prevailing in the exporter countries. This is not the same thing as differential application on the basis of trade relations. The long-term objective of developing a regional common free trade area may conceivably provide some support to such a move.

Technical barriers to trade, acting as non-tariff barriers have generated a few trade wars in recent times.

In May 2000, the Federation of Thai Industries was developing ammunition in the form of proposed non-tariff barriers for possible us against other members of AFTA (Asian Free Trade Area) which had erected non -tariff barriers against the spirit of the agreement. Members are to reduce tariffs among themselves to low levels of 0% to 5% by the year 2003. Already most of the reductions (80%) have been made. A major chunk being made at the beginning of the year 2000. Side by side, countries have allegedly set up non-tariff barriers. Singapore and Malaysia have stipulated new and stricter standards for electrical tools at the cost of the Thai industry.

The ASEAN Chamber of Commerce and Industry outlined in May 2000, US related non-tariff barriers which were hurting ASEAN export trade. Some of these were the US restrictions on wild-harvested shrimps, the proposed US bill banning imports of certain types of tropical timber, unilaterally modified rules of origin, stipulation of a single set of labeling conditions for gloves made from natural and synthetic rubber.

The European Union has indicated fresh rules to govern food safety effective from 2003, which are being looked at as new non-tariff barriers. These rules will enable EU to impose ban on import of any food product on the ground of the precautionary principle, with no need for scientific scrutiny. These are alleged to be too sweeping. They enable a ban on all food imports from a country and not only from specific exporters who are not able to confirm to standards set by EU.

The requirement of labeling products in local language has been alleged to be a non-tariff barrier. The exports to EU must carry labels in all the European languages of destination countries. This creates special problems of translation especially for small and medium firms. Thailand has threatened to retaliate by requiring labeling in Thai language for imports into Thailand.

The labeling of genetically modified (GM) food is another area of trade controversy. Facing stiff US resistance to the allegation of risk attached to GMO products, countries have moved on to the demand for labeling GMO food. With the wide publicity acquired by this issue, there is an increasing consumer awareness world wide about the possible health risks of GMO food. Hence, some firms have already started using the label " no GMO material used " in order to increase consumer acceptance for their products.

With the advent of biotechnology an increasing number of countries are adopting technical regulations as safeguards against risks from transgenic substances. Under the TBT agreement Canada has notified its intention to do so. These regulations are to provide for the health and environmental assessment of new substances from biotechnology that are foods, drugs or cosmetics, "that are microorganisms, cultured cells, or transgenic animals," or plants or products derived from them.

This vast and growing new area leading to TBT notifications from an enlarging number of members emphasizes the need for continuous globalbenchmarking of standards. There is a strong need for harmonization of technical standards between nations. In the absence of such harmonization, a transparency cannot be ensured and the process of trade liberation will inevitably suffer. At the same time within countries, firms must be able to interpret the standards and get a certification for their products in order to acquire importer acceptance. Thus the growth of certification agencies which specialize in particular fields must form an integral part of the future system of liberalized trade.

Article VI of GATT 1994 provides that a member country may impose a countervailing duty on goods which are dumped in the importing country i.e. sold at a price which is below its 'normal value', and it causes or threatens 'material injury ' to an established industry or retards the establishment of a domestic industry. A sale price is less than normal value if it is less than the comparable price, in the ordinary course of trade, for the like product when destined for consumption in the exporting country, or, in the absence of such domestic price, is less than either the highest comparable price for the like product for export to any third country in the ordinary course of trade, or the cost of production of the product in the country of origin plus a reasonable addition for selling cost and profit.

The anti-dumping agreement embodies a number of grey areas which facilitate its use as a non-tariff barrier. The concept of normal value is rather vague. Experience shows that in the conduct of anti-dumping investigations, there is a wide variation in interpretation of " cost of production". Consequently, there are frequent and vehement accusations of the use of countervailing duties as non-tariff barriers. A large number of cases with WTO's Dispute Settlement Body relate to anti-dumping actions of countries.

As of 30 June 1999, among the 1097 anti-dumping measures reportedly in force, the percentage of cases attributed to various countries were 31% by the United States, 17% by the European Community, 8% by Mexico and South Africa each, and 7% by Canada & India each.

The Agreement on Rules of Origin attempts to harmonize rules of origin on a non-preferential basis. The purpose is to ensure that such rules do not act as non-tariff barriers to trade. However, the work of harmonization is still in progress in the Committee on Rules of Origin. Consequently, rules of origin are frequently alleged to be used as non-barriers to trade. In May 2000, the ASEAN Chamber of Commerce and Industry appealed to the US Government to suspend its new rules of origin on 16 categories of textile and garment exports from South East Asian Countries till the adoption of harmonized rules of origin by WTO. The new US rules of origin enforced in 1996 require that Philippine garment exporters must produce yarn and textiles within their own country in order to be eligible for quotas under the Multi-Fibre Agreement (MFA). This new rule is viewed as unfair and a non-tariff barrier which hurts Philippine exports.

The new issues like core labour and environmental standards have been the principal bone of contention at the Seattle Ministerial conference in November- December 1999. In the face of cultural, economic and historical differences between countries, the South has vehemently resisted enforcement of uniformity in core labour and environmental standards. The North- South standoff has been heightened by the G-15 Summit at Cairo in June 2000, which categorically delinked core labour standards from WTO negotiations. The key question, which arises here, is whether in the first place core labour standards can at all be characterized as a trade issue. The G-15 would, while appreciating the importance of the issue as such, rather confine it to the domain of ILO.

These matters are linked with the larger question of the growing power and coverage of WTO. The North has tried to force the pace on new issues which enlarge the coverage of WTO, while the South favours a slower process of consolidation of the WTO and emphasizes the need to pursue the built-in-agenda, especially the liberalization of agriculture and textile sectors and the removal of various non-tariff barriers which work like de facto quotas.

## REFERENCES

Bhagwati, Jagdish. A Stream of Windows, Oxford University Press, 1999.

Gulati, Ashok and Kelly, Tim. Trade Liberalization and Indian Agriculture, Oxford University Press, New Delhi, 1999.

Krueger, Anne O. The WTO as an International Organization, Oxford University Press, New Delhi, 1999.

Messerlin, Patrick A. and Zarrouk, Jamel. Trade Facilitation: Technical

Nayyar, Deepak. Trade and Industrialization, Oxford University Press, New Delhi, 1997

Regulations andCustoms Procedures. The WTO/World Bank Conference on Developing Countries' in a Millennium Round, WTO Secretariat, Centre William Rappard, Geneva, 1999

Routledge, London and New York, 1996.

Srinivasan, T.N. Developing Countries and the Multilateral Trading System. Oxford University Press, 1998. Kaul

Trebilcock, Michael J. and Howse, Robert. The Regulation of International Trade.

WTO. Annual Report, 2000

# 12

## THE ROLE OF EDUCATION IN GLOBAL BUSINESS

*Hari Om*

With the globalisation of industries and economies, money, information, and goods flow freely around the world. Within nations, proper education is fast becoming an economic necessity for survival. The only thing that remains in place is the work force. Enabled by technology, most leading industries of the 21st century can be located anywhere, in any country, in any city. How are we going to get these industries to stay in India if they're already here, or move to India if they elsewhere? We're going to be able to do it with a highly skilled work force. Those skills will be our most effective weapon as we compete for business in the future global market place. The businessmen is coming to realise that education is to business what fertilizer is to farming. Thus in present global environment, the education will be increasing crucial to the global competitiveness of Indian work force. Infact, technology is preparing a world in which we may be learners all life long. The world of knowledge and information is fast moving from a paper culture to an electronic culture. The strategy to compete/survive in global market involves the key process of *continuous education* for everyone. For this 'Global Awareness Programmes' to teach about global business issues, global market trends, political trade agreements and trade barriers along with the use of case studies weal to be explored on such things as cross-border components of team building, expatriation, legal issues, financial issues, and effective cross-cultural teamwork.

The primary purpose of the education system is to impart knowledge and skills and, just as important, to transmit certain values. The resulting education package will vary enormously across regions and cultures. Achieving the primary objective involves a number of subsidiary ones: equitable access of education and training; producing the types of educational activities and equip individuals—economically, socially, and politically—for the societies in which they live (external efficiency); running institutions as efficiently as possible (internal efficiency); and financing education in ways that are both fair and efficient. Education improves occupational mobility, and voluntary compliance to law and social responsibilities. Education is needed, both to give workers more transferable, marketable skills and to develop informed citizens, capable of participating actively in civil society. In 1994-95, as per NIPFP estimates, central government subsidies on education amounted to about Rs.2,400 crore, constituting 5.6% of the total central subsidies of Rs.43,0478.8 crore. The state provided the bulk of subsidies on education. About one fourth of state subsidies are on education. However the share progressively falls for secondary and university reeducation. Discussion Paper on *Government Subsidies in India* points out that our subsidies system is not tangibly progressive. A significant portion of subsidies in higher education is appropriated by the middle to high income group, because shortages of seats in this sector are cleared by the quality based screening in the shape of entrance examination, interview, group discussions, etc., where the poorer sections of society are easily competed out. Further, the recovery rate as a whole in this sector is less than 1.5%. The recovery rate even in the University sector is as low as 1.25%.

Reform of education is therefore needed, and urgently. The state financed system on the basis of rigid formulas, allocating resources without regard to student or employer demand is highly inefficient. Although the provision of education is for the most part a public monopoly, it is poorly coordinated,. Programmes for professional development are fragmented, and scarce resources are often wasted on duplication of facilities. Nor did the administrators or teachers have any incentive to use the resources efficiently. The result is gross over staffing and high unit costs. In many ways education system has problems similar to those of state enterprises. The solution, although not the same, will involve some of the elements —for example, incentives to efficiency and greater responsiveness to market demand.

Priorities for reform lies in three principal areas : *Finance, Content, and Delivery.* The financing of education should provide incentives for efficiency. One way is to allocate public funds for training and higher education on the basis of enrollment, to make the system more responsive to demand—although such a policy needs to be accompanied by improved accountability. Reform of education financing is important not simply because it supports more efficient management of institutions (internal efficiency) but also because it can improve the content of education (external efficiency) by empowering the students to demand the education and training they need. Government must accept the responsibility for guaranteeing access to quality education; this may require inter-regional transfers to help offset widening regional disparities.

New curricula are central to reform content both to produce a more critical type of learning and to adjust to changing needs and values. It calls for raising the accountability of teachers. This must start with training new teachers and retraining the existing ones. Performance incentives need to be strengthened. The focus while making evaluation should be to test the capacity to use knowledge as well as to accumulate knowledge.

Improving the delivery of education is a complex process. It generally implies decentralisation, to make education more responsive to local needs; diversification of supply, including private suppliers, to promote competition and thus efficiency; and diversification of education practice to enhance individual choice. These incentives, however, require a major change in the role of the state, which has to establish a framework that includes methods of funding, accreditation of providers, and monitoring of quality, particularly in poor areas.

In higher education, due cognizance has to be taken of the fact that the country has an existing infrastructure which despite its problems, is still one of the best in the developing world. The country needs to capitalise on the advantage accruing from the infrastructure and nurture it in order to enhance competitiveness in the global market.

UGC is headed by full time Chairperson appointed by Government of India, Ministry of Human Resource Development. Members of the UGC are appointed by Government of India, Ministry of Human Resource Development for term of 5 years. They are not paid any salary. They are paid only TA/DA for their travel. In UGC members of the Commission are nominated on various committees for specific subjects/items. There is no model 'Code of Best Practices' for members of the Commission.

The funding of Central Universities Deemed Universities, Delhi Colleges etc. is done through UGC established in 1956 under the Act. For funding the Higher Education Institutions no Formal Financial Memorandum is signed between UGC and institutions. The terms and conditions of grant are prescribed and laid down in each sanction letter. The grants are provided by the council for Teaching, Research & maintenance of students. This is calculated with reference to the number of students being tought every year.

The Non-Plan grant is provided to Central Sector institutions on historical budgeting system i.e. on incremental budget system without taking into account the number of students being tought in each institution. Capital & Equipment Grant and maintenance of building grants are calculated on Formula basis. These are also related to teaching, Research etc. Capital & Equipment Grants are provided out of the Plan Grants based on the specific proposal/projects. UGC meetings are held 10-12 times in a year.

UGC follows a system of issue of sanction for each release. The payments are made on receipt of TR-42 bill. Payments are arranged through bank drafts. There is lot of delay in this system. There is no system of reconciliation. UGC doesn't have prescribed standard of uniform Accounting System. In the UGC an internal audit cell has been established recently. There are no prescribed check lists and audit code.

Approach Paper To Ninth Five Year Plan pointed the emphasis needed to be placed on consolidation and optimal utilisation of the existing infrastructure through institutional networking, restricting expansion to meet the demand of unserved areas through both traditional university system as well as through open university system. Grants-in -aid need to be linked to performance criteria to improve quality and inject accountability. Further, relevance will be achieved by restructuring the vocational bias content of the first degree course and industry linked inter-disciplinary post graduate teaching and applied research work. Fee will be restructured on Unit Cost Criteria and Paying Capacity of the beneficiaries. Additional resources will be generated by involving industry and commerce through contribution from community.

In view of the increasing and competitive pressures in which the Government has to operate, it has become necessary to introduce correctives to reverse many of the unsustainable past trends. Strategies may be formulated to set up appropriate incentives —to encourage the efficient response to market signals—while creating an effective social safety net that does not abandon the losers in the market place to destitution.

## *STRATEGY FOR THE NINTH PLAN*

Projects due for completion in the Eight Plan and in which less than 10% of approved outlay has been spent should be considered for discontinuation / shelving.

Projects which are near completion in the Eighth Plan should be taken up for accelerated completion with revised time and costs estimates.

Projects due for completion during the Ninth Plan or beyond as per approvals can be included as Plan projects for which no further details need be provided

For all other projects States and Central Universities would have to provide complete justification for their continuation with revised estimates of cost and time.

The existing schemes whose delivery costs are disproportionately high or which fail to make the desired impact should be considered for reorientation and discontinuation. It is necessary to shelve such schemes whose delivery costs, say 15-20% of the total cost of operating the programme.

To improve the information access on evaluation studies and findings of monitored data, efforts are required to be made to package the available information in user-friendly formats.

Institutional changes to bring transparency in implementation and operation of the programmes. For this purpose, avoidable barriers to full flow of information must be removed.

## REFERENCES

1. Bennelt, R.: *Managing People,* Kogar Page Ltd., 1989.
2. Mathis, R.L. and J.H. Jackson: *Human Resource Management,* West Publishing Company, 1997.
3. Narayan, B.: *Human Resource Management,* A.P.H. Publishing Corp., New Delhi, 1998.
4. Ramaswamy, E.A.: *Managing Human Resources,* Oxford University Press, Delhi, 2000.
5. Silvera, D.M.: *Human Reserouce Development: The Indian Experience,* New India Publications, Delhi, 1990.

# 13

# WTO REGIME AND INDIA

*Satender Kumar and Ravinder Goel*

India is a founder member of GATT (1947) as well as WTO with effect from January, 1995. Despite being part of multilateral trading system for nearly five decades it like other developing countries has generally been on the receiving end of the forum's agenda and not been able to receive the benefits the multilateral trading system was supposed to have delivered. Similarly the potential costs of globalisation to domestic economy have not been fully factored.

With a wider mandate of WTO (including services and intellectual property rights apart from goods) and experience of last five years it is important that we clearly understand the implications of positions we take or do not take and the positions other countries take or do not take on our national interests and draw suitable lessons for future participation in the multilateral forum. Failure to appreciate this aspect of negotiation process has resulted in a scenario where India will be removing all QR's (Quantitative Restrictions) on imports by 2002, while the developed US and EU will remove the quotas on textile and clothing imports by the year 2005 only. Similarly, despite heavily subsidised agriculture developed countries maintain high tariffs on import of agricultural goods while India is in the dock for removing its subsidies on agriculture as India agreed that it will not give more than 10 percent subsidies.[1] It may be mentioned that while agriculture in developed world is undertaken by affluent farmers, in India agriculture is practiced essentially by small farmers for subsistence purposes.

National positions in the WTO forum are usually well researched positions flowing from domestic compulsions of economies though presented in terms of equity and justice. No country will be able to effectively meet the debate if equally well researched alternatives are not presented. The latest example which highlights the need of such an approach is the issue of labour standards presented by developed countries in the WTO forum. It is fairly well known that the WTO Seattle Ministerial Conference in December 1999 collapsed because of the pressure of developed countries led by USA and EU to put the issue of labour standards in the WTO arena.[2] Despite strong opposition to the question by developing countries, the US and EU are still insistent on keeping the question in WTO framework. At a meeting concluded on 31 May 2000, US and EU once again "reiterated (their) common view that WTO agenda should include the social issues of labour and environment not as a matter of protectionism but as a matter of social justice and sustainability".[3]

The interaction of labour standards and international trade policy is by no means a new issue. Nonetheless it has assumed new dimensions since the Seattle Ministerial Meet. The purpose of this paper is to understand, analyse and evaluate the US/EU position and the options available to India and other developing countries for addressing the issues involved.

This paper is divided into four segments as follows:

Part-I explores the history of U.S. insistence on inclusion of labour standards as an element of international trade policy.

Part-II presents a view point and background to understand the U.S. position.

Part-III deals with the question of appropriateness of including labour standards in the WTO Agenda, and

Part-IV discusses initiatives that need to be taken to protect and promote the interest of India and other developing countries at the WTO forum.

**I. History of US insistence on Labour Standards**

The American insistence to include labour standards in the WTO agenda has a long history. A review of GATT/ WTO negotiating history shows that labour standards have been a favorite theme of US Government since the early days. It is important to note that issues of alleged unfair competition involving labour standards were addressed in Article 7 of Chapter II of the 1948 Havana Charter of the International Trade Organization (ITO). Since the GATT was conceived with a narrow mandate as compared to the ITO, it did not address labour standards, except in Article XX(e), which specifically provides for prohibition of goods made with prison labour. In 1953 the U.S. proposed (unsuccessfully) to add a labour standards article to the GATT. This proposal would have empowered GATT members to take measures against other countries under the provisions of GATT Article XXIII (Nullification and Impairment)6. The United States continued, in the 1970s and 1980s again unsuccessfully, to push for inclusion of a GATT article on labour standards in both the Tokyo and Uruguay Rounds of Multilateral Trade Negotiations.

The U.S. with some support from France, southern European Union members, Canada, and Japan continued to pursue the issue of trade and labour standards in the WTO framework and there was a concerted effort to add the issue to the agenda for the WTO Ministerial Meeting held in Singapore in December 1996. However, the ministerial meeting could not agree to the US argument. Despite the U.S. threat to veto the entire declaration if no mention of labour standards was made, Ministers only agreed to uphold internationally recognised core labour standards, but trade sanctions to enforce them were rejected. The Singapore Ministerial Declaration adopted on 13 December 1996 noted: "We renew our commitment to the observance of internationally recognized core labour standards. The International Labour Organization (ILO) is the competent body to set and deal with these standards, and we affirm our support for its work in promoting them. We believe that economic growth and development fostered by increased trade and further trade liberalization contribute to the promotion of these standards. We reject the use of labour standards for protectionist purposes, and agree that the comparative advantage of countries, particularly low-wage developing countries, must in no way be put into question. In this regard, we note that the WTO and ILO Secretariats will continue their existing collaboration."

**II. The Compulsions of the Developed World**

The increased competition from low cost imports from developing countries imposes an adjustment cost in terms of declines in output, wages, employment and working conditions in the developed import competing countries. However, they are not ready to pay the adjustment costs because of the specific characteristic of the globalisation process underway currently. It may be mentioned that this has not been the stance of the developed countries in the earlier period when a similar process was underway at the height of Gold Standard during the period 1890–1913.

Discussion on globalisation focus usually on three inter related aspects of trade, investment and finance. At least in the first two aspects namely trade and investment, globalisation 'then' i.e. under the Gold Standards is easily comparable with the process underway today. At the turn of century in the year 1900 the 16 most industrialised countries of the time exported some 18 percent of their GDP a figure which rose to over 21 percent in 1913. Broadly today also industrialised countries export nearly 1 in 5 dollars worth of their output. Similarly with respect to direct foreign investment, the accumulated stock of direct foreign investment at historic cost in 1992 was some 8.4 percent of world GDP whereas just before the outbreak of the first world war, a higher figure of 9 percent had been reached.[5]

The most striking difference between globalisation 'then' under the discipline of the fixed exchange rates of the Gold Standard and globalisation 'now' under a system of increasingly market-determined, flexible exchange rates has emerged in the area of international finance. The exploding growth in international finance is by far the most dramatic aspect of the ongoing process of globalisation without historic parallel. According the Bank for International Settlement (BIS), Basle, daily foreign exchange transactions volume worldwide was $ 1.971 trillion in April 1998. Of this staggering sum only a tiny share (less than 10 percent) is necessary for financing the trade in goods and services and capital transfer flows. Rest 90 percent or more transactions are purely financial or speculative in nature.

In qualitative terms also there are important differences. Under the Gold Standard the dominant nation states were the main actors involved in globalisation drive. Depending on the relative power and the perceived benefits, globalisation prior to first world war was a matter of diplomacy among the nation states. However, the main actors in the globalisation process today are TNC's, banks and financial institutions. These corporations have strong influence on the nation states from where they originate and the nation states pursue policies for their benefit. But the interests of the corporations are not identical with the interests of the nation states. Nation states are accountable to their electorates for general economic performance in terms of employment, balance of payments growth etc. The TNC's howeve move around the world according to their convenience and the process of globalisation remains significantly outside the control of nation states. Since they cannot control the mobility of capital which is mostly under the decision of big TNC's, they hope to improve their performance to the satisfaction of their electorates domestically by protecting employment at home through different means. Apart from the control on labour migration, various non tariff barriers erected against competitive imports from abroad, the quest to propagate labour standards at WTO forum with an implicit threat of trade sanctions emanates from this compulsion of developed world.[6]

The US campaign for inclusion of the labour standards in the WTO mandate is thus protectionist beyond doubt. The insistence by the US and some other countries to subject export of goods from developing countries (to their own markets) to social, labour and environmental conditions imposed by them is blatantly protectionist non-tariff barrier directed at exports from developing countries, particularly in relation to goods in which their exports are competitive. The US has also been unilaterally taking actions against what it perceives as a violation of labour standards. It imposed a ban recently on the import of 'Mangalore Ganesh Beedies' from India because they are said to be based on child labour. Interestingly the ban is based on a TV channel report in US.

### *The US own record*

While, there is concern in the United States that many of its developing country trading partners appear to be disregarding certain essential worker rights, it has been mentioned by Bhagwati[7] that the United States is itself open to criticism when it comes to the realization of several labour standards. He puts forth a view that it is "morally obtuse" for the United States to thrust on developing countries particular stipulations relating to worker rights, while not extending these efforts to its own problems in the proposed international standards.

***Nafta Supplemental Agreement***

In 1992-1993 Clinton administration has also negotiated a separate side agreement to NAFTA (North American Free Trade Association) covering labour and environmental issues.[8] The NAFTA supplemental agreement commits each party to the promotion of eleven broad labour conditions, ranging from freedom of association to migration policies. The agreement, unlike the current US demand, does not attempt to apply U.S. standards or common uniform criteria in its evaluation of labour conditions in other countries. Instead, the agreement contains different enforcement mechanisms for different standards. The complaint process consists of three stages-filing a petition with the domestic National Administrative Office, Ministerial consultations, and lastly consultation with the Evaluation Committee of Experts. Complaints pertaining to freedom of association, the right of collective bargaining, and/or the right to strike can only be taken to the second stage of the complaint process. More importantly, sanctions cannot be utilized to encourage enforcement of laws pertaining to these rights. Of the eleven labour principles, only the implementation of those pertaining to child labour, minimum employment standards, and occupational health and safety can be supported by sanctions.

It is interesting to ask whether the NAFTA labour side agreement might serve as a model for a global agreement that might in the future, be incorporated into the WTO. From a global point of view the NAFTA side agreement goes beyond what are considered to be core labour standards and emphasises the observance of existing national laws governing labour standards in the NAFTA member countries rather than the inter country harmonisation of these laws that proponents of labour standards favour. Further more, not all standards are subject to sanctions and those that are (i.e. child labour, minimum employment standards, and occupational safety and health) are precisely ones that have engendered much of the ongoing controversy in the global context.

**III. Appropriate forum for addressing labour standards**

There are some trade experts who hold the view that labour standards should be included in the WTO agenda . Freeman for example points out that "unlike trade economists who view any interference with free trade as the work of the devil, I would be pragmatic in this area. If trade negotiations are the only way to raise forcefully the standards flag in an international setting, why not? If trade sanctions can improve labour standards, that benefit must be weighed against the cost of lost trade. If trade sanctions can overturn an evil dictatorial regime and save human lives, go for it. Perhaps the standards issue will induce international trading groups to consider innovative ways that international trade might be used to finance improvements in standards."[9]

In considering whether or not the WTO is the right place to handle trade and alleged breaches of core labour standards, it is appropriate to note the conclusion reached in the OECD report on Trade, Employment and Labour Standards:

"Existing WTO provisions have not been designed for promoting core labour standards. Some of the suggestions under discussion would imply a reinterpretation of WTO practices and procedures while others would require to a greater or lesser extent re-negotiation and amendment of WTO articles. Extending the WTO's Trade Policy Review Mechanism procedure to include labour standards would fall into the former category while other proposals would fall into the latter."[10]

Further, the welfare gains from trade liberalisation have long been a hallmark of non-discrimination in the GATT/WTO system. It would be a significant digression from this precedent if countries with allegedly low labour standards were to be disallowed better market access on these grounds. For example, the US boycott of garments made by child labour from Bangladesh caused 50,000 children to loose their jobs and forced them to take up even lower paid jobs in other industries. Some were even pushed into prostitution. It is also important to note that if the labour standards are being violated it will be naïve to expect the market forces on their own bringing improvement in them. It may be conceded that there is need for intervention, but this should be indigenous in nature.

Historically, the issues of labour standards have been in the domain of the International Labour Organisation (ILO), which is often excoriated for the want of a system for enforcement of discipline to elevate labour standards. While the criticism may be true, it is oblivious of the evidence provided especially by the economies in East and Southeast Asia, that labour standards and social conditions are improved as countries achieve higher levels of economic development and per capita incomes. This makes out a strong case for policies to provide technical and economic help to promote economic progress and the concomitant effectuation of improved labour standards in low-income countries.

International organizations created over the years have, as Srinivasan[11] points out, specialized according to function. For example, he notes the particular rules and mandates that apply to such organizations as the: ILO, GATT/WTO, UNCTAD, World Bank; International Monetary Fund. The issue then is whether it is desirable and efficient to require that individual organizations assume responsibilities for rules for which the organizations were not designed. More specifically, he argues that issues of labour standards are best left to the ILO and should not be mandated to the GATT/WTO, which has been designed to articulate, monitor, and enforce the rules governing the international trading system.

Some observers might take issue with the above characterization of the GATT/WTO, arguing that it constitutes a forum for discussion and negotiation on trade related matters, and, in this light, should include issues of labour standards. But even if this were the case, there is a genuine possibility that the WTO could become overloaded if it were to take on labour standards and other new issues like the environment and competition policy. It is not without reason that developing countries were keen on focussing at Seattle on the implementation issue and mandated agenda of the WTO.

## IV. Issues for Indian initiatives

The US and EU insistence on labour standards only means that the question will have to be continuously dealt with in future. The 'greenroom' negotiating process and the disarray in which countries of South on the receiving end of the subject are, makes it imminent that the issue will be hoisted on the WTO forum if serious thinking on the subject is not undertaken. Merely rhetoric is not going help in keeping the issue out of WTO mandate in the new millenium. India, as a developing country, with leadership role, will have to take new initiatives based on sound theoretical framework and a strong backing and support of countries of the South.

### *Research Agenda for Third World Gains*

It is not sufficient, as generally has been the practice so far, for developing countries researchers and policy experts to go abroad to attend conferences in developed countries to understand the latter's position. It is imperative for developing countries to conduct their own research meetings and conventions and spread their conclusions and findings among developed country researchers and policy experts. But to embark upon extensive and independent research programmes and to propagate the findings in international fora is an expensive affair.

In view of the financial compulsions the researchers and the studies in the developing countries have to depend on the funds from the developed countries. Though foreign funds sometimes, play an important and a positive role in many research activities, yet it is more sensible to bank upon domestic funds on studies relating to the issues concerning WTO negotiations. The agencies funding the research may, sometime, exact a price for the funds they dole out, by influencing the outcome of the research. Pangariya[12] points out that this influence is exerted by offering funds to researchers who are favourably disposed to the view espoused by the funding agency in the first place. Alternatively, given their dependence on the funding agency, the researchers themselves are vulnerable to endorsing the agency's view. Yet another instrument the funding agency has at its disposal is the selection of research topics that are funded. For instance, funding on research on capital mobility has been plentiful, but no multilateral agency has funded research on the benefits of promoting labour mobility from developing to developed countries even though, prima facie, such mobility is enormously beneficial to them and the world. There is a serious view that international harmonisation of labour standard is not possible until the world has free mobility of business from North to the South and labour from South to the North. It may be mentioned that in the first phase of globalisation under the Gold Standard both capital and labour moved with relative ease. Between 1870 and 1914 some 50 million people left Europe of which two thirds went to the United States.[13]

Some decades earlier another 50 million people had left China and India to work as indentured labour on mines and plantations. Compared to those vast magnitudes of labour migration in relation to world population then, the present process of globalisation is decidedly a one-sided affair. The Indian government should mobilize opinion in the third world for international labour mobility and press hard to include the question of labour mobility in the coming WTO negotiations.

Similarly, it has to be realised that in a large number of traditional occupations children inherit the skills from their forefathers while working in closely knit families. It cannot be argued that child labour should be promoted, but there is need for carrying out serious research on the cultural impact of eliminating child labour practices on the society and families involved.

In the long run, it is incumbent upon large developing countries such as India to invest sizable human and financial capital to advance research of their own in the area of WTO issues. At a time when WTO agenda is speeding into areas where there is a clash between the interests and concerns of the North and the South, developing countries should strive hard to bring pressure to bear upon the ideas that govern negotiations. There is also need for active use of information technology to post the American and European public with the situation that prevails in the third world. Such efforts should also be directed towards Indian public and local N.G.O.'s so that they do not become victim of the opinion generated in the western world.

***Procedural Reforms***

Third world countries cannot afford to fight their battles on the ground chosen by the developed world or according to rules formulated by the latter. The WTO process of consultations and decision-making is characterised by the so-called 'green-room consultations'. The process is aimed at isolating and bullying third world negotiators, with the invitees to this process chosen in a non-transparent manner by WTO officials and the major developed countries. At Seattle, out of 135 members, only 23 members including India were, reportedly, called for green-room consultations, thus marginalising most of the third world countries.

Under the current practice Third World countries are forced to involve themselves in hard bargaining in a daunting atmosphere. They also individually face the responsibility of breakdown and trade retaliation, apart from concerted and deceptive campaigns in their capitals to remove the negotiators and replace them by those more acquiescent to the North.

It is important to put an end to this process, and ensure transparency and more open participation. Any country that has an interest on any issue and whatever its 'trade weight', should be able to participate. Otherwise Third World countries will continue to face the 'power' approach to negotiations favored by the major trading blocks and the WTO secretariat. It is undoubtedly difficult to negotiate with a large number of participants. But there is no reason why consultations and negotiations, as in other UN fora, cannot be open-ended, and participatory, open to any country that has an interest on a subject. Further, the green room process made sense when only trade issues were to be debated at GATT forum. Concessions were given or taken between countries which had a trade interest in a particular commodity. Today with non-trade issues on WTO agenda and the "single undertaking rule" obliging participating countries to accept or reject the WTO package as a whole, the green room process has no rationale.

### *Developing South-South Cooperation*

For the Governments of the south the most important

priority should be to forge a common front and this should be done without any further delay. Achieving such a unity needs an approach with wider vision that transgresses the compulsions of immediate expansion of exports or curbing of imports. Only such an approach among the countries of the South would help in creation of mechanisms for concentration and coordination at regular intervals to meet the incremental protectionist agenda of developed countries at the WTO forum. If such an effort is not mounted at this stage, and unity and solidarity are not achieved, the South will receive a major setback.

This effort for solidarity is not an attempt to form a block and cut the South off from the North, but rather an attempt to deal with the North in a way where the South and its interests are heeded. The developed countries concert among themselves, while discouraging any such moves on the part of the Third World countries. Only periodic and political level consultations within the South could help in maximising their commonality of interests and present a credible countervailing force. Any effort by any of the countries, big or small, to deal singly or in small sub-regional groups would fail to safeguard legitimate interests of these countries.

The Indian experience of Uruguay Round Negotiation and post WTO operations / functioning over the last five years clearly demonstrate that the alternative strategy of forming alliances on an issue to issue basis or at the level of G-15 countries has not yielded meaningful results. The phaseout of Multi Fibre Arrangement which restricts the global textile and clothing trade is heavily back loaded while India like other developing countries is being pressurised to throw open their yarn and fabric sector at the earliest. *(Recent research shows that in US markets quotas for clothing of Indian export interests will go only on 1 January 2005)*. Similarly European Union and Japan are raising new hurdles in the path of removing subsidies from agriculture where also the developing countries have a competitive edge.

This becomes all the more important in the light of constant efforts by US towards winning over a part of developing world in supporting its viewpoint at the WTO forum. It is with this view only that the US had suggested at the Seattle meeting to allow duty free entry to goods of least developed countries.

In the economic sphere, the Third World is facing the same dilemma that the States of Europe faced in the inter-war years over their security and demands from Hitler, and where each tried to buy peace at the expense of the other. The percepts of that period have been drubbed into the postwar political relationships in the community of Nations, but its implications have not been understood in the area of international economic relations. Surrender in the economic and trade domains is as dysfunctional as in the in the political and security regions. It only enhances hankering. The more countries capitulate now, the more they will be asked to succumb in the future.

The efforts at unity of the South on these issues will never succeed if they are directed towards total unanimity in the South. As many of those as are concerned about the independent growth processes of their countries should come closer and act jointly, remaining alive to the possibility of others from the South joining as and when they deem it fit. In any scheme of international cooperation and integration pooling of economic and political sovereignty for common benefits is an important element by participating countries. This is supplemented by selective harmonisation, equalisation and unification of economic regulatory structure so that the benefits are equally spread and shared without undue strain/cost on any member country.

## NOTES & REFERENCES

1. Utsa Patnaik 1999 – *The Cost of Free Trade: The WTO Regime and the Indian Economy* Social Scientist vol. 27, nos. 11-12 Nov.-Dec. 1999.

2. As of now no clear definition exists of what is included in the term 'core labour standards'. However, OECD has been stressing seven fundamental ILO conventions which should form the basis of consensus on the subject. These include prohibition of forced labour (No. 29) ; freedom of association and protection of the right to organize (No. 87); right to organize and collective bargaining (No. 98); equal remuneration for men and women for work of equal value (No. 100); abolition of forced labour (No. 105); non-discrimination in employment and occupation (No. 111); and minimum age of employment of children (No. 138). Organization of Economic Cooperation and Development. 1996. *Trade, Employment and Labour Standards: A Study of Core Workers' Rights and International Trade.* Paris.

3. See World Trade Scanner 14-20 June 2000, Page 551, for a report on the latest *US-EU Summit on WTO*. The meet was significantly led by US President Mr. Bill Clinton and European Commission President Mr. Romano Prodi.

4. Charnovitz, Steve. 1986. "The Influence of International Labour Standards on the World Trading Regime: A Historical Review," *International Labour Review* 126:565-84.

5. Deepak Nayyar 1996 Globalisation: The Past in our Present, address to Indian Economic Association, 1995, reprinted in Indian Economic Journal, Vol. 43 pp. 1-18.

6. Amit Bhaduri (1999) On the border of Economic Theory and History pp. 167-174 Oxford University Press, India.

7. Bhagwati, Jagdish. 1995. "Trade Liberalisation and 'Fair Trade' Demands: Addressing the Environmental and Labour Standards Issues," The World Economy 18:745-59 and Bhagwati, Jagdish. 1997. "Fast Track: Not So Fast," *Wall Street Journal* September 10.

8. Lemco, Jonathan and William B.P. Robson (eds.). 1993. *Ties Beyond Trade: Labor and Environmental Issues under the NAFTA.* Canadian-American Committee: C.D. Howe Institute (Canada) and National Planning Association (U.S.A.).

9. Freeman, Richard B. 1994. "A Hard-Headed Look at Labour Standards," in U.S. Department of Labour, Bureau of International Labour Affairs, *International Labour Standards and Global Economic*

*Integration: Proceedings of a Symposium.* Washington, D.C.: U.S. Department of Labour.

10. Organization for Economic Cooperation and Development. 1996. *Trade, Employment and Labour Standards: A Study of Core Workers' Rights and International Trade.* Paris.
11. Srinivasan, T.N. 1995. "International Trade and Labour Standards," in Pitou van Dijck and Gerrit Faber (eds.), *Challenges to the New World Trade Organization.* Amsterdam: Martinus Nijhoff/Kluwer.
12. Pangariya Arvind 1999 "WTO Negotiations: Invest in Research." *Economic Times* 20 October, 1999.
13. Lewis WA (1977) 'The Evolution of International Economic Order'. Ellot Janeway Lecture, Princeton: Princeton University Press.

# 14

# MANAGING RISKS TO FINANCIAL SYSTEM FROM VOLATILE CAPITAL FLOWS : INDIAN EXPERIENCE

*Nidhi Jain*

Financial flows can have an effect on the domestic financial system of recipient countries.One, a surge in financial flows may overheat the economy. Second, it may lead to a lending boom which can exacerbate macroeconomic and financial sector vulnerability. Third, it may increase volatility of asset prices and returns. Sharp increase in capital inflows pose inherent risks as observed in Latin America in 1994-95 and South-East Asia in 1997-98. Such flows may disrupt the economy if and when such flows get reversed or drastically reduced. Several countries that have received substantial flows have faced costly banking crisis. While the beneficial effects of capital flows were clearly visible, the risks came to the fore after the Asian crisis. In this context it is interesting to understand how India has minimised the risks such flows pose to financial system and maximised growth. This paper studies the policy approaches utilised by India to deal with effects of financial flows on financial system.

Unlike the South-East Asian meltdown in 1997, India has escaped relatively unhurt from the surge in financial flows and sudden outflows of financial flows. This is not a matter of chance - but due to sound management of financial flows.

A co-ordinated policy framework and careful calibration of policy instruments resulted in an effective management of financial flows in India without intolerable shocks to the performance of the economy. The Indian authorities have deployed a wide array of policies to regulate the surge in capital inflows. First, India has adopted a progressive approach to capital account liberalisation taking into account the overall macroeconomic conditions and the progress in the development of the financial and foreign exchange markets. Secondly, stability - oriented macroeconomic policies have been put in place to alleviate the impact of surging financial flows on the economy. Third, prudential supervision has been strengthened to improve the soundness of the financial institutions.The following policy approaches have contributed to the success achieved in managing volatile capital flows :

**(A) Capital Account Liberalisation**

Hasty capital account liberalisation without strong economic fundamentals, a well-functioning market mechanism and healthy financial institutions may cause immense damage to the national economy. The process of liberalisation of the capital account has been very gradual in India. India has adopted policy of cautious movement towards capital account liberalisation. It seeks to move over to capital account convertibility over time in a phased manner. Tarapore Committee's recommendation of achieving certain pre-conditions before liberalising the capital account are noteworthy. India seeks to meet the following preconditions : to reduce fiscal deficit GDP ratio to 3.5% by 1999-2000, achieve an inflation rate of 3-5% mandated by Parliament with empowerment for the Central Bank, maintain REER in a 5% band around a target level to be announced publicly, reduce average effective CRR to 3% by 1999-2000 and reduce gross NPA of banking system to 5% - before liberalising its capital account. Thus, one reason why India has avoided the risks posed by financial flows is because capital account liberalisation has been accompanied by actions to strengthen its financial system and because India has paid careful attention to co-ordinating the sequence, speed and timing of capital account liberalisation.

**(B) Management of External Debt**

India's management of external debt has hovered around building adequate reserves to tide over sudden outflows, monitoring maturity profile of external debt portfolio at a macro level and restricting short-term flows. As regards, *adequacy of reserves,* India has been steadily building up reserves by encouraging non-debt creating flows and de-emphasising debt-creating flows. India's foreign exchange reserves have been steadily increasing over the years. For instance, reserves increased in the range of $4.7 billion in 1996-97 ; $2.9 billion in 1997-98 and $3.1 billion in 1998-99 i.e. a cumulative $10 billion.1 However, between end-March 1996 and December 1998, India's total external debt increased by a mere $2 billion.2 Thus, India's policy of building and maintaining adequate level of reserves while at the same time constraining debt, especially short-term debt has helped India to ensure financial system stability.3

Further in India, with deregulation and liberalisation, adequate attention has been paid to the *maturity profile of external debt portfolio.* Appropriate maturity structure is not a micro decision in India that is left to the final borrower whose main consideration is cost. Rather it is recognised as a macro aspect and a stability issue. Accordingly, in India, from 1992, emphasis has been laid not only on the cost and size of debt, but also on the maturity. The desired maturity profile is taken into account in policy articulation and clearance of individual cases. The average maturity of our ECB is five years. Basically, consideration of the size, cost and maturity are embedded in the clearance mechanism for ECB.

A major source of vulnerability in the Asian crisis was the large stock of short-term liabilities of banks and corporates and their linkage to foreign exchange reserves. For example, short-term debt as a % of foreign exchange reserves rose from 89% (End-1993) to 153% (Mid-1997) for Thailand; Malaysia saw an increase in this ratio from 28% to 62% while for South Korea the ratio increased to 214% from 148% during the same period. In India, as opposed to East-Asian countries, we carefully monitor short-term debt. We maintain a difference in treatment between trade and non-trade related debt. The authorities sanction short-term debt over six months on a case-by-case approval of purpose, amount and terms, within a sub-ceiling of total external commercial borrowings ceiling. NRI deposits are controlled through specification of interest rate or interest rate ceilings for different maturities in respect of deposits in select schemes India's external debt scenario is healthy as short-term external debt is just 5%-6% of total external debt4 and less than 20% of country's foreign exchange reserves. India's approach to management of external debt has also helped India to avert the risks of financial flows and ensure financial stability.

## (C) Our Approach to Tackle Macroeconomic Risks of Financial Flows

India has tackled the macro-economic risks of financial flows by pursuing following policies: sterilisation through open market operations, sterilisation through other means, restrictions on financial inflows, liberalisation of the current account and selective capital outflow liberalisation.

The surge in financial flows to India since 1993 led to a spurt in foreign exchange reserves. This brought in its wake the problem of large increase in primary liquidity which resulted in unacceptable growth in M3 in 1993-94 (18.4%) with the attendant problem of acceleration of inflation. The problem of excess liquidity has been tackled by India through a combination of policy measures including a drastic reduction in the monetisation of the budget deficit, an increase in cash reserve ratio, resort to open-market operations and restructuring of non-resident deposit schemes to reduce the element of high cost borrowing. In 1993-94, as part of sterilisation policy, large open market operations were conducted by RBI equivalent to a cash reserve ratio increase of 2.8 percentage points. During 1993-94, RBI under took aggressive open market operations and sold government securities worth $ 3 billion to mop up liquidity. In 1994-95, a multi pronged strategy was followed. First, there was a phased increase in CRR of banks. Secondly, moderate OMO were conducted. Thirdly, the growth of foreign exchange reserves was moderated by discouraging short-term inflows and regulation of inflows under euro-issues. Further, Indian authorities have imposed direct or indirect controls on financial flows. India imposed guidelines to limit access of Indian companies to eurobond market. In May, 1994, India's Central Bank stipulated that any group of companies will not be allowed more than two euro-issues during a financial year and there must be a minimum gap of twelve months between two issues floated by a single firm. In addition, the guidelines stipulated that 85% of the receipts from these issues should be used within one year for import of goods and services. Indian government is also trying to sterilise the burgeoning foreign exchange reserves by liberalising current and capital account transactions to increase imports. Capital outflows, too, have been liberalised to some extent e.g. Foreign investors are allowed to repatriate dividends and capital freely but Indian residents are not free to take capital out of the country, a restriction which makes it easier to avoid panic overreaction in foreign exchange markets. Further, in managing our external account, we ensure a sustainable current-account deficit5. Policymakers in India have been extremely conscious (after the crisis of 1991-92) of the need to ensure that the current account deficit remains at an appropriate level. Price stability is also an important objective underlying monetary policy in India.

**(D) Strengthening of Financial Sector**

The East Asian experience shows that a loose domestic financial system and large financial flows are the worst combination. Weaknesses in the financial sector - was one of the several causes for the East Asian crisis. Banks were not subject to prudential regulation and supervision or asset liability management. This coupled with poor governance and lack of internal controls resulted in excessive leverage and excessive credit expansion directed to unproductive investments. Financial reporting and disclosure norms in these countries were far from satisfactory. This kind of regime encouraged large domestic credit expansion. The pegged exchange rate system also resulted in investments being financed by short-term external debt. Globalisation of the financial market was not accompanied by an appropriate information system. Lack of transparency delayed public realisation of the magnitude of the problem. Heavy lending against real estate put several banks into difficulties when land prices began to fall.

However, India has strengthened its financial system since the onset of financial flows. RBI has been making continuous efforts towards strengthening financial soundness by prescribing capital adequacy norms for banks and financial institutions, advising improvements in asset classification and accounting systems and establishing best practice norms for income recognition and provisioning against exposures faced by them. A Board for Financial Supervision has been set up for exercising integrated supervision both, on-site and off-site over banks, financial institutions and finance companies. Besides several steps have been taken to improve the audit system in general. There is mildly recognised transparency in operations of banks. We have taken various measures to ensure that the banking system does not get into a maturity mismatch bind. Liquidity position of banks is being closely monitored. We discourage banks investments in real estate and stock market, corporate exposure to debt especially external debt is within reasonable limits.

Prudential regulations in India pertain to capital adequacy, income recognition, asset classification, marking investments to market, portfolio concentration and large exposures, connected lending, country and transfer risk, market risk, risk management system in banks & internal controls.

Prudential supervision in India consists of both on-site and off-site supervision. On-site inspections are based on CAMELS (Capital adequacy, asset quality, management, earnings, liquidity and systems and controls). The domestic banks are rated on CAMELS model while foreign banks are rated on CACS model (capital adequacy, assets quality, compliance and systems). The OSMOS - Off-Site Monitoring and Surveillance system that is prevalent in India with respect to supervision consists of 12 returns (called DSB returns) focussing on supervisory concerns such as capital adequacy, asset quality, large credits and concentrations, connected lending, earnings and risk exposures (viz. currency, liquidity and interest rate risks). The supervisory intervention power rests with RBI and the process is triggered by the deterioration in the level of capital adequacy, NPAs, credit concentration, lower earnings and larger incidence of frauds which reflect the quality of control.

Further, RBI has made continuous efforts to impart greater transparency to the balance sheets of banks. Commercial banks in India are required to disclose capital adequacy ratios (both Tier/and Tier II Separately), percentage of NPA's to net advances, provision made towards NPA's, gross and net value of investments. From April 2000, banks are also required to disclose maturity profile of loans and advances, investments and lending to sensitive sectors.

The RBI has also accorded attention to strengthening

internal control systems in banks. Banks have been advised to introduce the system of concurrent audit in major and specialised branches and are required to set up audit committees to follow up on the reports of the statutory auditors and inspection by RBI.

Thus, we find that India has taken steps to strengthen supervision and regulation of financial system while liberalising its financial markets.6 Since attempts to liberalised financial markets in India have been accompanied by attempts to tighten the system for effective supervision and regulation, India has been successful in ensuring financial system stability during period of surge in financial flows and sudden out flows.

**(E) Position of Indian banks in respect of certain factors that increase financial sector vulnerability**

If an increase in bank lending consequent to surge in financial flow is associated with declining liquidity ratio's, increased exposure to real estate or stocks, increased exposure to foreign exchange risk, portfolio concentration, connected lending it reflects increased vulnerability of financial sector to banking crisis. How is India poised in respect of these factors?

India is favourably poised in these respects since to avoid portfolio concentration, India sets limits on lending to individual borrowers and group borrowers. Exposure to a single borrower can not exceed 25% of the banks capital funds (i.e. paid up capital and free reserves). The Mid-term review of Monetary and Credit Policy for 1999-2000 has introduced reduction in this from existing level of 25% to 20% effective from April 1, 2000. Existing level of exposures in excess of 20% as on October 31, 1999 are sought to be brought down to 20% over a period of two years (i.e., by end October, 2001). Group exposure can not exceed 50% of the capital funds of the bank. Additional 10% is allowed in respect of exposure to infrastructure projects (power, telecom, roads and ports).

Exposure of banks to real estate operations is limited in India to less than 1%.8 Of the gross bank credit amounting to Rs. 2,58,991 crore; Rs. 3,00, 283 crore and Rs. 3,42,012 crore at end March 1997, 1998 and 1999 respectively — Rs. 1,546 crore, Rs. 1899 crore and Rs. 1625 crore had been in the form of real estate loans. Thus, real estate loans by banks in India have been 0.60%, 0.63% and 0.48% of gross bank credit respectively at end — March 1997, 1998 and 1999.[9]

Further, India seeks to ensure adequate liquidity within the financial system by closely monitoring liquidity position of banks and requiring banks to maintain CRR and SLR as per section 42(1) of the RBI Act, 1934 and Section 24(2A) of the Banking Regulation Act, 1949 respectively. The method of computing these ratios has been defined in the respective sections of the Acts. The RBI has powers to modify CRR between 3% to 20% and SLR between 25% to 40%.[10] The RBI has advised banks to monitor liquidity through maturity or cash flow mismatches. RBI by enforcing liquidity risk management system on banks in India seeks to prevent financial institutions from facing a liquidity crisis in the light of financial flows.[11] As part of the liquidity risk management system, banks are required to bracket future cash flows in different time buckets. The banks are required to fix tolerance levels for various maturity mismatches depending upon the bank's asset-liability profile, extent of stable deposit base, nature of cash flows etc. Further, prudential limit on mismatches (negative gap) in cash flows during 1-14 days and 15-28 days should not exceed 20% of each of the cash outflows during these time buckets as per RBI guidelines. The RBI monitors the liquidity position of banks through a periodic return on structural liquidity. The objective of RBI is to move to fortnightly reporting by April 1, 2000.

As regards banks investments in stocks that exposes the banks to market risks, RBI has placed quantitative restrictions on the extent of exposure that banks can have in equity.[12] The overall ceiling of investment by banks in ordinary shares, convertible debentures of corporates and units of mutual funds etc. is limited to 5% of banks incremental deposits. This limit has been enhanced to the extent of banks investment in venture capital in accordance with the Monetary and Credit Policy Statement for 1999-2000. The banks in general are not allowed to trade in commodities. Recently, however, select banks have been permitted to deal in gold/silver/platinum. These banks must maintain 9% capital adequacy on all risk weighted assets including on the open position in gold/ silver/platinum that carries 100% risk weight w.e.f. 31March, 1999. To control banks exposure to 'market risk', investment portfolio of banks is classified into 'Permanent' & 'current' categories w.e.f. 1992. At present, banks are required to mark to market at least 70% of all approved securities and 100% of non-approved securities. The ratio of marking to market has been fixed at 75% of approved securities w.e.f. March 31, 2000. In addition, effective from March 31, 2000 government and other approved securities are to be assigned 2.5% risk weight instead of 'nil' risk weight as earlier and requisite capital has to be maintained thereon.

To avoid increased exposure of Indian banks to foreign exchange risk, banks are required to assign 100% risk weight to their open position in foreign exchange w.e.f. March 31, 1999. Besides, they are required to fix aggregate and individual gap limits for each currency with the approval of RBI. They are required to adopt Value at Risk Approach to measure the risk associated with forward exposures. The RBI monitors currency risk through a monthly return on maturity and positions for both on and off balance sheet items in foreign exchange.

Connected lending is India is governed by the regulations of Section 20 of Banking Regulation Act. In order to strengthen the provisions relating to connected lending and making their application more stringent, the Reserve Bank is seeking legislative amendment to empower it to take appropriate steps to safeguard against siphoning of bank's funds through connected lending and to initiate criminal prosecution in such cases.

That India has instituted adequate safeguards in respect of these factors implies that financial sector vulnerability has not increased in India with the onset of financial flows. Increased financial sector vulnerability in the presence of large financial flows is likely to lead to fiscal sector distress and crisis (instability in the financial system) once any untoward event occurs. Since in India, financial sector has been strengthened during the period of surge in financial flows, financial flows have not led to financial distress and banking crisis.

**(F) Management of Exchange Rate**

India has avoided another of the serious mistakes of several East Asian countries, most notably Korea, the Philippines and Thailand. These countries pegged their currencies to the US dollar in the early 1990's; then experienced inadvertent and sharp currency appreciation vis-à-vis Europe and Japan when the dollar strengthened after 1995; and then ran down foreign exchange reserves vainly trying to defend the overvalued exchange rate when market sentiment turned against the currencies in late 1996 and in the first half of 1997. By spending reserves in a failed attempt to defend the currency, the central banks also left their economies exposed to subsequent financial panic when short-term debts came to exceed the dwindling level of foreign exchange reserves. In the end, the currencies collapsed in any case, but only after a deep financial crisis had already gotten under way. Fortunately, the Reserve Bank of India has been more circumspect in exchange rate policy, letting the rupee weaken in the face of Asian crisis.

Free capital movement and pegged exchange rates are a dangerous mix. India has avoided this. India has a unified, market determined exchange rate regime since March 1993. However, the central bank intervenes to regulate the market. It is more a system of managed float. The primary objective of the Reserve Bank in regard to the management of the exchange rate has been to ensure that the external value of the rupee is realistic and credible as evidenced by a sustainable current account deficit and manageable foreign exchange situation. Subject to this predominant objective, the exchange rate policy is guided by the need to reduce excess volatility, prevent the emergence of debstabilising speculative activities, help maintain adequate level of reserves and develop an orderly foreign exchange market. The Indian market is not yet very deep and broad and is characterised by uneven flow of demand and supply over different periods. The market is also characterised by a few major players, and lumpy public sector demands, particularly on account of payment for oil imports and servicing of public debt. In this situation, the Reserve Bank has been making sales and purchases of foreign currency in order to even out lumpy demand and supply in the relatively thin forex market and to smoothen jerky movements. However, such intervention is not governed by a predetermined target a band around the exchange rate.

India has been able to keep the spill over effects of the Asian crisis to a minimum through constant monitoring and timely action, including recourse to strong monetary measures, when necessary to prevent the emergence of self-fulfilling speculative activities.

**(G) Capital Market Reforms**

The development of effective and efficient transaction infrastructure in capital markets is as essential as appropriate macroeconomic policy and prudential regulations and supervision for managing financial flows. In this respect, we find major changes have taken place in the capital market during the period of financial flows. In 1991, India's capital market did not have a statutory regulatory framework. The Securities and Exchange Board of India (SEBI) was given statutory powers in 1992 and has since laid down a structure of regulations governing various participants in the capital markets; including rules for insider trading, takeovers and management of mutual funds. The stock exchanges, which were earlier dominated by brokers and lacked effective supervision, are now much better governed. The focus of the new regulations is to ensure investor protection through transparency and full disclosure. The technology of trading has been modernised. There is now automatic matching of buy and sell orders with price time priority. The fully computerised stock exchange trading system ensures transparency for investors and assurance of the best price. The settlement system has also seen major improvement. Earlier, completion of a trade involved physical transfer of share certificates from seller to buyer followed by submission of the certificates to company registrars to effect changes in the register of stockholders. The process was vitiated by long delays, frequent loss of certificates, return of certificates because signatures of the seller on the certificates did not match with signature on record with registrars, and also the danger of forged certificates. In 1996, a National Depository commenced operations offering investors the facility of holding securities in dematerialised form and settling trades through book entries in the depository, eliminating delays and uncertainties in transfer of ownership. These changes are putting in place a set of capital market institutions which can generate confidence among investors. The present of FII's has been an important force in pushing the capital market to come closer to international standards.

The process of capital market reforms aimed at improving market efficiency, making stock market transactions more transparent, curbing unfair trade practices and bringing the Indian capital market upto international standards has helped to promote investor interest and ensure investor protection and has contributed to arresting the rise in volatility in domestic stock market. Another factor that has gone in India's favour is the fact that Indian stock market is not fully integrated with the world markets. Therefore, volatility spillover effects have been guarded against. Further imposition of ban on short sales by SEBI (as on June 15, 1998 — July 6, 1998) has helped India to counter volatility in share prices. In order to tighten the measures aimed at curbing volatility in share prices, SEBI prescribed additional volatility margins (AVM) (w.e.f. July 6, 1998).

## CONCLUSION

India has avoided the risks posed by financial flows to domestic financial system so far on account of its strong fundamentals and introduction of prudential regulation and supervision alongwith financial liberalisation. India, we find, has been pursuing sound policies in areas where serious concern has been expressed in the light of South East Asian crisis. India has managed to escape relatively unhurt since it does not have a number of vulnerabilities that charecterised the crisis-hit East Asian economies. Thus, India has been successful in ensuring financial system stability in the light of surge in financial flows and sudden outflows.

## NOTES

1. In the East-Asian countries, however, foreign exchange reserves dipped. For example, for Thailand the foreign exchange reserves

stood at $25.7 billion in December 1997 as compared to $37.2 billion on December 1996. In Indonesia, foreign exchange reserves fell from $18.6 billion (Dec. 1996) to $16.1 billion (Dec. 1997). For Malaysia, the decline was to $20 billion (Dec. 1997) as compared to $26.2 billion (as on Dec. 1996) and in Korea's case foreign exchange reserves fell from $33.2 billion (as on Dec. 1996) to $19.7 billion (as on December 1997).

2. Adequacy of reserves is linked not only to imports now but also to short-term liabilities, particularly short-term debt.
3. Central banks in both Thailand & Korea went out of their way to take gambles in forward markets until their reserves were gone. Lack of adequate reserves magnified problems as the East Asian crises unfolded.
4. In Thailand short-term debt constituted around 30% of external debt. A high level of short-term debt makes the country vulnerable because of continuous need of rollovers which can be extremely difficult at times of crisis.
5. When the CAD exceeds 5% of GDP, it is generally regarded as high and in most cases, where it persists over a relatively long period of time, it would turn out to be unsustainable. The sustainability of a large CAD depends mainly on how the capital inflows financing the deficit are used and whether the external liabilities associated with the capital inflows are consistent with the country's debt servicing capacity.
6. Financial liberalisation when accompanied by strict bank regulation & supervision prevents reversal in financial flows or a sharp rise in interest rates from breaking the banks.
7. It is important to note that liberalisation introduces greater competition leading to a squeeze on profit margins in traditional business and therefore requires restructuring and competence building in the Banking sector.
8. If funds are invested in unproductive sectors, they may give rise to rash of non-performing assets resulting in a fragile banking system and weakened macro-economic fundamentals.
9. In Malaysia in Mid-90's The real estate loans accounted for about 25% of outstanding bank loans & about 20% in Thailand & Indonesia.
10. The SLR ratio for banks has been reduced progressively from 37.5% to 25% on an incremental basis and the CRR, including incremental CRR from 25% to 10%. The CRR to be maintained by scheduled commercial banks is to be reduced by one percentage point from 10% to 9% in two instalments, effective from the fortnight beginning November 6, 1999 and the fortnight beginning November 20, 1999 respectively.

11. A sudden reversal of financial flow may cause financial institutions to face a several liquidity crisis. Similarly, if there is mismatching of maturities — the banks may be exposed to liquidity risk — the sudden inability to roll over debts.
12. One reason for East Asian crisis was banks exposure to market risk-borrowing to carry assets that are exposed to large fluctuations in their capital value : Stocks, commodities, foreign exchange or high risk instruments such as Brady bonds. Korean Fl's, e.g, had taken a large position in Russian bonds and Brazilian Brady bonds. When their prices fell sharply, the balance sheets of the Koreans had instantly a huge hole.

## REFERENCES

Calvo, G.A., Leiderman, L. and Reinhart, C.M. (1994), "The Capital Inflows Problem-Concepts and Issues", *International Center for Economic Growth, Occasional Papers,* No. 56, (San Francisco, California).

Folkerts-Landau, David and Others (1995), "Effects of Capital Flows on Domestic Financial Sector in APEC Developing Countries", in Capital Flows in APEC Region, (ed.) by Mohsin, S. Khan and Carmem: M. Reinhart, *IMF* Occasional Paper 122 (Washington: IMF), March, pp. 31-57.

Jain. N.(1998), "India Is In Asia But It Is Not Asia", *Chartered Secretary,*Volume XXVIII, No.10, April, pp.1016-1020.

Jain. N.(1998), "Policy Options In Managing Capital Flows", *Business Analyst,*Vol. 19, No.2, July-Dec, pp. 41-54.

Jain. N.(1999), "Restructuring Banking Sector ", in *Contemporary Issues in Finance,* edited by V.K. Bhalla, Anmol Publications Pvt. Ltd., New Delhi-2,pp 81-114.

Jain. N. (1999),"Restructuring Capital Markets ", *Chartered Secretary,*Volume XXIX, No.9, September, pp. 982-990.

RBI (Reserve Bank of India ) *RBI Bulletin* (various issues )

Reisen, H. (1996), "Managing Volatile Capital Inflows: The Experience of the 1990s", *Asian Development Review,* Vol. 14, pp. 72-96.

Subrahmanyam.G.(1994), "Management of India's Capital Inflows", *CEPAL Review* 53, August, pp.13-29.

World Bank (1997), "Private Capital Flows to Developing Countries - The Road to Financial Integration", *World Bank Policy Research Report,* New York: Oxford University Press.

# 9

# ADR/GDR ISSUES BY THE INDIAN COMPANIES

*Sanjay K. Singh*

American Depository Receipts (ADRs) are certificates, traded like normal shares in dollars, that represent shares of a foreign company held on deposit in a bank in its home country. First introduced in 1927, they allow American investors to circumvent restrictions on overseas trading, while giving foreign firms access to American equity markets without having to go through all the formalities of an initial public offering (IPO). Similarly, Global Depository Receipts (GDRs) trade in markets such as London and Luxembourg, but the US dominates the international financial markets.

**Indian Policy Framework**

The ADR/GDR are part of Foreign Direct Investment (FDI). With a view to encourage Indian companies to attract FDI, the Government of India has recently dispensed with the track record scrutiny of ADR/GDR issues.

The Indian companies now have free access to the ADR/GDR markets for raising money through ADRs/GDRs through an automatic route. Private placement of ADRs/DGRs are also eligible for automatic approval, if the issue is lead managed by an investment banker.

The automatic route for ADRs/GDRs also cover issue of

Employee Stock Options by Indian Software Companies/IT Sector Companies and business reorganisation/merger/demerger. The Indian companies, however, have to obtain the mandatory approvals under the FDI policy, Companies Act and Foreign Exchange Regulation Act.

The issue related expenses like underwriting commission, fees of lead managers, legal charges etc., are subject to a ceiling of four percent in case of GDRs and seven per cent in case of listing on the US Exchange. Issue expenses beyond the ceiling need the RBI approval.

The Indian companies, on completion of the ADR/GDR issue, have to furnish full particulars, including the amount of issue, number of underlying fresh equity shares issued, percentage of foreign equity level, detailed issue parameters to the Ministry of Finance and the RBI within 30 days of the completion of the issue.

**Accounting Standards**

The Securities Exchange Commission (SEC) of the US requires companies that are going public to disclose all material information about their business as per the US Generally Accepted Accounting Principles (GAAPs).

The Indian GAAPs, however, lack rigours of the US GAAPs. For example, according to the Indian GAAPs the audited third quarter 1999 results of Satyam Computers the net profits went up from Rs.19.81 crore to Rs.36.12 crores. However, under the US GAAP, the net profits are actually down from US$ 4.1 million (about Rs.17.60 crores) to US$ 3.96 million (Rs.17 crore).

The other striking contract between the GAAPs of India and the US is earnings per share (EPS). The EPS under the Indian GAAP has gone up from Rs.27.98 to Rs.34.07 (annualised) for the quarter ending 31—12—1999. However, under the US GAAP, the EPS for the corresponding period is down from US$ 0.63 (Rs.27) to US$ 0.37 (Rs. 16).

To ensure that relevant information is made available to the readers of financial statements, the US GAAP prescribes several disclosure requirements. Earning per share (EPS) data and segment information are some of the major disclosures. The object of EPS data is to measure the performance of the company over the reporting period. The company is required to disclose the basic and diluted EPS on the face of the income statement.

The basic EPS is computed by dividing the income available to the equity shareholders (after deducting any dividends on preference shares) by weighted average number of equity shares outstanding during the period.

The diluted EPS takes into accounted the diluted impact of convertible securities (such as convertible bonds), options, warrants and other such instruments, which may result in issue of equity shares in the future. Diluted EPS is computed in the same manner as basic EPS except that the demoninator (number of equity shares outstanding) is increased to include the number of shares, which would be outstanding if the convertible instruments were to be converted to equity. In addition, the numerator (income available to equity shareholders) is adjusted to add back interest/dividends on convertible instruments, net of the tax impact. This would reflect the fact that if the instruments had been converted to equity shares, interest/dividends would not be payable.

The US GAAP requires, in addition to disclosure of basic and diluted EPS on the face of the statement of income, specific disclosure regarding the effect of extraordinary items and cumulative impact of an accounting change on the EPS for the period.

The public companies are also required to disclose segment information in the prescribed manner. The object is to provide information about the different types of business activities in which the company is engaged and the different economic environments in which it operates. The segment information is intended to help the readers of the financial statements in better understanding the performance of the company, its future prospects and enabling investors make more informed judgment about the company.

An operating segment is a part of the company that engages in business activities from which earns revenues and incurs expenses and the operating results of which are reviewed by the chief operating decision maker for resource allocations and assessment of performance. An operating segment which contributes more than ten per cent of the total revenues, net income or total assets of the company is considered to be a reportable segment and information has to be made public about such an operating segment. The information to be disclosed for each segment include the following:

— factors used by management to identify segments;
— type of products and services from each segment;
—. details of segment assets; and
— reconciliation of segment data to entity.

The SEC has recently issued the Staff Accounting Bulletin on "materiality" to ensure that financial statements should disclose all material items, the knowledge of which may influence the decision of the user of the financial statement.

It states that the use of a percentage test along to determine materiality is not acceptable. Although a quantitative test can be used as an initial assessment, all 'facts and circumstances must be evaluated to determine materiality. Thus, there is no 'safe harbour" for materiality if a misstatement or omission of a financial statement item falls under a five per cent of earnings or income thereshold.

It sets fourth the type of 'facts and circumstances' that may render a quantitatively small misstatement of a financial statement item material. They are:

- whether the misstatement makes a change in earning or other trend;
- whether it hides a failure to meet analysts' consensus expectations for the company;
- whether it changes a loss into income or vice—versa;
- whether it concerns a business segment or division that plays a significant role in the company's operations or profitability;
- whether it affects the company's compliance with regulatory requirements, loan agreements or other contractual obligations; and
- whether it conceals an unlawful transaction.

It states that companies and their auditors must consider each misstatement separately and also the aggregate effect of all misstatements. Thus, if a single misstatement has a material impact on the financial statements as a whole, it cannot be cured by another misstatement which cancels out the impact of the first item.

The provisions of the Securities and Exchange Act of the US require that (i) a public company has to maintain and keep books and records which in 'reasonable details' accurately reflect the company's financial operation and results; and (ii) maintain internal accounting controls which provide 'reasonable assurance that transactions are recorded to permit preparation of financial statement in accordance with the GAAP. To prove a violation of these provisions, the Securities and Exchange Commission (SEC) needs to only prove that there is lack of reasonable assurance that the books and records are accurate or they reflect the company's operation in reasonable detail. The GAAP takes precedence over industry practice in accounting and auditing.

**Conclusion**

The good news is the good demand for the ADRs of the Indian companies in the US. The bad news is that the SEC of the US has made it mandatory for foreign issuers to follow the strict disclosure norms for ADRs. The Indian companies planning to issue ADRs after September, 2000 will have to follow the International Organisation of Securities Commission (IOSCO) disclosure norms. They will have to be more forthcoming in the description of business, property, legal proceedings pending against them, nature of the domestic capital market, trading in the NSE/BSE, exchange controls, taxation and compensation paid to directors. Under the new disclosure standards SEC has also made it mandatory that the audited financial statement submitted along with the offer document should not be older than 15 months at the time of offering or listing in comparison to period of 18 months earlier. In the emerging scenario, there is urgent need for internationalising the Indian GAAPs by providing for consolidiation of accounts, deferred tax accounting, segment accounting and related party transaction in the Indian accounting system.

## REFERENCES

1. Bhalla, V.K.: International Financial Management, Anmol Publications Pvt. Ltd., New Delhi, 1999.
2. Guidelines for ADR/GDR issues by the Indian Companies, p. 213-14, Chartered Secretary, February, 2000.
3. Lessard, Donald R., (ed.), *International Financial Management: Theory and Applications,* Wiley, New York, 1985.
4. R.B.I. *Report on Currency and Finance,* various issues.

5. Materiality Twirl, Morrison & Forster, *The Economic Times*, 02-10-1999.
6. Shepiro, Alan C., *Multinational Financial Management*, Prentice-Hall, New York, 1997.
7. UNCTC, *World Investment Report*, New York, United Nations, 1999.

# 16

# GLOBAL INDUSTRIAL CHANGE: THE ROLE OF INVESTMENT

*Ravi Gupta*

The world economy has undergone rapid changes over the past two and a half decades. Developing countries and economies in transition alike faced a diversity of external shocks and challenges in their pursuit of higher economic growth. In developing countries, the debt crisis and the sharp fall in commodity prices during the 1980s took centre stage on the policy agenda. In the economies in transition, the shift from central planning to a market economy during the late 1980s has presented a major challenge to policy makers. The increasing pace of globalization and technological developments in recent years have further modified the policy agenda of those countries and economies, with investment re-emerging as a key concern in economic development.

Successful countries include those in East and South-East Asia and, more recently, China, where rapid growth has been sustained by high rates of investment and industrialization. Those countries tend to invest an increasing proportion of their resources in the development of technological and human capital. On the other hand, many countries in Latin America and sub-Saharan Africa have recorded declining per capita income and investment rates that have generally fallen over the years as compared with rising trends in consumption.

Many of the countries in sub-Saharan Africa, in particular, face widespread poverty and bear a heavy burden of debt. Moreover, they remain highly dependent on agriculture as their main source of foreign exchange and have the smallest manufacturing base among developing countries. With regard to the economies in transition, the efforts to move from a system of central planning to a market economy in Europe and central Asia recorded yet another set of results unique to the economies concerned. Unlike China, those economies registered sharp falls in income during the early years of reform and many are still struggling to recover from recession.

Thus, global economic and industrial change has resulted in wider disparities in economic performance among developing countries and economies in transition. The challenge facing policy makers and the international community is to close the widening gap in order to avoid the social problems that will be created if the gap persists.

**Foreign direct investment**

FDI constitutes a relatively stable element of international private capital flows that is insulated form short-term and cyclical pressures, since it primarily reflects the long-term strategies of transnational corporations. For developing countries and economies in transition, FDI has become not only the single largest source of net capital inflow, but also the single largest source of net capital inflow, but also the only source showing a continued upward trend. The volume of FDI flows into those countries and economies almost tripled between 1990 and 1995. As a result, the share of developing countries in global inflows of FDI rose from 21 per cent during the period 1988-1992 to 32 per cent in 1995, while that of economies in transition increased from 0.8 to 3.8 per cent.

The main feature of FDI in developing countries is its highly concentrated flow into a few of them. In 1995, almost

80 per cent of such FDI went to no more than 12 countries, with China accounting for more than 40 per cent of total inflows. Of the 12, nine were middle-income economies, including Indonesia, Malaysia and Thailand in Asia, Argentina, Brazil, Chile and Mexico in Latin America, and Hungary and Poland, two economies in transition in central and eastern Europe. With the exception of China, low-income countries are virtually excluded from world FDI flows, accounting for less than 5 per cent of the total of such flows into developing countries in 1995.

**Major concerns about foreign direct investment**

Despite the growing importance of FDI as a source of investment finance, concerns have been raised about the net benefits of FDI to host economies. The benefits may come in the form of improved use of resources as a result of the transfer of capital, technology and human skills to subsidiary or affiliated companies. Through linkages with foreign companies, local partners, suppliers and distribution and service companies can become more efficient. The affiliate may have easier access than local companies to foreign markets through trade with other companies in the parent group or through the sales network and marketing efforts of the parent company. The presence of the affiliate may force local rivals to become more competitive, and the training and know-how provided may benefit other business when its staff moves on to other employment.

The main concern about FDI is that transnational corporations will use their market power to generate huge profits that benefit their shareholders rather than the host economy. If local competitors are driven out of business, the growth of industry in a country could be impeded, especially if a foreign company subsequently pulls out. The potential for earning immense profits is increased if local prices are controlled rather than determined by the market, thus giving the transnational corporation access to local resources at below the internationally prevailing price. Subsidies and other incentives to investment represent added costs to the host country. Because of concern about exploitation by large companies, many developing countries restricted or prevented FDI before the 1980s.

Empirical evidence is overwhelmingly positive with regard to both the direct benefits of FDI in improving technical efficiency and its spillover effects. There is also evidence that, except for very poor countries, which lack a minimum threshold stock of human capital, FDI contributes more to growth than domestic investment in developing countries, because it involves the transfer of technology and leads to a more than proportionate increase in total investment. Other evidence, however, shows that FDI is only beneficial in stable, open economies in which prices and capital flows are not distorted by government intervention. In more managed economies, by reducing total investment and growth, it could be counter-productive.

**Portfolio Equity Investment**

The growth of portfolio equity investment (PEI) in developing countries has been explosive since the end of the 1980s, fuelled mainly by the rapid liberalization of the financial sector in many Developing countries. It has also been boosted by the strategy of portfolio diversification increasingly applied by large investors in many industrialized countries, by low interest rates in those countries, and by significantly improved macroeconomic fundamentals in many developing countries and economies in transition. In addition, investors in portfolio equity have been attracted by higher yields than typically achieved with investment in domestic stocks. As a result, during the period 1990-1993, the volume of PEI rose more than tenfold to become the fastest-growing component of private capital inflows into developing countries and economies in transition. In 1993, PEI was also the second most important source of private capital for those countries and economies. During 1994-1995, however, PEI fell drastically to a level less than half of that reached in the peak year.

Developments in 1994 and 1995 confirmed that FDI and PEI, as the two forms of non-debt-creating flows, differ significantly, although they are driven by many of the same forces such as globalization, financial integration and improved macroeconomic conditions in recipient countries. Unlike FDI, PEI is characterized by much greater susceptibility to cyclical factors and contagion effects. Unlike FDI, PEI is traded on liquid markets, thus enabling investors to move funds quickly between markets in different countries.

Flows of PEI like those of FDI, are available to a very limited number of developing countries and economies in transition. Only 10 countries — all in either Asia or Latin America — accounted for 85 per cent of total flows of PEI in 1994 and an estimated 80 per cent in 1995. Flows are also highly concentrated in middle-income countries with access to international markets, although some low-income countries, such as Bangladesh, China, Ghana, India and Pakistan, have raised some finance through PEI.

PEI flows to emerging markets have two main forms, namely international equity issues and direct purchases in local markets. In 1994 and 1995, around half of total PEI was made in the form of international equity issues. Industry usually accounts for between one third and a half of the total placements, the remainder being distributed between financial institutions and public utilities, mainly telecommunications and energy producers. In 1995, the largest issuers in the industrial sector of emerging markets included conglomerates form the Republic of Korea, such as Samsung Eelctronics and Pohang Iron and Steel Co., as well as Petronas of Malaysia and the Jilin Chemical Industrial Company of China. Made either directly or through equity funds, direct purchases by foreigners in local stock markets accounted for another half of total PEI in emerging markets in 1994 and 1995. Similar to equity issues, they were highly concentrated in Asia and Latin America.

**Potential Problems with Portfolio Equity Investment**

If foreign investment is desirable, why do capital controls continue to be so popular in many developing countries? The main concern about PEI is that it may be destabilizing. A sudden large inflow could cause both an appreciation of the exchange rate and inflation. The desire to prevent such an appreciation in the face of substantial net capital inflows has typically led to very active intervention by the central bank and rapid increases in international reserves.

Inflows may also be undesirable if the financial sector is underdeveloped, in which case it could allocate funds inefficiently, or if funds are used to finance an inefficient public sector. A large outflow could cause a depreciation of the currency and increase the perceived risk of investment; the 1994 currency crisis in Mexico is an obvious example of such a problem. Accordingly, there is a general consensus in the literature on sequencing of economic reform that the capital account should be liberalized last.

The view that portfolio investors have no interest in controlling or managing companies and generally seek stakes that are small enough to sell easily is part of what worries critics of stock markets. On the other hand, professional investors of all types generally maintain a large proportion of their portfolio in long-term core holdings of large company shares, and those holdings do not suddenly change, even in falling market.

Empirical studies have found no evidence that growth in foreign portfolio investment causes increased volatility in emerging stock markets. Volatility did increase in a number of markets in East Asia and Latin America after internal financial liberalization, but that occurred in the 1970s or early 1980s, well before the surge in foreign portfolio investment. Yet doubts remain. Foreign portfolio investment tends to be concentrated in a few shares in each market and, given such a concentration, any collective behaviour on the part of mutual funds can have a considerable effect on the prices of the shares concerned. The high degree of volatility of Hong Kong and the contagion effect of the behaviour of mutual funds. It is likely, however, that the higher proportion of trading by individual domestic investors in emerging markets is the primary reason for the greater volatility of those markets.

## REFERENCE


1. Bhalla, V.K.: *International Financial Management*, Anmol Publication Pvt. Ltd., Delhi, 1999.
2. Bhalla, V.K. and R. Shiva Ramu: *International Business and Management*, Anmol Publication Pvt. Ltd., Delhi, 2000.
3. IMF: *World Economic Outlook*, Various issues.
4. World Bank: *Private Capital Flows to Development Countries, World Bank Policy Research Report*, Oxford University Press, New York, 1997.
5. UNCTC, *World Investment Report*, 1999.

# 17

## ELECTRONIC COMMERCE

*A.K. Saini*

The Indian economy was opened up to the world in 1991, which laid the foundation for a series of economic reforms. This process presented vast avenues and totally transformed the business. The companies abroad were permitted to tap Indian markets and the Indian companies could access the outside markets resulting in globalisation of business process. The companies were given liberty to expand their business operations at global level with the removal of bureaucratic hurdles to a large extent. In order to be globally competitive, Indian business organisations cannot afford to remain behind their competitors in other parts of the world in the use of technology for carrying out business operations and transactions. This gives rise to several issues which become more complex with rapid developments in the fields of information and the communication technologies which have transformed the whole world into a global village.

The state of the art Internet technologies like Electronic Data Interchange (EDI), Electronic Fund Transfer (EFT), Smartcards, etc. are transforming the key business processes. The Internet is revolutionising commerce. It provides the first affordable and secure way to link people and computers spontaneously across organisational boundaries. This has given rise to innovative enterprises - virtual companies, markets, and trading communities. The effective use of these technologies and the easy availability of Internet provide a boost making Electronic Commerce (E-Commerce) a reality.

## WHAT IS ELECTRONIC COMMERCE

Electronic Commerce popularly called E-Commerce is often used interchangeably with IBM's coined term "E-Business". Certain people and businesses in a much broader sense rather than just the shopping use the term "E-business". Some people also use the term "Internet Commerce" to mean electronic commerce that specifically uses the Internet or the web for data transmission.

E-commerce actually began in the 1970s. Larger corporation and banks for applications such as Electronic Funds Transfer (EFTs) and Electronic Data Interchange (EDI) through the creation of private communication network to share information with trading partners and suppliers used it. The process called Electronic Data Interchange (EDI) transmitted standardised data that streamlined the procurement process between businesses so that paperwork and human intervention were nearly eliminated. It was the foundation of electronic commerce. Apart from buying and selling, businesses engage in many activities that keep them in business such as identify product demand, promotion, accept orders, billing, delivery of the product, accepting payments and supporting the customers in using the product, etc. All these functions if performed using the Information technology is referred to as Electronic Commerce.

In its simplest form, it refers to shopping on the part of the Internet called the World Wide Web or the Web. But web shopping is only a small part of the E-Commerce picture. The term also includes online stock transactions, downloading software without going near a store, etc. For most businesses, it's not really about selling at all but about improving relationships among suppliers, distributors and customers.

Electronic Commerce can be defined as any form of computerised buying and selling, both by consumers and from company to company, which facilitates choosing the goods, ordering, delivery, after sales support and payment". E-Commerce refers to the paperless exchange of business information using a suite of technologies such as Electronic Data Interchange (EDI), Electronic Mail, Electronic Funds Transfer (EFT), Credit cards, Facsimile (FAX), Electronic Bulletin Boards (BBS) and Database services, etc. It can also be defined as the process of two or more parties making business transactions via computer and some type of network, e.g. Internet or some private network.

E-Commerce is the application of information technology (IT) to support the exchange of goods and services. The E-Commerce buzz that we hear on radio, see on TV, and read in the newspapers refers to online retailing - using the web to sell goods, services and information to consumers. The E-Commerce provides an environment where time differences and location do not matter. The Internet is the basic driving force for the conduct of E-Commerce. The scope of E-commerce has expanded from its conventional meaning of EDI to include the more basic commercial activity of buying and selling

## TYPES OF E-COMMERCE

E-Commerce can broadly be divided into three categories:

Inter-organizational: between different business entities. This could take place either on the Internet or on the Extranet which lets only a select few to participate in the transaction. e.g. supply chain management, payment management.

Intra-organizational: within an organisation or a business entity. The goal is to link the constituents together and increase the flow of information within the organization. Examples of it include human resource or department web sites that disseminate information and services through an Intranet.

Retail: directed at the consumer. e.g. for selling , buying and payments.

However at micro-level of operations, the classification could be of four types:

— Business-to-Business
— Business-to-Consumer
— Consumer-to-Business
— Consumer-to-Consumer

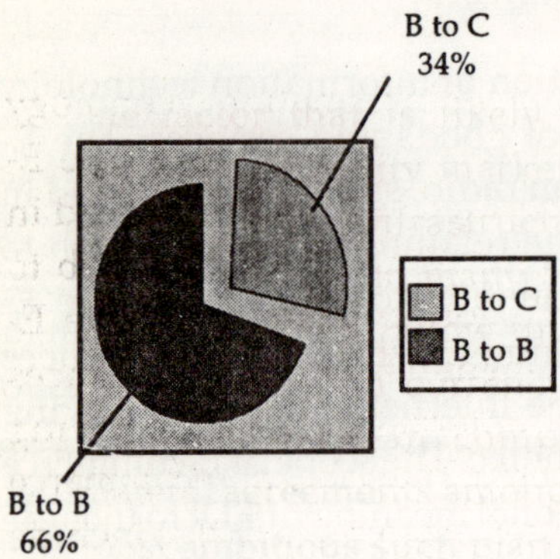


Year 1998

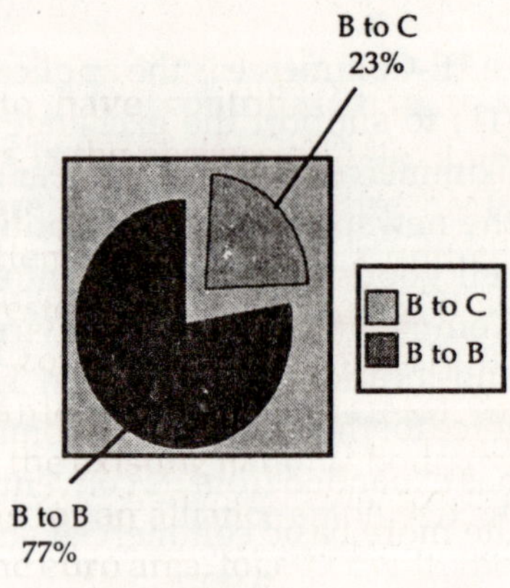


Year 2002

(Source: IDC)

**INTERNET and the WEB – An Integral part of E-Commerce**

The Internet is a worldwide network of thousands of computer networks. It is a large system of interconnected computer networks that spans the entire globe. Using Internet, we can communicate with other people throughout the world via e-mail, read online version of newspapers, magazines, academic books and journals, join the discussion groups on almost any conceivable topic, participate in games and obtain free computer software. The Internet provides an inexpensive and information-rich, shared network interconnecting very large number of people and computers across the world.

The popularity of Internet can be gauged from the fact that it has become a mass media within a span of less than 5 years. Radio, which was the first media targeted for masses reached 50 million in 30 years i.e. it became a mass media in 30 years. Television became a mass media in 13 years. Internet zoomed to 100 million in just 5 years. (*Note: A media becomes a mass media when it reaches 50 million people*).

The Internet originated in late 1960s but the Internet revolution is a phenomenon of the nineties when it moved out of the research institutes into the bedrooms of individuals across the world. Since the Internet has allowed commercial enterprises to connect, its growth has become phenomenal. According to a recent estimate the current size of the Internet is 250 TB (terabytes) and is growing at an annual rate of 60%. The number of Internet users around the world is estimated at about 200 million at present but growing @80% per annum. Around the world, the growth in users, nodes and servers will certainly lead to a virtual information explosion. The quantity of data will witness an exponential growth. The quality of the data will also become more sophisticated including rich content consisting of voice, data and graphics inputs.

World Wide Web (www) also called the Web, is a recent addition to the Internet (since early nineties). Its popularity has increased dramatically because it is easy to use, colourful and rich in content. Simply speaking, the Web is a series of interconnected documents stored on computer sites or web sites. When we use a computer and computer software called browser to visit a site on the web, we get a display of home page. A home page generally gives the name of the organisation or individuals sponsoring the site having a list of highlighted words, buttons or pictures which provides a link to a number of interconnected documents. The Internet and the web sites are not the same, although many people think the two are one and the same thing. The Internet is the network itself and many activities other than the World Wide Web takes place on it. Older services like e-mail, Gopher, File Transfer Protocol (FTP) and Usenet news group are available separately as well as they are integrated into the World Wide Web. People use the web for many reasons, They use it to locate product information, share research, exchange e-mail, get news, financial information, do trading of shares, do research, look for jobs, chat with others, transact business, take courses and pursue social and political agendas, etc. Today all kinds of businesses provide information about their products and services on the Internet. Many of these organisations use the Internet to market and sell their products and services. The potential is enormous.

The use of Internet for E-commerce is on account of the following benefits:

- Customisation
- Interactiveness
- Attention
- Timeliness
- Market Coverage
- Scalability
- Low transaction Cost for User

The Internet is favoured over other alternative means of communication due to the following features of Internet:

- Ubiquitious
- Open To Everybody
- Easy To Use

— Inexpensive As Compared To Other Technologies
— Flexible To Handle Wide Array Of Applications
— Global Reach

Internet is defining the way we communicate with each other, live, play, work and conduct business. It s challenging he set norms of doing business. Today, a person just needs a computer, a browser and access to the Internet and he can buy flowers, computers, airline tickets, a book of his choice and even a jeans specially cut out for him. The recent development of Wireless Application Protocol (WAP) promises to make the Internet mobile i.e. it is accessible through the cell phones and can browse the WAP enabled sites. Just a month ago a Hyderabad based IT Company, Visual Quest India launched indiawapservice.com, India's first comprehensive WAP mortal (mobile portal). The site combines the power of Internet with the convenience of mobile computing and throws open several new opportunities for retailers, businessman and customers. The predominant language on the web is English although sites in other languages are appearing with increasing frequency. Once the language barrier is overcome, the technology exists for any business to conduct e-commerce with any other business or consumer anywhere in the world. The sky is the limit.

## THE INTERNET – INDIAN SCENARIO

The Internet, which came to India in 1985 with the Educational and Research Network (ERNET) project of the Department of Electronics, Government of India, was initially made available to IITs but extended to other research and educational organisations. In August 1995, Videsh Sanchar Nigam Ltd. (VSNL), a Public Sector Undertaking, started offering Internet service to individuals. This opened up a hitherto unexplored market. VSNL is India's window to the world.

It was soon realised by the government that a single international gateway access provider like VSNL would not be able to handle the growth in Internet traffic and keep up with the technological innovations. The obvious problems would be: Congestion, Quality and Service. The government therefore in accordance with the recommendations of the IT Task Force decided to open up the Internet to private sector i.e. privatisation of ISP or Internet services were thrown open to private sector in 1998.

As on today the Internet Service Providers in India include:

— VSNL - the undisputed leaders with around 70% market share and offers a number of options / slots
— MTNL - the second govt. controlled agency with slightly lower tariffs than VSNL.
— Satyam Info - the first private ISP in India
— Bharti BT mantraonline) - the first private ISP with international gateway
— ETH (Dishnet Dial) – Joined the ISP Club in late 1999.
— Jain Studios (Freedialin.com) – the latest entry in the ISP scene offering unlimited free Internet service.

The privatisation has lead to increased competition, which will ultimately pave way for lower tariff, more sophisticated products and services such as E-Commerce. For 500 hours Internet connection, the charges have reduced from Rs.15000 in 1995 to Rs.2700 in the year 2000.

The Andhra Pradesh and the Karnataka government has undertaken a project to setup about 13000 community Internet centres to be called as "Dhabas" in the state to provide easy access to computers and the Internet. Out of this about 1500 centres would be setup in the current year and rest in the next three years. Other state governments are also working towards bringing IT revolution and reaping the benefits of IT through Internet.

## REQUIREMENTS FOR ELECTRONIC COMMERCE

In order to conduct E-Commerce or E-Business, the essential requirements are different for different participants. A consumer, who wants to buy some goods electronically, requires: the Internet connectivity and a national or International Credit Card for Payment i.e. a fast and reliable payment system. A business on the other hand requires: a web site providing interactive access to the consumers for selecting and ordering the products. For this he must have an updated catalogue of goods with Items codes, names, expected delivery times, rates, pictures, and a host of other features. He should also have some foolproof system for authentication of credit card payments. Apart from this, he should also have Logistics and Shipping systems for delivery of goods to the consumer. However for all these cyber transactions, the Cyber Laws, Taxation Laws, etc should be well in place.

## TRADITIONAL COMMERCE TO E-COMMERCE: CHANGING SCENARIO

The use of electronic data communication technologies primarily those that are part of the Internet and the web shall improve existing business processes and identify new business opportunities. In certain cases, business processes use traditional commerce activities very effectively and those processes cannot be improved upon through technology. Products that buyers prefer to touch smell or examine closely are difficult to sell using electronic commerce e.g. perishable food products, high fashion clothing, etc. Branded merchandise and products such as books or CDs can be easily sold using e-commerce. Therefore the situation varies from business to business and we have to study the specific business under consideration. E-commerce alters the traditional concept of time and space. The company can access new customers all over the world very efficiently , around the clock, seven days a week. This expands the market address and potential for higher sales. It also gives customers the opportunity to browse and shop at their convenience and at their own pace.

E-Commerce through Internet is likely to result in new industrial order or economy, which can be, referred as Paperless Economy. The Net Economy is using Internet as a backbone i.e. Internet is used for conducting critical activities of the company such as sell, buy, market, exchange data and information, etc. The basic tool i.e. the Internet is not just another marketing channel or advertising media. It is not just another way to speed up transactions. It will rather result in changing the relationship between consumer and producer in a number of ways. This has given rise to another area called electronic Customer Relationship Management (eCRM). Some of the changes brought about by the adoption of e-commerce are:

**Virtual Corporation -** Opportunity for the use of external business partnership - might have no physical location. Two or more parties can create a partnership that relies completely on electronic transactions.

**Global Market Access by Smaller vendor -** global markets, traditionally open only to large companies, will be accessible to smaller vendors due to lower need of resources to operate aboard. E-Commerce breaks the geographical boundaries. These boundaries will no longer bind a company's aspirations to be a global player or in restricting the scope of its market.

**Transformation of the retail store -** growth of Home Shopping and direct-from-manufacturer sales causing lower prices by reducing commission, rent etc.

**Pressure on Customer Service, Development Cycle and Costs -** stronger need for rapid, direct delivery. The value chain will become less and less tolerant of the need for inventory and storage. Greater competition will be unavoidable. Might cause stronger need for electronic cash.

**New Standards** - lead to many new formal & defacto standards for Components, Packaging, interfaces, documentation etc.

**Unhindered Growth of business** – business can grow to any limits with least resource inputs. The need to increase the sales staff or hire commercial space to grow is no longer required.

The organisations should not blindly follow the trends and join the e-commerce bandwagon. It must first analyse whether its business activities are suitable for such adoption of electronic means. Some businesses are highly suitable for e-commerce while some may never lend themselves to e-commerce. Business Processes, which are suitable for various types of commerce, are given below:

| *S.No.* | *Electronic Commerce* | *Traditional Commerce* | *Combination of and Traditional Commerce* |
|---|---|---|---|
| 1. | Sale/Purchase of Books, CDs, Music | Sale/Purchase of High clothing | Sale Purcahse of Automobiles |
| 2. | Online Deliver of Software | Sale/Purchase of Perishable food products | Online Banking |
| 3. | Advertising and promotion of Travel services | Small-Denomination transactions | Matching services |
| 4. | Online tracking of shipments | Sale of expensive jewelry and antiques | Sale/Purchase of Investment and Insurance products. |

Most organisations calculate Return on Investments (ROI) after adopting new technology. This is difficult to do for investments in information technology or e-commerce due to the fact that the costs and benefits are difficult to quantify.. Costs, which are function of technology, can drastically change during the short-lived e-commerce implementation projects.

E-commerce has profoundly affected the conventional business practices as is evident from the above examples. In the PC industry, DELL and Compaq, the leading MNC brands in the world are selling PCs directly over their website. A customer has to log on to their website, select their specifications and place an order and key in his credit card number. Only then Dell manufacturers the customised PC delivering it to his doorstep in a few days. Dell in this process is doing a business of over $10 million (over 40 crores) per day which is around 70% of its PC sales. Almost 100% of the Oracle software sales would take place over the Internet within a year. Everyone will be able to purchase software through "Oracle Store". This will result in eliminating $500 million of cost from Oracle's operations. Other vendors are now looking towards exploring this untapped market on the Internet.

Although Internet represents only a minute fraction of the total purchases, its growth is exponential. As reported by Jupiter Communications, that 10 million people in the US had bought something over the Net in 1997, over 17 million did so in 1998 and around 35 million made purchases in 1999. This is directly because the number of users using the Internet everyday is rising from 4% in 1996 to over 55% in 1999. The trend is clear and is rising exponentially

## INFRASTRUCTURE FOR ELECTRONIC COMMERCE IN INDIA

E-Commerce requires easy and inexpensive availability of Internet. VSNL which had the monopoly of providing Internet connectivity had about 45000 Internet subscribers in

1997 which has grown to over 5 lakh mark till 1999. According to third Annual PC industry analysis carried out by Skoch Consulting Service, a Delhi based research firm, the total number of installed PCs in the country will reach 5.7 million by December 2000 indicating a growth of 70%. The number of Internet subscribers is projected to reach 13 lakh mark indicating a growth of 160%.

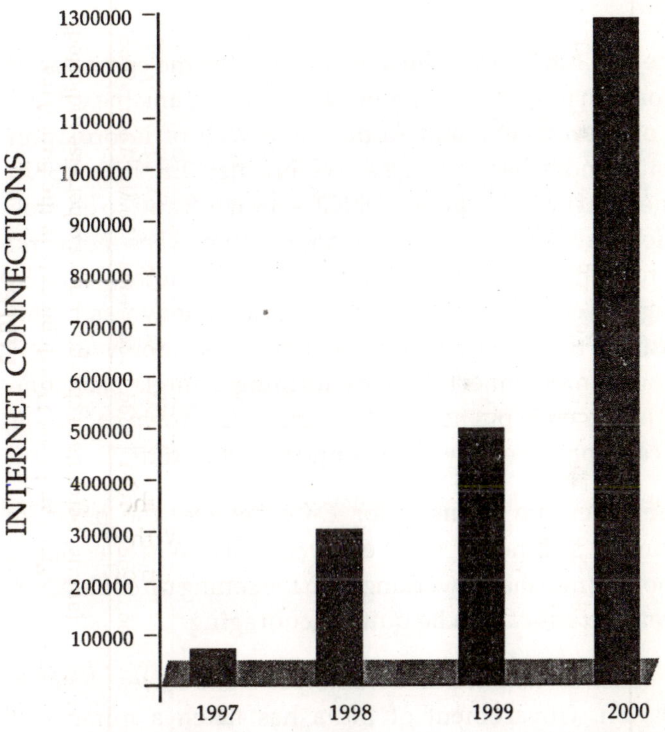


Figure: Internet Connections in India (Source: IDC)

This number is minuscule compared to the US where around 40% of the population is on the Internet. Despite such a growth in the users, the services are far from satisfactory. The number of hosts which provide the facility of webpage and website hosting/launching in India is only 16253 as against over 3 million in USA and 1.8 million in Japan. This penetration will reach a standstill if we do not promote other modes like cable and even internet through mobile phones (WAP) which has already entered the market. The cable system has been tried successfully in Orissa and most of the cable service operators are eyeing to harness the rich potential by bringing the middle-class on the net through the existing cables.

The NICNET and ERNET were setup in the early 80s, so as to form an information highway that would link the various parts of the country and form single web of information. Presently India has networks like NICnet, ERNET, VSNL, Banknet, SAILnet, BHELnet, ONGCs network and so on most of which are built around a single organisation. These networks were not able to communicate with one another thereby making the communication across various networks highly expensive. VSNL, as the international carrier is the only network that could interconnect these by forming a single backbone. VSNL has recentiy put its own network (with its own backbone) in place to provide easy interconnectivity in India.

The other pre-requisite for E-Commerce, the payment mechanism still needs to be evolved fully. With the banks also moving into the networking with the setting up of BankNet, the scenario appears to be quite encouraging.

In order to take the E-Commerce to the lowest level of population, Government of India has taken a number of decisions to boost and strengthen the information infrastructure in the country. Some of these are:

- DOT to focus on building additional capacities for the National Information Infrastructure.
- License fee for private ISPs to be waived for the first two years.

— Tariff for both Internet and other data services have been lowered for faster dissemination.

— Aim to help users get Net connection within one to two weeks anywhere in the country.

— DOT to continue to provide Internet service but focus increasingly on providing the national backbone to enable interconnectivity among private ISPs.

The government of India is busy chalking out plans and measures to strengthen the e-commerce boom in all possible ways.. It is necessary for them to first create an environment and setup necessary infra-structure for a smooth trade through the worldwide web and promote it to replace the age-old documentation system and time consuming transaction, before thinking of any controlling measures. The e-commerce or trading through the net will put an end to all the formalities as one is negotiating or bargaining straight with his/her client or customer. All those third parties and middlemen are swept out in this trading process. In order to meet the growing demand of Internet, it is essential to develop and strengthen the infrastructure to support the entire network using optical fibers for communication, making telephone easily available, etc. Therefore the government decided to privatise the Internet business in India and strengthens the telephone systems apart from exploring cheap and easier means of accessing the Internet such as Internet on Cable Network, etc.

## NEED FOR ELECTRONIC COMMERCE

E-Commerce is shrinking the world. Distant markets suddenly are within easy reach, saving business time and money, prospecting and presenting new business opportunities based on better, more thorough information. A Company that incorporates electronic commerce as a major component of its marketing strategy stays at least in line with, if not ahead, of the competition.

What really pushes a business organisation to move to a paperless environment? There can be numerous reasons to place the organisation on the e-commerce bandwagon. Although these reasons are specific to every organisation but some of the common ones are listed below:

— Competition – The organisation is either forced by the competition or it can pre-empt the competition by moving ahead of others in joining e-commerce. An excellent example is Dell Computers that was the first to start sale of computers through the Internet thereby reducing cost. It also provided a facility to the customers to assemble the computer choosing different hardware components such as Memory, Hard Disk, CD Drive, Monitor, etc. IBM, Compaq and other manufacturer's had to change their marketing strategy to find ways to reduce operational costs by adopting the e-business model of sale through Internet.

— Global Reach – The Internet has crashed the geographical boundaries and the entire world has shrieked to a global village. This permits the customers to make purchases from any part of the world without actually visiting the place. This widens the reach of the companies to the entire globe. This further translates into 24 hour, seven days a week and 365 days in a year business for the company. For example, books can be purchased from Amazon.com from any part of the world, AT&T allows the customer to receive the bill and authorise payment electronically from any part of the world.

— Customer Service – Personalised and Customised services through Internet is one of the greatest advantages e-commerce offers. The customers can customise the product according to their own taste such as: online newspaper. The customers can be updated on the status of order placed by them when it goes through various stages of processing such as pacing, shipping, etc. Pre-sale and Post-sale support is an important ingredient of the e-commerce package.

— Value Addition - A product has to go through various stages of value addition from manufacturers to the consumers and at each stage the cost is added up making the product expensive for the consumer. This business chain can be shortened through the adoption of e-commerce thereby making the product cheaply available to the consumers.

— Nettish Products – The products which are more suitable for purchase through the Internet as their delivery takes place through the Net are referred to as Nettish Products, e.g. E-mail, E-Greetings, Software, Chat Software, etc.

The fall in operational costs, higher quality, integration of supply and distribution chain, improvements in efficiency levels and etc. are too attractive for any business to ignore. Business is increasing on the Internet because it provides cost-effective alternative. According to a study in France, it has been established that use of EDI alone could lead to net savings ranging from 20 to 80 percent.

E-commerce offers the above benefits over other traditional means of conducting business. The explosive growth of Internet clearly indicates that the Internet shall become an essential medium for conducting business. Financial institutions are offering a wide range of on-line services such as on-line banking and securities trading. Electronic shopping malls have sprung up throughout the Internet. Above all, the Internet offers worldwide access to consumers, at a fraction of the traditional costs. Retail products, for example, can now be offered globally from one easily updated site with consumers having 24 hour access to products and services. E-commerce is likely to transform and expedite business transactions, reduce transaction cost, increase the velocity of money and hence the velocity of business on global basis.

## ELECTRONIC COMMERCE REVOLUTION IN INDIA

In India, e-commerce is just fledgling but its advantages and convenience are soon to be realised A large number of Indian companies are fast jumping into the E-commerce boom which has completely revolutionised the global business organisations in the developed world. Every day we find a new headline informing of a new E-Commerce pact or venture covering all kinds of organisations. The dotcom has become the word of the day. Today you can order anything and everything on the Internet from air travel tickets to cars, books, computers, readymade garments, hotel reservations, bouquets, to vegetables, music, etc. all from the comfortable confines of your bed room through a PC. It is very difficult to find an organisation that is not using the Internet. Almost every one of them has got a web-site on the Internet, which is being used for conducting e-commerce in some form, or the other.

The famous shirt maker of Mumbai "Charag Din" launched its website so that large number of its loyal clientele outside Mumbai could make purchases through the Net. A company called TriSoft Design has completed a project thereby connecting over 700 shops in the Connaught Place area on the Net for shopping thereby creating a Virtual Indian Mall on the Internet. Wintech Computers – a software consultancy firm is implementing an on-line shopping project in Mumbai thereby setting up the country's first web based electronic super market chain. They plan to put-up about 70 outlets in Mumbai. The customer doesn't have to pay for shopping through the company. The product range includes books, gift items, flowers, jewellery, consumer electronics, etc. The two biggest concerns for a consumer while shopping on the Internet are whether they will get the same quality of the product and will the delivery take place efficiently and fast. These genuine concerns will be addressed by the outlets of the company and by having tie up with the vendors who can guarantee quality and service. Both VSNL and the MTNL and host of other companies are working on offering on-line E-commerce solutions (like EFT) by connecting banks and number of business houses.

On the government front, the recent decision of the US government to make all federal purchases paperless, is likely to give a boost to E-Commerce Trading in general and India in particular as US is the largest trading partner of India. The developing countries are forced to opt for this electronic trading environment, in dealing with their paperless counterparts in the US and other parts of the world. If the Indian business houses do not conform to global standards, they are bound to loose. India is slowly gearing up to take advantage of the new rules of the business game i.e. E-Commerce through the privatisation of Internet. Further, the European Union (EU) assembly recently endorsed a proposal drafted by its civil service and executive branch , the European Commission, to regulate and promote E-Commerce.

The Indian corporates will have to suffer the consequences of this "dual trading environment" (paperbased and paperless) for some time. They electronically manage information when dealing with their multinational counterparts. They also keep their paperwork intact for the slower movers on the road to electronic commerce. This would multiply their operational costs during the transition period and there is no other option.

The EDI that plays a crucial role in E-Commerce is widely

used in the banking sector for inter-branch and inter-bank transactions. Indian Customs EDI System (ICES) which provides paperless transactions in the customs house also makes use of EDI. An exporter, for example, can log onto the ICES, electronically submit forms and get the requisite clearance on his screen, without moving out of his house. Not only would this tremendously expedite processing of forms, it would also reduce the corruption in various departments, according to electronic commerce experts. The system is integrated with other agencies like DGFT, Airports Authority of India, Apparel Export Promotion Council and the Punjab National Bank.

The Directorate General of Foreign Trade (DGFT), which issues all types of licenses for import and export has connected all its zonal offices with the headquarters using the EDI system, and is now effectively interacting with trade, industry and related organisations. Further E-Commerce projects are also proposed in the Export Guarantee Corporation of India (ECGC), at several ports in India. The integration of EDI into the computerised Marine Container handling System (MACH) and the Integrated Cargo Management System (ICMS) is also under implementation. The Government is committed to introduce EDI at all customs houses, ports, airports and other government regulatory agencies by the end of year 2000.

MTNL, the public sector telephone agency is also planning to provide E-Commerce and Web hosting services through its Internet backbone. MTNL is gearing to provide services for the business-to-business and business-to-government transactions. They already have the software and are working on the proper mode of encryption, as it would be a public network. Infact, they are in the process of implementing the firewalls. MTNL is working in collaboration with National Centre for Software Training (NCST) on the E-commerce initiative and desires to be a total solutions provider including secure online payments and facilitating trade transfer. MTNL is one of the first companies to offer the ECS for payment of telephone bills.

In India, E-commerce and its fastest growing component "Net-business" is still largely an uncharted territory. As per findings of survey by KPMG, E-Commerce in India would be restricted to business-to-business operations. It may take some time to percolate to the level of individual consumers, given the low level of prevalence of the plastic money (i.e. credit cards, etc.). According to a survey by National Association of Software and Services Companies (NASSCOM), the apex association of the software industry, e-commerce in India is likely to cross Rs.300 crore during the current financial year. During 1998-99, e-commerce transactions were to the tune of Rs.131 crore and only Rs.12 crore of this was from the retail (B2C) sector and the rest constituted B2B transactions. International Data Corporation (IDC) predicts that by year 2000 E-commerce in India will be in the range of $160 million. Another survey by Indian Market Research Bureau (IMRB) predicts that by the year 2001, E-commerce in the B2B sector in India will be in the range of Rs.25000 crores. On the higher side the market size could be as big as Rs.50,000 crores. The survey predicts that in the B2C sector, the market size will be in the range of 4200 crores on the lower side and Rs.16,000 crores on the higher side. However in India much change is still needed to create a favorable environment for increased Internet diffusion and for increasing public trust in the E-business paradigm. It is evident that the potential benefits offered by E-Commerce are far from realised. The undisputed fact is that the Internet is going to be more and more popular.

So Net-Shopping has finally arrived in India and we have to keep pace with this. Those business which are prepared to move onto the Internet bandwagon and transform their business to take the advantage will survive and others will move into oblivion in a short span of time thus proving that the Darwin's law-the survival of the fittest still prevails

So Net-Shopping has finally arrived in India and we have to keep pace with this. Those business which are prepared to move onto the Internet bandwagon and transform their business to take the advantage will survive and others will move into oblivion in a short span of time thus proving that the Darwin's law-"Survival of the fittest" still prevails

## COSTS OF ELECTRONIC COMMERCE

Some of the more important costs and benefits especially as they relate Electronic Commerce activities on the Net are as follows:

a. The Web Hosting Cost - The first-cost, a company face when it decides that it wants a web presence, is the hosting cost. Hosting determines where the files and images associated with the web site are going to reside. Large companies or those who want that total control tend to perform this function in-house while small businesses or those who do not consider this function a core competency will out-source the service with an Internet Service Provider (ISP). It is hard to break down hosting costs for companies that perform the services in-house because a lot of the costs get absorbed into general overhead. In any event we have to account for such things as the salaries of the staff who run the operation, the connection to the Internet, domain registration & equipment. The costs for out-source hosting will be high compared to the in-house hosting.

b. Design and Development Costs - Once we have found a place to host our web site, the next task is to design & develop it. Again this can be performed in-house or contracted out. The costs involved in both will vary depending on size & complexity of the web site.

c. Maintenance Costs – This cost relates to maintaining the web site.

d. Opportunity costs - There are also opportunity costs. This is especially true for small business if they put up the web site themselves. Resources (time and money) are scarce and decision-markers need to ask if they could be better used elsewhere. Consumer or end-users of web sites also face costs. There is a lot of misinformation on the web.

## BENEFITS OF ELECTRONIC COMMERCE

While there are certainly plenty of costs associated with E-Commerce, there are also a lot of benefits. E-commerce can increase sales and decrease costs. No longer a company needs army of people and expensive real estate to setup a global presence. It has been found that the firms use the Internet to improve enterprise information and workflow, redefine the way they communicate with customers, and leverage global resources. Some of the companies like Cisco Systems, Amazon, Onsale and BidnAsk, all US based, are developing new business models with E-Commerce. CISCO and General Electric are leveraging the Internet to redefine marketing channels and customer communications to provide rich information, receive orders and gather detailed customer profiles. Rather than questioning company's personnel, customers seek out detailed product and technical information at the web site and company is saving a lot of revenue on this account.

Inexpensive Internet access allows small and large firms to access expertise, information and resources worldwide at low costs. This lowers information and entry barriers across various industries, allowing firms to better leverage resources and compete globally. For example, amazon.com, which is a bookstore on Internet, is using e-commerce quite effectively. Amazon offers a catalog of over 2 million books to buyers at any time, anywhere. It has posted a 35% monthly sales growth and garnered a well recognised brandname in cyberspace. Amazon incurs virtually no direct warehousing, sales and rental costs because it automates order processing, and wholesalers and suppliers ship most products directly from their warehouses to buyers. By not operating retail facilities or intermediate warehouses, Amazon accumulates savings to pass on to customers.

The advantages of E-Commerce for business-to-business are:

— Lower purchasing costs
— Reduced Inventory Control
— Lower cycle time
— Efficient customer service
— Lower sales and marketing costs
— New Markets (Sales opportunities)
— Smooth business operations and
— Reduced Document processing costs

Another benefit is that it helps the colleagues even if they are located at dispersed offices, collaborate, with each other and work as one cohesive team in the service of the customer. The customers can have constantly updated product information, price lists and product support information.

Some of the cost-effective uses of E-Commerce are:

**MARKETING:** The company's web site can be used as a marketing tool by providing information such as prices and specifications to a global audience 24 hours a day. The business negotiations can also be held on Internet. With a minimal investment, a small or home based business can make its corporate presence felt. The Internet can also be used for market research through a mailing list for supporters and advocates. Every person who visits the company's website or has subscribed to mailing list is sent an electronic-mail. This provides a fast and cheap media for pre-testing the product launch.

**ADVERTISING:** This exploits the web's natural advantages as a low cost medium for disseminating information and processing transactions. Advertising offers an excellent example of this. The cost involved in advertising in a web site is very much less compared to giving advertisement in a newspaper.

Therefore E-Commerce can be useful to target potentially interested customers and to communicate with them. Internet advertising is likely to complement other advertising media. In India, almost all the multinational barring few Indian companies have created their home-pages where they provide complete information about the company and its products. An Internet ad provides a direct link to web site to get more information or for buying the product.

**SALES:** Customers can order electronically from their computer sitting in the confines of their home without actually visiting the market and spending time at a discounted price. Related benefit includes error reduction because orders don't have to be re-keyed into order entry systems and increased efficiencies through the automation of the business processes.

**BUSINESS COMMUNICATION:** Apart from above, the E-Commerce also offers a low cost, secure method of business communication.

**BRAND EQUITY:** Another benefit of web-sites is that information based industries excel here on the Net. For example, Amazon.com has considerable brand equity for essentially being a virtual company.

## ELECTRONIC COMMERCE: EMERGING OPPORTUNITIES

Rapid and unprecedented growth of the Internet and the World Wide Web makes Electronic Commerce the business opportunity of the future. The traditional patterns of commerce have had to change as electronic customers have much greater opportunity to select a supplier taking into account factors such as value, price and quality. Benefits for both sides include the more convenient locations and times for ordering, faster buying, potential availability of product information and the possibilities for customized service.

The ability to buy and sell at any time and from any location is changing the business landscape. E-commerce is a round-the-clock advantage for the customer. It allows fast and flexible execution and response to market opportunities. The web enables a company to introduce a new product, get immediate customer reaction, refine & perfect it, all without incurring huge investments in a physical distribution infrastructure. The growing online economy is characterized by greater choice of products, purchasing options and increasing competitions. According to a study conducted by Forrester research in 1997, the total value of goods & services traded between companies over the Internet will reach $ 45 billion in the year 2000 and around $327 billion in the year 2002.

The E-commerce route is specifically suitable for:

— New businesses, which have no existing, structure to be changed.

— Technology Companies to improve electronic route to promote their services such as Services, Software, etc.

— Media companies which would benefit from the fast distribution of information together with low setup costs.

## ISSUES FOR E-COMMERCE

The entire electronic commerce depends heavily on the availability of high speed data communication networks, availability of personal computers to a large segment of the population and easy and inexpensive access to the Internet. At the back-end it also requires efficient, reliable payment mechanism (credit cards etc.), and an awareness and acceptability of these payment mechanisms by the masses.

Further, the co-existence of a conventional and electronic trading environment, tends to multiply the costs. Thus, those companies dealing with the business houses already using E-Commerce will have to move to a paperless environment and they will possibly be inclined to deal more and more with other companies who are conforming to the same paperless standards. India, which is passing through a transitional phase is faced with a number of problems in using the E-Commerce for conducting business globally. Some important problems are:

— Inadequate infrastructure of DOT/MTNL
— Availability of only a single national backbone in the public till sometimes ago
— Problems of Congestion, Quality and Service
— Unreliable telephone links and Overloading of lines
— Inadequate telephone network
— Difficulties in getting Internet Connection which have eased largely with more ISPs

## CHALLENGES OF E-COMMERCE

India needs a framework to encourage and stimulate the growth of e-commerce in all its forms. The good news is that these all are getting fixed. Cyber laws governing se-commerce transactions are now getting in place with the passage of "IT Bill" in the Parliament. The Information Technology Act 2000 (which is yet to be notified) is expected to provide security of the transactions on the Internet. To further boost the e-commerce, the Govt. of India has opened the gates for foreign companies by allowing 100% foreign direct investment in e-commerce to start with. The companies would have to divest 26% of their equity to Indian public over a period of 5 years. With these, the era of e-commerce will dawn in a big way. The potential inhibitors to the widespread adoption of E-Commerce in India are:

**LEGAL BARRIERS:** The major legal barriers to EDI implementation are the admissibility of EDI generated documents and their acceptability as evidence in court. The Government has setup a committee to study the legal requirements for EDI, review the current laws in India, identify those that need to be amended and recommend legal policies, amendments and administrative regulations that may be required to legalise EDI transactions. For example: Indian Evidence Act, Intellectual Proprietary Act, etc.

**RELIABLE ELECTRONIC PAYMENT SYSTEM:** For purchases made on the Internet, they must be paid. This requires on the part of an e-business organisation to offer flexible payment options to the customers that are safe, convenient and widely accepted. Electronic Payment System (EPS) is a method of paying for an on-line purchase (tangible or intangible) of goods or services in a paperless mode i.e. without actually holding cash or issuing a cheque. Electronic payments are an efficient means of payment, offering improved security, assurance of value, require lesser manual intervention, and offer reduced cost and easier record storage and handling. The business has to therefore find out (identify) which choice among various options works the best for the company and for the customers. The four technologies or payment systems that are used on web-sites offering shopping facility are-Electronic Cash, Software wallets, Smart Cards and Credit/

Debit cards. Each of these systems has unique properties, costs, advantages and disadvantages. Some of these are already popular and widely accepted for payment while others are still growing and are in the evolving stage and their future is unclear. For an organisation, they must understand the merits and de-merits of each method before making a wise decision on payment system to be adopted by them.

Electronic cash distribution and payments can be handled by e-wallets, smart cards or through proprietary; limited use scrip (e.g. flooz). Electronic cheques are the encrypted representation that resembles e-cash. This mode for online payments though small at present but is growing quite rapidly. Credit & debit cards are the most popular forms of e-payments. A recent survey indicates that over 80% of the Internet purchases are paid for with credit or Debit cards. Debit cards draw the payment directly from the bank account in the same way as cheques do.

All Electronic Payment Systems have some issues that must be resolved to allay customer fears and give them confidence. Some concerns about electronic payment methods include - Privacy & Security, Independence, Portability, Divisibility and convenience. Of these issues, privacy and security are primary concerns to be addressed. A customer wants to know "Is the transaction not private and secure. Can the electronic currency be copied, reused or forged"? If the answer is 'Yes', the customer will not use the system.

**SECURITY CONCERNS:** Since Internet is 'Open', 'untrusted' and 'global network', security of data sent over the public networks is a primary concern. In general, the businesses and individuals interested in E-Commerce face four primary issues in terms of security:

i) *Privacy:* Assurance that the transaction is private between sender and the receiver and the transaction can be read only by the intended receivers. This can be achieved by using data encryption techniques. The resolution of this issue is likely to be market driven: If individual privacy remains a major consumer concern, E-Commerce will not flourish as predicted.

ii) *Authentication:* Verification of both the sender and the receiver's identity with proof of transactions and receipt of messages are done. It ensures that the transactions have been generated by a specific known source.

iii) *Integrity:* Assurance that the transaction received is identical to the one that was sent by the sender. It can be ensured by end-to-end message authentication.

iv) *Non-Repudiation:* Proof that a transaction actually took place between identified parties and the message has not been modified en-route.

The Internet as a media does not support any of the above issues, hence technologies are being developed to permit sharing of information on above four counts. Some of the solutions ensuring security of the transactions are: Firewalls, Tunnels, Encryption (Public and Secret keys), Digital Signatures, Digital Certification, etc. The Secured Socket Layer (SSL) designed by Netscape, is the most commonly used security design protocol. It has become a standard and is being supported by large number of Web Servers and Web Browsers.

The rising frauds in the area of electronic banking, e-commerce and other forms of cyber usage such as Internet abuse, Cyber terrorism have given rise to global threats. Central Bureau of Investigation (CBI) is training its personnel to develop the expertise in navigating through the cyberspace and understand the cyber criminals and crimes. The types of Cyber crime (i.e. which is related to computers) include:

— Hacking of ATMs
— Misuse of Computer in organisations for siphoning off money
— Illegal transaction through Computers
— Hacking information from sensitive sites
— Collecting and sending sensitive data which affect national security

**TAX FRAMEWORK:** E-Commerce in general and business in cyberspace in particular grows, tax administration faces new complexities. It is therefore imperative that Indian tax authorities must address themselves to the implications of this development. This requires tax sharing agreement between various countries. A number of multi-lateral organisations and trade bodies like World Trade Organisations are involved in deep discussion on the global framework adopted for taxation of cyber transactions involving huge sums of money.

## FUTURE TRENDS

The availability of Internet access through the mobile means using the Wireless Application Protocol (WAP) will set a new trend in popularising the adoption of e-commerce among the masses. The emergence of Extranets is likely to provide impetus to E-Commerce. An Extranet is a part of one or more organisations intranets that has been expanded onto the Internet. The project of providing Internet connectivity to homes on the TV sets through the local cable television connection is underway. The cable modem route is considered to be the most suitable and the best way to take the Internet to the masses. This will result in widespread adoption of E-commerce in India in the retail sector selling.

Assuming that the future communications networks have the capacity to transmit as much data as is required - in highly secure conditions; and cheaper hardware and software solutions are available to make full use of these communications facilities, what we need is a willing community to emorace new work practices.

## SUMMARY

Although still in the embryonic stage, e-commerce is big potential world-wide for Business-to-Business and Business-to-Consumer sector and this is true in India too. E-commerce is growing explosively on the Internet. By encouraging e-commerce we will gain, besides lower prices and better quality of information without cost and responsibility of maintaining it. Companies need to replace their manual and paper based operations to electronic alternatives, redefine and simplify information flows and use these information flows in a dynamic way. The E-Commerce is unaffected by time zones, geography or location, language barriers and business hours which offers real benefits. Although India has to go a long way to realise the true potential of Internet for conducting E-Commerce, a lot depends on the initiative of the government to build the necessary infrastructure, but it can surely be said that E-Commerce is the way to a better future.

## REFERENCES

1. Bajaj, K K. and Nag, "Electronic Commerce", Tata McGraw Hill, 1999.
2. Economic Service, "Electronic Commerce-Efficient Commerce",Vol XXI No.16, April 1997, p37.
3. Hamilton, Scott., "E-Commerce for the 21st Century", Computer Vol.30 No.5, 1997,p 44.
4. Schneider P. Gary and James T. Perry, "Electronic Commerce", Course Technology Thomson Learning, 2000.
5. The Economic Times, "Electronic Commerce Now", July 8, 1997, p14.

6. The Economist, "Survey:Online Commerce", May 10-16, 1997, p59.
7. Express Computer, May 24, 1999.
8. Web-site: http://www.cybercash.com/
   http://www.webshop.com/
   HYPERLINK
   http://www.altavista.com/
   http://www.altavista.com/
   http://www.rediff.com/

# 18

# VALUE-AT-RISK: AN EMERGING TECHNIQUE IN RISK MANAGEMENT

*Navjot*

In an economy, finance is the conduit between savings and investments. Naturally the CEOs always had to cope with the fact that the cost of such transmission may vary. Indeed there is nothing new about the price variability; what is new is price volatility. Since the mid-1970s, a potent mix of fast interlocking markets and a revolution in information technology has increased the speed, frequency, and magnitude of price changes in both commodities and financial markets, which in turn have multiplied both opportunity and risk for the CEO. Not surprisingly in the developed capital market, much innovative energy has been devoted to devising instruments and mechanisms that enable the CEO to survive this turbulence. With the globalisation of the economy world over, the concepts like capital adequacy, asset classification, and income recognition have pride in the glossaries of the financial sector. Post Daiwa/Baring episodes, the focus of supervisory concern has been shifted from asset quality to risk management. Instead of merely addressing the credit quality issues, financial sector in general and banking sector in particular is laying emphasis on overall risk profile. Varieties of risks are created and are required to be managed to encompass credit/interest rate / pricing / environmental / legal/systemic / currency / reputation risk.

Here an historical fact from a book called "Measure of Reality" is worth noting. The fact goes like this: some 900 years ago, dull people in a barbaric state of civilisation populated Europe. Europe was much less advanced than the Arab world. Then 400 years afterwards, Europe embarked on a wave of imperialism that seems to have no precedent in history. The book asks, "How did this happen?" The thesis of this book is that this change happened as Europe started to "measure" the material world. What happened was a change in the mentality that induced people to start measuring space and time. It was the beginning of clocks, measuring space, measuring the material world and the environment that led to huge technological progress in Europe and explains why Europeans and specifically Westerners seems to have been able to conquer all other civilisations they met. In a way Value-At-Risk is along the same line. What we are doing is trying to measure the risk in a systematic way. VAR is an extension of the idea of measuring things. The good thing about VAR is that it measures risks in a way that most people can understand it.

VAR is the emerging technology that tries to bridge the gap between recognition of risk and measurement of risk. Risk measurement has always been important in the modem approaches to finance. The importance of risk measurement has been underlined by the "derivative disasters" of the early 1990s. Internal systems, which allowed Nick Leeson (Barings) and Robert Citron (Orange County) to adopt their positions appear incomprehensibly inadequate. If systems existed which could measure the risks of these positions, and report them to the top management, then these positions would never have been allowed. The usefulness of risk measurement is not limited to the fraction of financial portfolios, which have led to well-publicized ruin. At the core of modem finance is the link between risk and return. Every position on a financial market assumes certain risks, in the hope of obtaining certain returns. This process would be more competently executed if the risks could be accurately quantified. The usefulness of such quantification applies in the normal day-to-day operations of thousands of companies, and not just in the few situations where spectacular losses are in the offing.

Commercial banks, Investment banks, Insurance companies, Non-financial firms and Pension funds hold portfolios of assets that may include stocks, bonds, currencies and derivatives. Each institution needs to quantify the amount of risk its portfolio may incur in the course of the day, week, month or year. For example, a bank needs to assess its potential losses in order to set aside enough capital to cover them. Similarly, a company needs to track the value of its assets and any cash flow resulting from losses in its portfolio. An Investment fund may want to understand potential losses on its portfolio, not only to allocate its assets better but also to fulfill its obligations to make set payments to investors. In addition, credit rating and regulatory agencies must be able to assess likely losses on portfolio as well, Since they need to set capital requirements and issue credit ratings.

Bank is exposed to interest rate risk and foreign exchange risk in many currencies, in many different forms (for example, deposits, loans, swaps, futures, forward exchange contracts, options,) for many maturities in many different operating centres, in many countries. It aims to measure the potential loss from its exposure to each type of risk in each of its treasury operations and for the group as a whole. While it is a huge multidimensional problem, the bank wanted a risk management system that was relatively simple, easy to understand, easy to explain (internally and externally) and reasonably robust. The answer was found in Value-At-Risk.

Value-at-Risk is an estimate of the largest loss that a portfolio is likely to suffer during all but truly exceptional periods. More precisely, the VAR is maximum loss that an institution can be confident it would loose a certain fraction of the time over a particular period: Though it was initially used to measure the market risk, its application areas have increased in number as well as in scope. In the basic sense, the VAR refers to the maximum amount of money likely to be lost over some period at some specific confidential level. It also refers to the estimation procedure to produce the VAR figures. It also refers to the methodologies that can be used to estimate other types of risks such as credit risk, cash flow risk as well as value at risk. Finally, the VAR is also an approach to risk management, wherein the VAR figures are used to restructure the company and for taking similar management decisions. Consider a bank with a portfolio of assets that would like to characterise its potential losses using VAR, for example, the bank could specify a horizon of one day and set the frequency of maximum loss to 98 percent. In that case, a VAR calculation might reveal that the maximum loss is $1 million. Thus on average, in 98 trading days out of 100, the loss on the portfolio will not exceed $1 million over a one day horizon. But on 2 trading days in 100, losses will, on average, exceed $ 1 million.

VAR can be used to assess the potential loss on a portfolio of assets generally. The users can specify any horizon and frequency of loss that fit their particular circumstances. But the method of calculating VAR depends not only on horizon chosen but also on the kinds of assets in the portfolio. One method may yield good results with portfolios consisting of stocks, bonds and currencies over a short horizon, but the same method may not work well over longer horizons such as a month or a year. If the portfolio contains derivatives, methods that differ from those used to analyse portfolios of stocks, bonds or currencies may be needed.

VAR uses standard statistical methods employed in other

scientific and professional fields. One of the key advantages of VAR is that it looks at risk over time, based on historical data, rather than simply providing static snapshot of a portfolio or balance sheet. Most VAR models assumed that the changes in the value of the portfolio, on average, are random and their frequency distribution can be estimated using a normal or Gaussian, statistical curve. Depending on the nature of the portfolio and the time period of analysis, however, a log normal distribution may be appropriate.

The four most commonly used models are:

**Historic Simulation**

This requires data on the financial prices underlying the portfolio and use of financial price changes of say, the last 100 days to create 100 new sets of prices. Defining the current value of prices as $P_0$ the historical approach produces a set of 100 new prices. The analyst is to re-value the portfolio at each set of prices creating a distribution of possible portfolio value changes. One is to sort the portfolio changes low to high (losses to gains) and for a 97.5% level of confidence, select the point halfway between the third and the fourth largest loss.

**Estimated variance/covariance**

The analyst is to calculate volatilities and correlations of changes in the prices underlying the portfolio's instruments/ assets. Then the *deltas* (change in price for a given unit change in underlying price) of the instruments in the portfolios are to calculated. The analyst is to use the correlations, volatilities, notional values, and deltas to calculate the volatility of the portfolio, assuming that changes in prices are normal, then VAR at 95% confidence level would be 2.

The call by Banking Supervision for market capital requirements highlighted a growing preoccupation with the measurement and management of market risk. Against this background, J.P. Morgan made freely available its daily estimates of the volatilities and correlations of key interest rates, exchange rates and equity indices, along with a comprehensive technical description of its methodology.

**Fixed Scenarios**

Under a fixed scenario model, instead of revaluing a portfolio against historical market data, the portfolio is revalued against some set of fixed scenarios. Fixed scenarios are also referred to as stress simulations, as in G30 derivatives Recommendation 6. For example, in one shift, it might be assumed that the US dollars long bond yield jumps 80bps and the yen/US dollars spot rate tumbles to 92bps. These are the types of scenarios that traditional Asset Liability Management (ALM) group use in presentations and analysis for senior management.

Any such set of scenarios can be assembled. From these scenarios an implied volatility of the portfolio could perhaps be calculated.

While computing catastrophic portfolio simulations can be useful in providing an understanding of the non-linear portfolio risks, deriving volatility from scenarios is questionable. It is interesting to note that what constitutes a catastrophic scenario depends on the current position held in the portfolio. The same scenario can be catastrophic for one party and highly lucrative for another. Thus, unless precise position is known, it is not even possible to construct worst case scenarios. Moreover, the mere choice of scenarios introduces the statistical bias into the sample. The history of some firms has shown that people are not good at predicting outlying cases, and therefore the portfolio SD is likely to be underestimated. While fixed scenarios can provide insights into how a given portfolio or balance sheet behaves, the model is not a likely candidate for producing accurate estimates of VAR.

**Monte Carlo Simulation**

Use macro models of markets to simulate the finance prices underlying the portfolio via the Monte-Carlo method (i.e. search for random elements of market models and generate random numbers to feed these elements); create at least 5,000 possible trails of the financial prices. Combine these financial price changes with the current prices to create 5,000 new sets of financial prices. Revalue the portfolio for each new set of financial prices and sort the resulting portfolio value changes from low to high.

At present there is no methodological market standard (an initial recommendation from the BIS in 1993), but whilst alternative models are not only feasible and were subsequently endorsed by the Basle Committee in 1995. The methods should incorporate (as recommended by the committee) both qualitative and quantitative standard criteria. The three methodologies i.e. Historic Simulation, Risk Metrics, and Monte Carlo Simulation are valid ways of determining VAR, for a portfolio (without options); the three methods would produce very similar figures, if not identical.

Risk Metrics and Monte Carlo are computationally complex. Risk Metrics is essentially a variance/covariance analysis using an extensive database of prices and volatilities in financial asset accompanied by correlations among them. Given the spread of prices and correlations, approximately 56,000 data points are available from which those relevant to one's portfolio can be drawn and used with appropriate software to determine VAR. One shortcoming of Risk Metrics is that it remains unable to accommodate fully the changing price sensitivity of options (i.e. gamma and vega). It is based on the assumption that all distribution in market factors and market values are zero mean and normal.

Like Risk Metrics, the Monte Carlo approach necessitates

the determination and correlations and volatilities of the instruments/assets in the portfolio, and the simulation program requires extensive running to produce the array of price change scenarios necessary to be statistically relevant. It produces direct simulation of future distributions.

The Historical method is computationally and conceptually simpler and is independent of any calculated factor such as correlation that are not directly market observable. To determine VAR, the historical method analyses "actual" distribution of probable changes in market values devised from historical price activity. There are no limitations on the shape of the distribution and in many instances distribution of market value changes can deviate from normal.

The concept of VAR is considered as an emerging technique because in the last decade, the economies world over have witnessed the globalisation and internationalisation, with the result that this interconnectivity make trouble in one region more potentially calamitous elsewhere than ever; so if Russia would sneeze, Brazil might also catch cold. The world in the last few decades started recognising this fact and has started a move towards risk measurement and risk management.

The study of this concept is important because the media, mainly in the developed economies (the concept being new is not common in underdeveloped economies like India) is flushed with the arguments both in favour as well as against Value-At-Risk. In such a scenario, it is very difficult for a corporate to judge the exact nature of this technology around which lot of controversial issues is raised. The insight into the concept can help in clarifying the ways in which VAR can be implemented for corporates. This topic is of the interest of Transnationals, Bankers, Derivative dealers, Regulators, Academics etc. The Transnationals for instance would like to know their capital at risk at any point of time, so that it can take steps to hedge that risk. Banks can determine the level of capital that may be applied to various businesses. The derivative dealers can evaluate the diversification benefits of alternative asset classes and managers and the incremental risk that they add to the portfolio. It is important for the regulators also to study different aspects of VAR, the Basle committee has, for instance has recently introduced an amendment to capital accord to incorporate market risk. The topic is also of the interest of academicians who would like to explore different dimensions of this emerging concept.

VAR is not very popular in India. The reasons for this are two: 1) this concept is of recent origin and is in the first phase of its life cycle; 2) there is a lack of data and skills in this area of finance. However there is a strong sense of promoting the application of VAR technique in Indian organisations with the ultimate goal of disclosing the VAR of the organisation in the balance sheet. If this happens, it would help supervisors. The supervisors would be able to make better peer-group comparisons, fix a cap on the overall amount of risk for an organisation, say a bank and also practice differential supervision; for instance by varying the capital requirement according to the riskiness of the institution. But VAR implementation in India can be done only in the phased manner, due to data and skill constraints. It means that a beginning should be made immediately in some segment though the application to the whole balance sheet might take quite some time.

## REFERENCES

Barry Schachter: "An Irreverent Guide to Value at Risk." Financial Engineering News, Vol. 1, 1997.

Dr. Satchidananda S. Sogala: The Value-At-Risk: Methodologies and its Relevance to Indian Banks, IBA Bulletin, June 1994

Gregory P. Hopper: Value at Risk: A new Methodology For Measuring

Portfolio Risk, Federal Reserve Bank Of Philadelphia, July/ August 1996.

Rod A. Beckstorm, Don Lewis, Chris Roberts: VAR: pushing risk management to the statistical limit, Capital Market Strategies, November 1994.

Warren J. McLeland: "What's all the Fuss about?" Treasury Management International, September *1995*.

Quarterly Bulletin: Bank of Japan, February 1997.

Colin lawrence and Gary Robinson: "How Safe is the Risk Metrics?" Risk, Vol 8/Nol/January 1995

Bank of International Settlement (BIS 1992, page 25)

# 19

# FINANCIAL DECISIONS UNDER UNCERTAINTY—AN INFORMATION THEORETIC APPROACH

*Chandra Prakash Gupta*

Nothing is so certain in life as *uncertainty* is. As we are grow and evolve, the World around us becomes more complex and sophisticated and thereby more uncertain! The straight implication of it is that it has made *the future* highly blurred and fuzzy and as a consequence, a decision-maker is constrained to take sound decisions. But, the survival of any system depends upon how sound its decision making is. Therefore, efforts should be made to reduce future uncertainty and accordingly, any attempt that can assist in understanding it, measuring it, and controlling it to the extent possible should certainly be welcomed.

Uncertainty is all pervasive but the present article is concerned with it only in the area of financial decision making. And, as such a humble effort is made here to improve the quality of financial decisions under uncertainty using some widely used principles of Information Theory. It's main objective is to *show* how the principles of Entropy and Maximum Entropy are useful to a finance manager in taking better decisions especially when he/she has incomplete information about future.

What follows is planned as thus—Section-I provides necessary a brief discussion on uncertainty and preliminaries related to the basic principles of Information Theory-Entropy and Maximum Entropy; Section-II shows some areas of Finance where these could be used to improve financial decision making; and finally, conclusion.

## SECTION - I

Uncertainty is a multi-dimensional reality and hence, it is not a single monolithic concept. It exists in *shades* - it may be *probabilistic* or possibilistic; determinate or indeterminate; crisp or fuzzy.[1] Inspite of the different facets of uncertainty, it is understood usually in *probabilistic* sense and hence, is modeled through Probability Theory. The main cause of such uncertainty is *lack of information* that makes 100% certain prediction for future impossible. Here, we shall mean uncertainty in the sense of probabilistic uncertainty.

The degree of probabilistic uncertainty in a decision making situation is directly related to lack of information—the higher is the degree of lack of information in a situation, the higher is the degree of uncertainty[2]. Therefore, a measure of such uncertainty should be based on the degree ot *lack of information* and Information Theory provides us Entropy that measures of lack of information. Shannon (1948)[3] defined **Entropy** while developing the mathematical theory of communication as thus—

$$S_n = -\sum_{i-1}^{n} p_i log\, p_i$$

where

$S_n$ = Shannon measure of Entropy for a situation where n outcomes are expected to occur.

$p_i$ = Probability of i[th] outcome.

Some of the important properties of Shannon's Entropy are -

1. $S_n$ is permutationally symmetric. It does not change if $p_1, p_2 \ldots\ldots, p_n$ are re-ordered among themselves.
2. $S_n$ is a continuous function of $p_1, p_2 \ldots, p_n$ for all $p_i$ lying between 0 and 1.
3. The entropy does not change by the inclusion of an impossible event.
4. $S_n$ is never negative.
5. $S_n$ is zero when outcome is known with certainty otherwise it is positive.
6. $S_n$ is a concave function of $p_1, p_2 \ldots, p_n$.
7. The maximum value of $S_n$ is for the uniform distribution, i.e. when all the probabilities are equal, the entropy will be maximum and it is equal to log *n*.
8. If $\mathbf{p} = (p_1, p_2 \ldots, p_n)$ and $\mathbf{q} = (q_1, q_2 \ldots, q_m)$ are two independent probability distributions of two random variables, X and *Y*, then the entropy of the joint distribution is the sum of the entropies of the two distributions, i.e. $S_{pq'} = S_p + S_q$.

Estimation is an essential prerequisite for decision making under uncertainty and one problem of such estimation is of determining an appropriate probability distribution given a set of information. The solution of it is not straight as the information is incomplete. For this, Jaynes (1957) suggested a principle called — **Maximum Entropy Principle (MaxEnt).** Its basic objective is to derive scientifically a probability distribution that is compatible with given set of *incomplete* information.

Let $X$ be a random variable taking values $x_1, x_2 ..., x_n$ with the corresponding probabilities $p_1, p_2 ..., p_n$ which are *unknown*. Further, there are $C(p)$ constraints imposed by the available information and $\boldsymbol{p} = (p_1, p_2 ..., p_n)$. Then, the principle of Maximum Entropy (MaxEnt) says —

Find $\boldsymbol{p}$ that

$$\text{Max.} \ -\sum_{i-1}^{n} p_i \log p_i$$

s.t.

$$C(\boldsymbol{p})$$

$$\mathbf{p} \geq \boldsymbol{0}$$

MaxEnt provides a reasonable choice of selecting a particular probability distribution from among infinity of solutions. That is to say, we may find infinite solutions satisfying $C(\boldsymbol{p})$ and $\boldsymbol{p} \geq \boldsymbol{0}$ and each of these would have different amount of uncertainty. But, Jaynes suggested that out of all such distributions, one should select that probability distribution which has maximum entropy. Thus, MaxEnt helps in selecting one probability distribution out of many. It is a scientific method in a sense that it does not allow anyone to make any scrupulous assumption about information that is not available. It makes use of all information and allow us to say something with *truth*. It is also a natural extension of Laplace's famous *principle of insufficient reasoning*[4].

A large number of probability distributions are derived in the related literature (for instance, see Guiasu(1977)) for different sets of information and for different nature of random variables. Some important results are summarised below which would be useful for a finance manager.

R1. If X is a discrete random variable with values $x_1, x_2 \ldots, x_n$ and with the corresponding probabilities $p_1$, $p_2 \ldots, p_n$ having only natural constraints of non-negative $p_i$'s and the sum of probabilities is unity, then MaxEnt provides the following probability distribution:

$$p_1 = p_2 = \ldots p_n = 1/n$$

R2. If X is a continuous random variable taking values in the interval [a, b] and having only natural constraints, then MaxEnt provides the Uniform Probability Distribution with the following density function:

$$f(x) = \frac{1}{b-a}$$

R3. If X is a continuous random variable with mean , *m* and having natural constraints, then according to MaxEnt, *X* follows the Exponential Probability Distribution, i.e.

$$f(x,m) = \begin{cases} \frac{1}{m} e^{\frac{x}{m}} & x \geq 0 \\ 0 & x < 0 \end{cases}$$

R4. If *X* is a continuous random variable with mean, *m* and standard deviation, *s*, and having natural constraints, then MaxEnt suggests that *X* follows the Normal Probability Distribution with mean, *m* and standard deviation, *s*.

R5. If information is available about means, variances and covariances, then according to MaxEnt, the compatible probability distribution will be the Multivariate Normal Probability Distribution.

Thus, the above results show that a decision maker can derive some underlying probability distribution using MaxEnt and thereby can take better decisions than those what he/she could take otherwise.

## SECTION-II

A clear understanding about uncertainty and risk is essential for better financial decisions. But, unfortunately, finance managers are not able to appreciate the points of relation and distinctions between them and therefore, at times, they use both interchangeably. However, a better understanding of the principle of Entropy establishes clearly distinction between them. In Finance, uncertainty is to be understood in terms of *lack of information* while risk should be in terms of *variability* in outcomes. Besides this, entropy provides a well established measure of uncertainty, which a finance manager can use to compare the uncertainty involved in different decision making scenarios.

It is discussed in the sequel that how one can apply the principle of Maximum Entropy for a number of financial decisions. The discussion is planned to be brief. The financial decisions selected are Capital Budgeting Decisions, Security Analysis, Portfolio Theory and Arbitrage Free Pricing.

### Capital Budgeting Decisions

Capital budgeting decisions are very important financial decisions for a firm as they ensure optimum allocation of its economic resources among various economic activities and determine its earning capacity. These decisions are for long term and they involve decision making in distant future.

Therefore, a finance manager often has incomplete information in such decisions. In case, he/she knows only outcomes of a project and nothing else; then the uniform probability distribution could be used. Then, Expected NPV ( or some other measure of profitability of the project) and associated Variance could be determined as measures of Return and Risk and accordingly, a decisions could be taken. If only ranges of cash-flows are known, then one can do necessary analysis using the Uniform Probability Distribution, a result from R2. If the finance manager knows only the mean cash-flows over the project life, then the Exponential Probability Distribution can be used and all analysis related to probabilities and risk can be done accordingly. If cash-flows are randomly and independently distributed over the project life and only means and standard deviations are known, then the Normal Probability Distribution can be applied using R4. If each period cash-flows' means, variances and covariances are available, R5 suggests the use of the Multivariate Normal Probability Distribution.

From above, it is clew that in some cases when underlying probability distribution is unknown, a finance manager can derive a suitable probability distribution using MaxEnt. This results in two advantages — *one,* he/she is not supposed to introduce any subjective assumption in deriving a probability distribution; and *second,* it provides a unique probability distribution *(only in some cases and not always)* which is compatible with the existing information set. These, in overall, will increase the quality of financial decisions.

**Security Analysis**

Ultimate objective of the Security Analysis is to determine return and risk profile for each security. Since return is measured in terms of Expectation and risk in terms of variance, it is necessary for the security analyst to know the underlying probability distribution. In cases where probability distributions are unknown, risk and return could not be found out and consequently, a decision may not be taken. If taken, then it must be after introducing a number of subjective assumptions, which is not good for scientific and objective decision making. Here, MaxEnt can be of much use in deriving a suitable probability distribution from the given information set. Depending upon the availability of information, a security analyst can have a probability distribution using Ri- R5.

**Portfolio Theory**

One of the important issue of Portfolio Theory is — *'how to construct an efficient frontier?'* It is important because unless and until one has efficient frontier before him/her, he/she could not select optimum portfolio. Various theories have suggested various ways of obtaining an efficient frontier. But, the most important contribution due to Markowitz is that of *Mean- Variance Efficient Frontier.* One way to derive the Markowitz efficient frontier is — Minimise Variance of a portfolio subject to a given level of return from it. That is to say:

$$Min. V = \sum_{j-1}^{m} \pi_j (x_1 r_{1j} + x_2 r_{2j} + \ldots + x_n r_{nj} - x_1 \bar{r}_1 - x_2 \bar{r}_2 - \ldots - x_n \bar{r}_n)^2$$

$$= \sum_{j=1}^{m} \pi_j (R_j - \bar{R})^2$$

where

$$R_j \sum_{j=1}^{m} \pi_j r_{ij} \qquad \bar{R} = \sum_{i-1}^{n} x_i \bar{r}_i$$

s.t.

$$\bar{R} = E$$

$$\sum_{j=1}^{n} x_i = 1$$

Here,

$\pi_j$ = *the probability of the $j^{th}$ outcome for $j = 1, ..., m$*

$R_j$ = *the return on investment when/h outcome arises*

$R$ = *the mean return on the investment*

$r_{ij}$ = *return on the ilk security for $i = 1, ..., n$ when $j^{th}$ outcome occurs*

$x_i$ = *the proportion to be invested in the $j^{th}$ security; and*

$r_i$ = *the expected return on the $i^{th}$ security.*

The above model states - minimise the variance of a portfolio consisting of *n* securities and subject to constraints of a given expected return, *F*, and the summation of proportions equal to unity. It involves choosing $x_1, x_2, ..., x_n$ such that the variance among $R_1, R_2, ..., R_m$ is minimum.

That is to say, make $R_1, R_2, ..., R_m$ as equal as possible among themselves. Any departure of $R_1, R_2, ..., R_m$ from equality might be considered a measure of risk. Hence, same purpose could be achieved if we choose $x_1, x_2, ..., x_n$ so as to maximise the entropy measure

$$Max\ Entropy = -\sum_{j=1}^{m}(\pi_j R_j)\log(\pi_j R_j)$$

$$= -\sum_{j=1}^{m}\pi_j(x_1 r_{1j} + x_2 r_{2j} + ... + x_n r_{nj})\log[x_j(x_1 r_{1j} + x_2 r_{2j} + ... + x_n r_{nj})]$$

*subject to*

$$\sum_{j=1}^{m}\pi_j(x_1 r_{1j} + x_2 r_{2j} + ... + x_n r_{nj})$$

$$x_1 + x_2 + ... + x_n = 1$$

and $\quad x_i \geq 0 \text{ for all } i = 1,...,n.$

This formulation shows that alternative approaches to define and derive efficient frontier are possible[5]. Though it can not be claimed to be a better formulation than that of mean-variance, yet it provides another interesting dimension to view portfolio problem.

**Arbitrage Free Pricing**

Presently, pricing of financial products is by and large based on the assumption that competition for financial gains will eventually eliminate any arbitrage opportunities from the financial markets. An arbitrage opportunity is said to exist when an investment strategy that costs nothing can earn income on such investment. When coupled with other assumptions about the stochastic process governing the movements of asset prices, a fundamental duality theorem in financial economics shows that this *no arbitrage opportunity* assumption is equivalent to existence of a set of *risk neutral probability measures*, which satisfy a number of linear constraints. These risk neutral measures are widely used in pricing *contingent claims*, such as options. Stutzer(1996) in the paper —'Thermostatics in Financial Economics' showed that MaxEnt could be used to derive a *canonical risk neutral probability measure* which could, then, be used for pricing.

Stutzer (1996) conjectured that the absence of arbitrage opportunities requires the existence of a probability measure, Q, under which the Q-expected returns of all risky assets must equal the risk free rate, r. Measure Q is labeled as canonical risk neutral probability measure which could be derived by solving the following MaxEnt problem:

$$Mas\ S = -\sum_{j=1}^{K} Q_j \log Q_j$$

*subject to*

$$E_Q[R_i]=r,\ i=0,1,\ldots,N$$

*where*

$R_i$ = *return on $i^{th}$ asset and there are N+ 1 assets with 0 as risk free asset and Kfuture outcomes.*

Thus, computation of expectations taken with respect to such canonical measure provides an alternative means of deriving some asset pricing formulae.

## CONCLUSION

The basic objective of the article is to show that some Information Theoretic concepts especially Entropy and Maximum Entropy can be fruitfully employed to improve the quality of financial decisions under uncertainty. It has also shown that these concepts can provide alternative formulations for problems like deriving an efficient frontier and risk neutral probability measure for pricing contingent claims in Finance. Understanding well the concept of Entropy equips a finance manager to understand *uncertainty* better and how it is different from risk which is used in the sense of variations in the returns/cashflows. How one can derive a probability distribution when the information is incomplete is also discussed. Such derivation is more scientific and objective in nature. And, it is believed that this would help in a big way in improving the quality of decisions in the areas of Capital Budgeting Decisions and Security Analysis.

## NOTES

1. For a detailed discussion on the nature and type of Uncertainty, see Gupta (1992)
2. To understand a distinction between Risk and Uncertainty, refer to a detailed discussion in Gupta (1984).

3. Shannon (1948) introduced the concept of Entropy but later on many scholars have defined it differently. However, we shall be discussing only Shannon's Entropy and for others, one may refer to Kapur and Kesavan (1992).
4. The principle of insufficient reasoning postulates that the uniform probability distribution is the most satisfactory representation of our knowledge when we know nothing about the random variable except that each probability is non-negative and the sum of probabilities is one.
5. Alternative formulations using entropy are discussed in Kapur and Kesavan (1992). Not much work is done in this direction and hence, it could be pursued further.

## REFERENCES

1. Gupta, C.P. (1984): Negative Parameters in Decision Analysis; A dissertation submitted to the University of Delhi, India. (Unpublished).
2. Gupta, C. P. (1992): Capital Budgeting Decisions under Fuzzy Environment; A thesis submitted to the University of Delhi, India. (Unpublished).
3. Jaynes, E. T. (1957): Information Theory and Statistical Mechanics; Physical Reviews, 106: 620-630.
4. Kapur, J. N. and Kesavan, H. K. (1992): Entropy Optimization Principles with Application; Academic Press, INC.
5. Shannon, C. E. (1948): A Mathematical Theory of Communication; Bell System Technical Journal, 47: 379-423.
6. Stutzer, M. (1996): Thermostatics in Financial Economics; in Heidbreder, G. R. (1996): Maximum Entropy and Bayesian Methods; (Ed.); Kluwer Academic Publishers; 375-390.

# 20

# RISK ADJUSTED RETURN ON CAPITAL

*Harminder Singh*

Since the late 1980, a number of large U.S. banks have evolved into a collection of focused and semiautonomous lines of business, each with a different product, customer, distribution, or geographic mandate. This decentralized organisational structure has created issues concerning performance measurement, risk management, and resource allocation. As these issues emerged and gained urgency, banks found they needed new ways to measure and evaluate the performance of different lines of business.

Most banks have moved quickly to develop measurement systems that would permit them to construct income statements by line of business, but the development of business balance sheets was delayed. Construction of complete balance sheets required the allocation of equity capital to each line of business, and until the late 1980s most banks either did not allocate capital or allocated it on an undifferentiated basis, according to the amount of assets employed. While the construction of income statements permitted banks to measure the contribution of businesses in dollar terms, it did not permit them to do so relative to the capital resources consumed by the business or the risk incurred. Gradually, however, banks came to recognize the need to allocate capital on a risk-adjusted basis.

Today most of the sophisticated global banking institutions have incorporated this framework into both their lending and capital markets Wading businesses. In part this was the result of regulatory initiatives that imposed risk-driven capital requirements on a bank-wide basis, but also banks came to realize that businesses with few assets, such as transactions-processing businesses could be significant users of capital. Failure to allocate capital based on the amount of risk involved can lead to serious performance measurement errors.

Development of RAROC methodology began in the late 1970 initiated by a group at Bankers trust. Their original interest was to measure the risk of the bank's credit portfolio, as well as the amount of equity capital necessary to limit the exposure of the bank's depositors and other debt-holders to a specified probability of loss. Since then, a number of other large banks have developed RAROC or systems like RAROC with the aim, in most cases, of quantifying the amount of equity capital necessary to support all of their operating activities-fee based and trading activities, as well as trading lending.

It has been suggested that the most important role of a financial institution's senior management is to provide allocation of capital to the institution's individual business units. Surprisingly then, it is not uncommon to discover among otherwise advanced institutions that this process of capital allocation is performed on a relatively arbitrary basis. Most companies relate the decision in one form or another to observed returns, but frequently little rigour exists beyond this.

The key concept behind a risk adjusted performance measure is that in order to compare the returns of an arbitrary group of assets or business units, a measurement of the risk which has been run in order to makes those returns, must be taken into account. Where significant risk is taken, the return should be scaled down accordingly, prior to comparison with a lower risk undertaking.

RAROC is aimed at portfolio managers who wish to determine what the risk/return characteristics of each constituent of their portfolio are. It does this in the first instance by drawing upon a comprehensive historical database of correlations and volatilities for each of a large number of so-called 'risk factors'. A risk factor might be anything from exposure to one month dollar LIBOR, through to exposure to changes in an index. Drawing upon the historical characteristics of such risk measures permits RAROC to characterize the risk profile of a portfolio of assets. This profile is then used as input to a Monte Carlo simulation model.

This model generates large numbers of projected scenarios providing what Bankers Trust refer to as a 'statistical map of potential gains or losses'; a measure of the risk and return characteristics of the portfolio/ and its constituent assets. This provides the ability to relate risks directly to returns, providing a basis for investment, and ultimately capital allocation decisions between assets within the portfolio.

The use of RAROC by major money-center and regional banks in USA is to formulate capital structure targets and to evaluate performance is a major change from traditional practice. Banks have long relied on measures such as return on assets (ROA) and return on book equity (ROE) to evaluate their own performance, both at the consolidated level and for individual operating units. And capital adequacy has been determined primarily by banks' ability to meet minimum capital requirements set by regulators. Neither the regulatory requirements nor conventionally applied ROA or ROE measures are adjusted in any systematic way for differences in the risks of the bank's various activities. The Basle guidelines, for example, effectively assign the same capital requirement to all commercial loans, regardless of their degree of risk, while requiring no capital for taking deposits and positions in Treasury bonds.

**Hurdle Rate**

Initially, most banks designated a single bank-wide hurdle rate as the appropriate measure against which to compare business return on equity. Usually this bank wide hurdle rate-equaled management's objective for return on equity for the bank as a whole. Over time, however, banks began to recognize that a single bank wide hurdle discriminated against low-risk businesses and in favour of high-risk ones. Low-risk businesses would have difficulty in meeting a bank-wide hurdle rate, while high-risk businesses would not. As banks recognized that their businesses varied in their riskiness, and therefore in the amount of capital allocated to them, they began to apply hurdle rates that reflected differences in business risk. Increasingly banks are moving away from a single bank-wide hurdle rate to specific rates for each line of business, based on the perceived riskiness. Some banks have resisted using differentiated hurdle rates, arguing that allocating different amounts of capital adequately addresses difference in risk. This argument fails to distinguish between the different roles of capital for creditors and for investors. To creditors, capital is a shield that protects them against losses. Investors, on the other hand, view equity capital as a scarce resource to be invested where the risk-adjusted returns are highest. Thus, allocating different amounts of capital addresses the concerns of debt-holders, depositors, and regulators, while applying differentiated hurdle rates addresses the desire of shareholders to be adequately compensated for the risks borne.

RAROC systems allocate capital for two basic reasons: (1) Performance evaluation and (2) risk management. For performance-evaluation purposes, RAROC systems assign capital to business units as part of a process of determining the risk- adjusted rate of return and, ultimately, the economic value added of each business unit. The economic value added of each business unit is simply the unit's adjusted net income less a capital charge (the amount of equity capital allocated to the unit times the required return on equity). The objective in this case is to measure a business unit's contribution to shareholder value and, thus, to provide a basis for effective capital budgeting and incentive compensation at the business unit level.

For risk management purposes, the overriding goal of allocating capital to individual business units is to determine the bank's optimal capital structure. This process involves estimating how much the risk (volatility) of each business unit contributes to the total risk of the bank and, hence, to the bank's overall capital requirements.

Using capital allocations for both capital budgeting and management performance evaluation raises the question of what is the appropriate measure for gauging the risk. Bank of America allocates capital according to the nonhedgable risk that originates in a business unit; For example, I lending activities, the net income of loans is calculated assuming "matched duration" finding, i.e., the loan is funded in a way that removes the interest-rate risk associated with the loan. This process also removes from the capital calculation volatility arising from risks that can be easily hedged. The treasury unit is responsible for hedging interest rate and currency risk. This process reduces the risk assumed by line managers (through variability in their compensation) and focuses their attention on risk that they can potentially influence. As a result of this process, most business units are allocated capital based on credit risk and business risk (volatility arising from operational errors) and not based on volatility arising from hedgeable risk.

At Bank of America, the capital share for each business is obtained by multiplying economic capital by the same, corporate-wide cost of equity capital- the so-called "hurdle rate." A project or business unit is then evaluated according to its expected "residual income" — or what Bank of America calls the "economic profit."

Economic profit is calculated as earnings (net of taxes, interest payments and expected credit losses) less a charge for the cost of equity capital. The amount of capital allocated varies with the contribution of the project to the overall volatility of the earnings of Bank of America (the project's so called internal beta.)

In addition, RAROC systems are used to evaluate the performance of business units for purposes of compensating line managers. At many banks, including Bank of America performance is evaluated according to the "residual income"— or what Bank of America calls the "economic profit" — of the activity. The objective of this calculation, again, is to provide an ex-post measure of the value added by a particular activity, one that allows the economic profit of "off-balance-sheet" activities to be compared to that of traditional asset based activities. The value added associated with each activity can then be used as a basis for determining incentive based compensation for line managers.

At most firms, today, credit risk management, market risk management and operational risk management are all handled separately by different managers with different goals. RORAC can blend these different elements of risk into a single risk framework, giving business managers a decision-support tool that takes a comprehensive view of these different risks for strategic and tactical decision making. Institutions that seek to implement this discipline can find themselves bogged down by either a lack of infrastructure or disjointed business management process. Before RORAC-related models and calculations can be effectively implemented, companies must build the tools necessary to identify risk on a company-wide basis.

## REFERENCES

Nigel Webb, "Hotter property" The Banker June 1996.

Lawrence, D. "Measuring and Managing Derivative market Risk", International Thomson Business Press, London, 1996.

Kimball, Ralph, C, "Innovations in Performance Measurement in Banking," New England Economic Review, May/June 1997.

Cocks, G. Measuring Market Risk within a Bank, Journal of Applied Finance and Investment, Vol. 1, No 2, May/June 1996.

Christopher James, "RAROC Based Capital Budgeting,and Performance

Evaluation: A case study of Bank Capital Allocation." A publication by The Wharton Financial Institution Center, University of Pennsylvania.

Merton, R. and A. Perold, 1993. "Theory of Risk Capital in Financial Firms." Journal of Applied Corporate Finance, 6: No.3.

# 21

# EXCHANGE RATE SYSTEM AND PRIVATE CORPORATE TREASURERSHIP

*Chander Kanta Gupta*

The turmoil in financial markets which started in Thailand in July 1997, spread to other countries of the region and had global ramifications, evoked lot of discussion at all levels - international, regional, national and institutional levels. One of the arguments was about the choice of exchange rate regime. In the light of this, the present paper tries to analyse the exchange rate arrangements in the Post World War II period and tries to explore the new dimensions added to the corporate treasurership in the global business world. The paper deals with exchange rate arrangements in the world in the Post World War II period in Section I. Section II deals with Corporate treasurership in the global operations and last Section deals with futures, options and derivatives.

## SECTION I

### Exchange Rate and Significance

The exchange rate is basically regarded as the price of one currency in terms of another. The exchange rate is an important economic variable of an economy as it links a nation's domestic economy to the international market. The changes in exchange rate leads to changes in reserves, credit, debits, balance of payments of a country; credit rating, interest rates, external commercial borrowings foreign exchange accounting and corporate reporting, bilateralism and multilateralism, currency translation mechanism, international accounting, harmonisation and uniform financial practices, transaction currency and transaction costs, inter-country comparison, etc. The increased importance being attached to the exchange rate is due to the internationalization of business operations, the continuing growth in the world trade, the trend towards integration of world economies through trade, financial flows, technology spill overs, information networks, etc.

In the Bretton Woods System, we had gold convertibility of the dollar and for the system to function successfully, it was essential that confidence was maintained in the US dollar. So long as central banks knew that dollars could be converted into gold at $35 per ounce, the banks would willingly hold dollars in their reserves. But it was quite obvious from the beginning itself that the gold convertibility of dollar was bound to become increasingly less feasible as dollar liabilities rose over time relative to the U.S. gold stock. Throughout the period US dollar was the only currency that was freely convertible into gold. The Bretton Woods System had started facing problems during 1960's when the US liquid liabilities began to outstrip US reserves, the deterioration is particularly marked from 1968 to 1972 leading to the collapse of the system.

With the breakdown of Bretton Woods System of Fixed Exchange Rate, the monetary system became a hybrid and a whole host of exchange rate regimes co-existed between currencies. We had currencies floating on a managed basis, some currencies freely floating and others moving in and out of various types of pegged-rate relationship. Table 1, it is observed that in 1975, nearly 80% of the countries (which were members of IMF) had pegged their exchange rate. As against this in December 1997, the figure has gone down to 36%. This indicates that over the past decades many countries have shifted from fixed exchange rate system (Pegging to a single currency, such as Dollar, French Franc, or any other currency or to a basket of currencies) to a more flexible arrangements.

**TABLE 1**

**No. of countries under Fixed and Floating exchange rate systems since the end of the Bretton Woods System.**

| *Classification Status* | *Dec. 31, 1975* | *Aug. 31, 1980* | *Nov. 1, 1986* | *June 30, 1995* | *Dec. 31 1997* |
|---|---|---|---|---|---|
| Pegged to | 105 | 95 | 91 | 67 | 66 |
| Independently Floating | | | 20 | 48 | 53 |
| Total no. of countries | 136 | 139 | 150 | 158 | 181 |

*Note:* Pegged to include pegged to single currency, SDR, other currency composite.

Total No. of countries - Countries Members of IMF.

*Source:* Calculated from Annual Reports on Exchange Arrangement and Exchange Restrictions,IMF, Various issues.

The basic arguments in favour of flexible exchange rates are following: floating exchange rates ensure balance of payments equilibrium; floating exchange rates ensure monetary autonomy; and floating exchange rates insulate economies from external stocks.

Though there are many argument in favour of flexible exchange rate regime but flexibility has limitations and disadvantages as well. The flexible regime can lead to volatile behaviour of exchange rates. Thus increases the uncertainty about the future exchange rates and this can hinder the growth of trade across borders particularly by small and medium sized companies which cannot afford to take risks. Though this argument was relevant twenty or thirty years ago, but now given hedging instruments, the risk could be reduced.

Given the arguments for both fixed and flexible regime, Jeffrey A. Frankel has rightly said, "No single currency regime is right for all countries or at all times". Though there is no perfect exchange-rate system. What is best depends on a particular economy's characteristics. The factors which should be taken into account in choosing the exchange rate regime are: 1) size and openness of the economy; 2) inflation rate; 3) labour-market flexibility; 4) degree of financial development; 5) credibility of policy makers; and the capital mobility.

## SECTION II

Traditionally the role of treasurer was to arrange the raising of funds whenever needed; but in today's world he plays a very important role in the corporate management. It is his duty to ensure the funds are raised economically and used in the most efficient and effective manner.

**Normally the responsibilities of a Corporate Treasure Centre around:**

1. *Investment Decision:* It relates to allocation of capital that would yield maximum expected benefits in future.
2. *Financing Decision:* He decides when, where, how and in which currency to acquire funds to meet the firm's global investment needs. He strives to obtain the best financing mix or optimum capital structure for the firm. and also attempts to maximise the wealth of its owners by maximising the value of share.
3. *Dividend Decision:* The Corporate Treasurers provides input for deciding about the dividend payment. Whether the firm should distribute all profits or retain them or distribute a portion and retain the balance. Tax considerations are also highly relevant in this area of his responsibilities.

4. *Liquidity Decision:* Managing current assets efficiently and safeguarding profitability, liquidity and risk are also his areas of work.
5. *Profit Maximization:* Maximisation of share holder's wealth and return on investment decisions and evaluation exercises are also conducted by him.

With the collapse of the Bretton Woods System and unprecedented pace of globalisation, (due to pervasive adoption of the free market ideology, economic expansion of developing countries, advances in communications, removal of barriers to trade, capital and knowledge transfers and globalisation of the financial markets) the corporates in the international business face larger risk than the domestic companies; like - political risk, foreign exchange risk, risks due to war or revolution, prevalence of terrorism etc. Of all the additional risks, the corporate-treasurers are more concerned about the exchange rate risk. The exchange rate risk arises due to fluctuation in the exchange rates.

The three types of foreign exchange risk that may affect a firm are:

1. *Transaction* exposure arises when a company has receivables or payables in a foreign currency resulting from a transaction with a company in a different country.
2. *Translation exposure* arises as a consequence of recasting the financial statements of foreign affiliates into the home country.
3. *Economic or operating exposure* is the risk that a company's operations will be affected by an unanticipated change in exchange rate.

The floating rate system brought volatility into the currency equation and required firms to manage their exposure to foreign exchange rate fluctuations more carefully. Treasurer must be well-equipped to cope with multiple currencies and interest rates. The Corporate Treasurer should have working knowledge of the language of the countries in which his operations are most significant. The treasury professionals in multinational corporations should be able to converse in the language of other international treasurers and bankers. In addition, the treasurer must be skilled in foreign exchange risk management and should have good knowledge of instruments used for risk minimisation - knowledge about financial derivatives. He should possess expertise in foreign investment decisions, capital budgeting and long-term funding from international capital markets and be aware of non-financial implications of financial strategy. In international capital market, a variety of sources are available, hence the corporate treasurers must acquire a broader knowledge about the various ways of raising funds and their suitability to their corporates bodies and associates. Treasurers should be able to forecast (take into account) relative inflation, as relative inflation has a dominant influence on interest rates and exchange rates. In addition a Corporate treasurer should be able to forecast the expected loss or gain due to currency depreciation, appreciation or speculative bouts. Hence globalisation has brought new challenges to Corporate treasurship function and at the same time development in the financial markets has opened new way to minimise risks through new financial instruments futures, options and derivatives and multinational corporate treasurer is expected to have an expertise in future, options and derivatives to hedge the foreign exchange risk.

## SECTION III

### Futures, Options and Derivatives

There are different types of risks involved in the financial market. The *unique* risk is that a particular investment will go bad through default or calamity. Diversification strategies are the one way to manage this risk. The other type of risk is the market risk - the market risk is associated with changes in the factors like price, level, interest rate, political stability, exchange rate, and so on. *Hedging* is the best defence against market risk. Hedging is done to protect the investment from the outside risk that is not in one's control that is the day-to-day market risk. The *futures* and *options* are the most commonly used *derivatives* instruments. Derivative is a financial contract whose pay off structure is determined by the value of an underlying asset. Futures contract is a binding agreement to buy or sell something in the future. The unique feature of a future contract is that the counter party is always known and is always the same. The other party is always the clearing corporation. Contracts are originated for a specific delivery time in the future and are so denoted in the market, hence the name futures. Futures contracts are traded on commodity exchanges or other futures exchanges. People can buy or sell futures like other commodities. When an investor buys a future contract (he takes a long position) on an organized future exchange, he is, in fact assuming the right and obligation of taking delivery of the specified underlying item on a specified date. Similarly when an investor sells a contract (he takes a short position) one assumes the right and obligation to make delivery of the underlying asset. In futures, it is not necessary to hold on to a futures contract until maturity - one can easily close out a position in futures contract. Most of the futures contracts are cancelled by parties by engaging into reverse trades. The buyer cancels a contract by selling another contract while the seller does so by buying another contract. Important point is that a clearing house guarantees the performance of the futures contracts, the parties in the contracts are required to keep margins which are adjusted on a daily basis to account for the gains or losses, depending upon the price at which the future contracts are being traded in the market. This is known as the marking of the market; it involves giving a credit to the buyer of the contract if the price of the contract rises and debiting the seller's account by an equal amount. Similarly the buyer's balance is reduced when the contract price declines and the seller's account is accordingly updated. And the profit or loss on a contract is settled daily and not on maturity of the contract.

Options offer another way to offset risk exposure with the added feature of not requiring the hedger to forgo all of the advantages that may accrue from favourable changes. An option on a future represents a right to buy or sell a specific futures contract at a predetermined price at any time prior to the expiration of the option. For the right, the purchaser of the option pays a fee known as the premium. An option which allows its purchaser to buy a futures contract at a given price called strike price is known as a call option while an option which allows its purchaser to sell a future contract at a given strike price is called a put option. The value or premium of an option varies. The higher is the uncertainty or volatility, the higher would be the value of the option. When an option is purchased a premium is totally paid. Options are also standardized contracts and traded on exchanges. The trading in options is regulated by the exchanges that ensure the honouring of such contracts. There are a wide variety of underlying assets on which options are written.

The long evolution of futures market dates back to the establishment of the Osaka Rice Exchange during the 17th century. However financial futures (financial futures is a term that describes contracts in interest rates sensitive instruments such as treasury bills, Eurodollars, foreign currencies, stock indexes, etc.) are relatively new innovations that begun in 1972 with the inauguration of the International Money Market at the Chicago Mercantile Exchange with the introduction of foreign currency futures contracts. One of the prominent features of global financial markets in the last ten years has been the rise in the importance of derivatives markets both in size and breadth, size (contract traded) breadth (in terms of the types of risks traded). Foreign currency futures and options are a new form of financial instruments that are used to manage foreign exchange risk or take speculative position on currency movements.

The daily trading activity in foreign currencies and their derivatives is significantly greater than that of all the other financial instruments and their derivatives. World trade, foreign investments and international capital flows have certainly contributed to this trading activity. More importantly however, financial deregulation (lifting the capital controls) along with technological advances in electronic transfer, have offered traders the opportunity to seek the highest return adjusted for risk globally. The large volume of trading along with volatile currency prices, offer both, speculation opportunities and also demand for hedging.

The volume and mobility of global finance capital has increased significantly. In 1986 about $188 billion passed through the hands of currency traders in New York, London and Tokyo everyday. By 1995, the daily turnover reached almost $1.2 trillion (BIS Report). Currently it is around $2 trillion. Historically most trading in foreign exchange was the result of international trade, as buyers and sellers of foreign goods and services needed another currency to settle their transactions. But now the trade in currency has very little to do with international trade which accounts for just two percent of the global currency movements. Thus the present process of globalisation of finance is no longer complementary to international trade and investment but has gained a life of its own. In the current phase, financial flows are rarely associated with the flows of real resources and long-term productive investments. These flows are largely liquid and are attracted by short-term speculative gains and can leave the country as quickly as they come.

## CONCLUSION

All this clearly demonstrates the fast changing role and responsibilities of Corporate functionaries of all sort, in general, and Corporate Treasurer in particular. With unprecedented fast pace of information technology, communications 24-hour trading and minimal role of governments, a multinational corporate treasurer has to be adequately, trained, updated knowledge of financial and investment operations and global resource allocations, deployments and re-deployments. As such he has tons of challenges and opportunities of innovative and diverse types.

## REFERENCES

1. Bank for International Settlements: Annual Report, 1996.
2. Financial Times Survey, May 27, 1986.
3. IMF: Annual Reports on Exchange Arrangement and Exchange Regulations, Various Issues.
4. Keith Pilbeam: International Finance, Chapter II.
5. Prasana Chandra: Fundamentals of Financial Management, Chapter I.
6. Paul Ginzing: The History of Foreign Exchange.
7. Paul Ginzing: The Case Against Floating Exchange Rates.
8. Robert W. Kolband and Ricardo J. Rodriguez: Financial Management.
9. Robert Fraser: The World Financial System.
10. Scammell W.M.: International Monetary Policy, Bretton Woods and After. Chapters 5, 6 and 9.
11. Shapiro Alan C. Multinational Financial Management.